# POLITICS
# AND PUBLIC POLICY
# IN HAWAI'I

# POLITICS
# AND PUBLIC POLICY
# IN HAWAI'I

Edited by Zachary A. Smith
and Richard C. Pratt

STATE UNIVERSITY OF NEW YORK PRESS

Published by
State University of New York Press, Albany

For information, address State University of New York
Press, State University Plaza, Albany, N.Y., 12246

Production by Diane Ganeles
Marketing by Theresa A. Swierzowski

Library of Congress Cataloging-in-Publication Data

Politics and public policy in Hawai'i / edited by Zachary A. Smith and
    Richard Pratt.
        p.    cm.
    Includes index.
    ISBN 0-7914-0949-X (acid-free).—ISBN 0-7914-0950-3 (pbk. : acid
-free)
    1. Hawaii—Politics and government—1959–  2. Hawaii—Economic
policy.   3. Hawaii—Social policy.      I. Smith, Zachary A. (Zachary
Alden), 1953–  .      II. Pratt, Richard, 1941–  .
    JK9395.P66   1992
    996.9′04—dc20                                             91-13267
                                                                 CIP

10 9 8 7 6 5 4 3 2 1

# CONTENTS

List of Figures — vii

List of Tables — ix

Preface — xi

Introduction — 1
*Zachary Smith and Richard Pratt*

*Part I: The Policy Environment*

1. Policy Control: Institutionalized Centralization
   in the Fiftieth State — 13
   *Norman Meller*

2. The State Economy — 29
   *David L. Hammes, Ronald A. Oliveira,*
   *and Marcia Sakai*

3. Social Dynamics of the Aloha State:
   The Population of Hawai'i — 51
   *Jeffrey L. Crane and Alton M. Okinaka*

*Part II: Policy Processes*

4. Blood Runs Thick: Ethnicity as a Factor in
   Hawai'i's Politics — 67
   *Dan Boylan*

5. Policy in Hawai'i: The Budget — 81
   *Deane Neubauer*

6. Resolving Policy Conflicts in Hawai'i through Mediation — 99
   *Peter S. Adler*

*Part III: Policy Issues*

7. Environmental Quality in America's Tropical Paradise    113
   *Richard J. Tobin and Dean Higuchi*

8. Dealing with Scarcity: Land Use and Planning    131
   *David L. Callies*

9. The Politics of Housing in Hawai'i    147
   *Kem Lowry*

10. Planning for Rapid Transit on Oahu: Another Great
    Planning Disaster?    165
    *Karl E. Kim*

11. Tourism in Hawai'i: Economic Issues for the 1990s
    and Beyond    185
    *James Mak and Marcia Sakai*

12. Crime and Justice in Hawai'i    201
    *A. Didrick Castberg*

13. Education in Hawai'i: Balancing Equity and Progress    215
    *Thomas W. Bean and Jan Zulich*

14. Hawai'i Labor: The Social Relations of Production    229
    *Edward D. Beechert*

15. *Kupa'a 'Aina:* Native Hawaiian Nationalism in Hawai'i    243
    *Haunani-Kay Trask*

Contributors    261

Index    267

# LIST OF FIGURES

Figure 2.1 Growth in Real Products 1970–1988      35

Figure 2.2 Distribution of Total Employment and Gross
State Product in Hawai'i by Sector (1986)      41

Figure 11.1 Visitor Arrivals and Real Expenditures      192

Figure 12.1 Hawaii Judicial System      207

# LIST OF TABLES

Table 2.1 Export Trade to Japan and Asia                                    33

Table 2.2 Import Trade from Japan and Asia                                  33

Table 2.3 Hawai'i Statewide Employment by Industry                         36

Table 2.4 Income of Families (in 1980 Constant Dollars)                    39

Table 2.5 Per Capita Revenue, Expenditure and Debt of
State and Local Government (1986)                                           43

Table 3.1 Hawai'i's Resident Population, by Selected Years                  53

Table 3.2 Population by Selected Island                                     53

Table 3.3 Visitors to Hawai'i by Selected Years                            55

Table 3.4 Ethnic Background (1988)                                         57

Table 3.5 Language Spoken at Home in 1980                                  57

Table 3.6 Percent of Adult Population Affected by Specific
Health Risk Factors (1987)                                                 58

Table 3.7 Health Risk Factors by Ethnicity                                 58

Table 3.8 Annual Mean Income (Before Taxes) of Households
and Families, 1982–84 and 1985–87                                          60

Table 3.9 Median Family Income of Major Ethnic Groups
(1980)                                                                      60

Table 3.10 Poverty Status of Families and Unrelated
Individuals, 1969 to 1987                                                   61

Table 3.11 Ethnic Distribution of Hawai'i's Population,
Arrests, Murder Arrests, Murder Victims,
and Drug-Abuse Arrests (1986)                                              62

Table 3.12 Hawai'i Adult Incarceration and Arrest Rates
(1980)                                                                      62

Table 4.1 Selected Districts: 1986 Election     68

Table 4.2 Ethnicity and Party     71

Table 7.1 Relative Commitment of States to
Environmental Protection     127

Table 9.1 County Government-Assisted Housing Production     151

Table 10.1 Population, Registered Motor Vehicles, and New
Car Sales, Island of Oahu (1950–87)     168

Table 10.2 Population and Motor Vehicle Projections,
Island of Oahu     171

Table 11.1 Visitors to Hawai'i by Country/Region (1989)     190

Table 12.1 Major Offenses, State of Hawai'i, 1989     203

Table 12.2 Major Offenses by County, 1989     204

Table 12.3 Representation of Ethnic Groups
in Hawai'i's Prisons     210

# PREFACE

The idea of creating a book about public policy in Hawai'i was in the back of our minds long before we began to talk to one another about the project. These islands are simply too interesting a place to live without wanting to write about how things are done here in comparison to other places. As it happened we began to get serious about the endeavor at almost exactly the same time, but independent of one another. When we learned of our mutual interest, the book was well on its way.

As everyone who has published a book knows, the good will and good work of many people are required to go from conception to completion. The contributors have made our jobs easier by producing strong drafts of their chapters and then responding graciously to what must have at times seemed zany suggestions for revision.

The book never would have been completed without the efforts of Reshela DuPuis and Shannon Tangonan, who worked in the Public Administration Program at the Manoa campus. Both gave the best kind of attention to the substance and detail of the project and deserve a great deal of credit for whatever is good about it.

ZACHARY SMITH
Northern Arizona University

RICHARD PRATT
University of Hawaii at Manoa

# INTRODUCTION

This book provides interpretations of Hawai'i's contemporary policy issues and their social, economic, and political frameworks. One of our purposes in putting it together is to afford people not living in the islands insights into the world which exists behind Hawai'i Visitors Bureau posters. Inevitably, examination of a community will reveal a tension between its fondest images of itself, given to outsiders to obtain their travel dollars or their admiration or to residents to bolster community solidarity, and the realities of day-to-day life. This tension appears to be far greater in Hawai'i than elsewhere. Here it is harder and harder to reconcile the images of paradise and its presumed leisurely lifestyle with the actualities of an ongoing struggle between Oahu's accelerating urbanization and rapid statewide economic development, and with the commitment of residents and native Hawaiians to hold onto what each group sees as irreplaceable physical and cultural qualities.

A second goal of this book is to provide those who live in Hawai'i with a vehicle for talking to each other about who they have become and what they are becoming. We do not agree with a number of positions taken in these chapters, but whether or not we agree, our intention is to provide information and interpretations that can act as points of departure for talking about our collective realities and options.

Apart from our concerns to pull together image and reality and create a dialogue, there are a number of factors that converge to make the fiftieth state's political life and policy processes of interest to a wide range of readers. One of these is its name. Hawai'i is one of the most familiar locations in the world with a renowned image as a modern paradise. Clothing announcing "Hawai'i" can be seen virtually anyplace on earth. Over the past ten years, familiarity in the United States has increased and become highly differentiated. Now one should not be surprised in a small midwestern town to see a T-shirt reading "Maui" or advertising the name of a bar or restaurant along that island's coast.

Further evidence of increasing interest in the islands is the frequency of travel to Hawai'i. In 1990 more than six million people came here. On any given day, about one out of every ten people in the islands is a visitor. Inevitably many of these visitors become curious about the life that exists beyond the tourist enclaves.

Hawai'i warrants attention because it is America's only island state. The significance of this rests only partly in the obstacles or opportunities provided by the remoteness of the islands with twenty-five hundred miles of ocean between them and the West Coast. It is also relevant that the ocean involved is the Pacific. During the 1980s, conventional wisdom came to hold that the industrial world was on the threshold of the "Pacific era." If such a shift of attention from Europe to Asia and the Pacific does occur, is it unreasonable to expect we may learn something useful from Hawai'i about dealing with people from those societies and cultures we so poorly understand? Hawai'i is, after all, the most Asian of all the American states. It is, moreover, the only state in which Caucasians are a distinct minority, comprising well under thirty percent of the population.

The islands are a topic of interest because the themes that describe their past are distinctly different from those used to describe mainland states. Hawai'i is, for example, the only American state to evolve from a sovereign kingdom. A well-developed Hawaiian society existed long before Captain James Cook first brought Western culture to the islands in 1778. The Hawai'i of today is built not on Western institutions and customs, but on those of the early population of the islands, which may have been as large as the one million who now live there. These ways are foreign to Western minds. Missionaries and men of commerce fought for these people's souls and for their land, and the results of that struggle continue to shape Hawai'i.

Finally, Hawai'i is of interest because its special social and political history has created distinct institutions. Since admission to statehood in 1959, it has had the most centralized system of governance of any American state. It is, for example, the only state that has no incorporated villages, towns, or cities. It is unique in having the only system of primary and secondary education run by a single statewide board. It is the only state in which the institutions of governance evolved downward from a centralized authority rather than—with classic American reluctance—upward from local jurisdictions.

Because Hawai'i's history is so rich and varied, a great deal has been written about it. The most well-known works are Lawrence

Fuchs's *Hawai'i Pono: A Social History,* published just after statehood in 1961, and Gavan Daws's *Shoals of Time,* published seven years later. There are many others however, ranging from those broader in scope, such as the works produced in the 1950s by Ralph Simpson Kuykendall, to the more highly focused studies of individual islands, island districts, towns and families, such as Marion Kelly's study of the Big Island's Ka'u district. There are also important histories written by Hawaiian people. Probably the best known of these is by David Malo, who wrote in the early nineteenth century.

A number of studies have dealt with specific social or political issues. The most famous, Andrew Lind's *An Island Community: Ecological Succession in Hawaii,* published in 1938, deals with social tensions and patterns of assimilation prior to World War II. More recent notable works include Noel Kent's *Islands under the Influence* (1983), an analysis of the mechanisms by which outsiders came to exert control over the economy and policy-making process, and *Land and Power in Hawai'i* (1985), by George Cooper and Gavan Daws, a detailed description of the systematic acquisition of land, which enriched those who not much earlier had championed land reform.

Despite Hawai'i's superficial notoriety (and other more substantial reasons to expect that interpretations of contemporary politics and policy would be of interest to many readers) there is little analysis available. Testimony to this is provided by the fact that Tom Coffman's *To Catch a Wave,* a study of John Burns's 1970 election to the governorship, remains the most widely used textbook in classes on Hawaiian issues, despite its 1973 publication date.

Even today, people living on islands twenty-five hundred miles from the society with which they most identify can come to feel both inferior and unique, and these orientations become attached to attitudes about policy. Which of these feelings are reasonable in a given situation? Put a different way, what can people in Hawai'i learn from other places, and other places from Hawai'i? To take a case in point, to what extent is the juxtaposition of image and reality in Hawai'i's budgetary process different from that in other places, and what can we learn from those places? What is unusual about the way in which the struggle over land—as a source of wealth and as a means for controlling development—takes place in Hawai'i as opposed to the same struggle in America's nonisland states? How are the grievances and forms of protest of native Hawaiians different from and connected to other native Americans? We hope this book will shed some light on these issues for residents and for those with an interest in the fiftieth state.

We have divided the book into three parts comprising fifteen chapters. In part 1, "The Policy Environment," three chapters provide an overview of political, historical, social, and economic developments in Hawai'i. Norman Meller begins with a discussion of the historical basis for, and continuance of, centralization in the governance and administration of the island. Hawai'i is unique in the degree of centralization of power at the state level, and Meller examines some policy ramifications of this centralization. In chapter 2, David Hammes, Ronald Oliveira, and Marcia Sakai present an economic history of the state, comparing economic activity in the island with that of the mainland and discussing the constraints facing an island economy. In chapter 3, Jeffrey Crane and Alton Okinaka survey social characteristics of contemporary Hawai'i, including population dynamics, income differentials, and social class differences, and find significant social inequalities in the islands, which will continue to have policy implications. Just as social differences shape the public policy process, economic conditions affect the financial ability of a state government to respond to problems.

In part 2, titled "Policy Processes," the next three chapters examine unique or unusual attributes of the policy-formation process in the islands. Chapter 4, by Dan Boylan, contends that ethnicity is a pervasive, although usually denied, influence in politics and public policy, and ties to it the decline of the two-party system in the state. In chapter 5, Deane Neubauer takes us inside the budgeting process and argues that what appears to be a single systematic process actually masks highly politicized activity which shapes public policy. The final chapter in part 2, by Peter Adler, summarizes the uses of alternative ways of settling public conflicts and illustrates the use of mediation to resolve a difficult struggle over shrinking water reserves. Adler suggests that several factors have caused Hawai'i to be in the vanguard of the movement to find alternatives to traditional litigation in dispute resolution.

Part 3, "Policy Issues," consists of nine chapters that examine what we feel are the most pressing public policy issues in the state. In chapter 7, Richard Tobin and Dean Higuchi provide an overview of environmental problems. Hawai'i has a fragile ecosystem which has been radically altered since Westerners first arrived in the islands. Habitat destruction, water pollution, waste disposal, and other environmental problems can be expected to be public policy issues in Hawai'i's future. Chapters 8 and 9, by David Callies and

Kem Lowry, respectively, link issues that are among the most important facing Hawai'i's people: land use and planning and affordable housing. Callies reviews the legal and social issues involved in Hawai'i's regulation of land uses and development practices and argues against using voter initiatives in land-use decisions. Lowry in turn suggests that Hawai'i, especially Oahu, is moving toward market-driven housing development and away from a statewide planning process, and he raises questions about the wisdom of this shift in the face of Hawai'i's housing crisis. In chapter 10, Karl Kim analyzes another issue related to land scarcity: transportation. In an island environment with limited open space, transportation takes on a significance far greater than in most mainland states.

In chapter 11, James Mak and Marcia Sakai take a look at the economics of Hawai'i's greatest source of income: tourism. Tourism's dominance during the last twenty years may continue over the next twenty, but, they argue, its charact er is changing and it seems to be entering a new phase. Mak and Sakai explore the conditions favorable to future growth in this all-important industry. In chapter 12, Didrick Castberg summarizes crime and the criminal justice system in the islands. Although many of the crime-related problems in the islands are similar to those encountered on the mainland, the state has special concerns: notably an enormous illegal industry and a prison population that is disproportionately native Hawaiian. In chapter 13, Thomas Bean and Jan Zulich look at the educational system, unique in its statewide centralization of educational activities. Bean and Zulich discuss both the current controversy about decentralization in primary and secondary education and efforts to gain more autonomy at the University of Hawai'i. Chapter 14, by Edward Beechert, summarizes Hawai'i's labor history and interprets recent trends and developments in the configuration of labor that promise to alter social and class differences in the islands. Finally, in chapter 15, Haunani-Kay Trask argues strongly that native Hawaiians have begun to do what they must to counter the assaults made on them and their culture since contact in 1778 and to restore the native people to their rightful relationship with the land.

We do not agree with some of the positions taken by the authors contributing to this volume. Our intention in putting this collection together has not been to provide arguments everyone should accept or that neatly tie everything together, but to stimulate interest in, and discussion of, public policy in Hawai'i. To that end we want to share some of our reactions in reading these chapters in the hope that this will encourage a more critical reading of these writers.

Norman Meller (chapter 1) describes Hawai'i as a state with an usual degree of centralization and raises for us—in addition to his question about county home rule—the issue of whether there should be more localized governance. In particular, should Hawai'i have incorporated townships? For example, should Kailua-Kona on the Big Island be able to raise money, elect officials, and exercise greater control over its internal development? Should an elected council for the rural district of Ka'u have authoritative input into the process of deciding whether or not the state's proposed spaceport is developed there?

David Hammes, Ronald Oliveira, and Marcia Sakai (chapter 2) make the case that Hawai'i's best economic strategy is to capitalize on its geographical advantage as a trading hub in the Pacific. Given Hawai'i's fragile ecology, limited land space, and already rapidly increasing population densities, this raises for us questions about the validity of continued growth. Are there alternatives to further inclusion in the global market and the increased vulnerability to global economic forces inclusion this implies? Or is such inclusion inevitable no matter what the long-term consequences are for people in Hawai'i?

Jeffrey Crane and Alton Kinaka (chapter 3) make it clear that economic inequalities are contributing to the increasing rigidity of social class differences. Haunani-Kay Trask (chapter 15) paints a picture of native Hawaiians typically being placed at the bottom of island society politically, economically, and socially. And Didrick Castberg's data (chapter 12) show that native Hawaiians are highly over-represented in the prison population. Is there a connection between the issues these authors discuss? If so, is it worthy of more public concern than it has received? Although argued with moral force, is Trask's case for sovereignty a useful response to the inequalities Crane and Okinaka describe? Is it best for native Hawaiians to recover indigenous rights, or is increased participation in the traditional American democratic process a more realistic path to self-determination?

In chapter 4, Dan Boylan contends that, as political party competition has declined, ethnic voting has become more important. We want to ask whether voting on the basis of ethnic affiliation is more, or less, harmful than other ways voters decide. Is it better or worse to vote on this basis than in reaction to high-priced media campaigns sponsored by special interests or out of residual loyalty to a party perhaps too long in power. Of more significance, in a state where people are preoccupied more and more with earning enough money to meet living costs, what kind of investment in understanding candidates and issues can people be expected to make?

Deane Neubauer (chapter 5) tells us that, despite its systematic and objective appearance, the state budget is really several interwoven processes: the governor's budget, the legislative budget, and the agency budgets as reshuffled by the Department of Budget and Finance. Taken together, these reflect the state's underlying politics of centralization and control. Would it be better, from the standpoints of fiscal responsibility and policy coherence, if less effort were put into making the process appear objective and more into making it comprehensible and accessible to concerned agencies and publics?

In chapter 6, Peter Adler gives expression to his belief that there is something about Hawai'i's setting and culture which fosters the use of alternatives to court-related conflict resolution. If that is true, what might be done to build upon those attributes and go further in avoiding Americans' excessive reliance on lawyers and litigation as a way to resolve disputes?

After reviewing the state's environmental issues, Richard Tobin and Dean Higuchi (chapter 7) show that, controlling for its size, Hawai'i is far below average in what it devotes to environmental protection. They also contend there is a need to learn from other states before something happens which further threatens the islands most crucial resource: its natural setting. If they are correct that little is being done and the possibility of serious or catastrophic damage is real, what would have to happen for the need for environmental protection to be taken more seriously?

David Callies (chapter 8) concludes, among other things, that the formal planning process involving notice, hearings, and the input of professional planners is superior to the ad hoc planning procedures produced when land-use decisions are made by voter initiative. We might add that the relatively hidden planning process, which involves negotiations between local government officials, developers, and planners, responds to political pressures (such as campaign contributions to elected officials) to which most people may not be privy. This can produce plans that enrich a minority of insiders to the detriment of other, less privileged interests. Gavan Daws and George Cooper provide numerous examples of this less-than-desirable planning process (even identifying the beneficiaries of the process) in their book *Land and Power in Hawai'i*.

Kem Lowry (chapter 9) points to some interesting aspects of the conflict between controlled development and the construction of affordable housing. One thing he notes is that, although most people are for containing development by the more efficient use of already developed areas, people living in an area chosen for higher densities are inevitably against it. The result is both urban sprawl and high housing costs. What, if any, are the alternatives to this apparent trap?

Although Karl Kim (chapter 10) believes that a rapid transit system is a good idea for urban Honolulu, he is very careful to spell out the argument against that alternative and for expansion of the current bus system. Are there any realistic alternatives to either a rapid transit or bus system? Should the state, for example, create much stronger economic rewards for carpooling, or for not driving during rush hours, or for not owning a car?

James Mak and Marcia Sakai (chapter 11) raise several critical issues about today's tourism in the islands. One of these is about the benefits and costs of further growth of the industry. They ask who gains by continued tourist development. It is economic growth, but at what cost? It seems to us that, as a new convention center and still more hotels are planned, the down side of an economy based on tourism has not had any significant impact on the public policy debate in Hawai'i. What is required for the costs of such growth to be considered before overdevelopment threatens the industry's viability and further alienates residents?

Thomas Bean and Jan Zulich (chapter 13) describe the highly centralized system of educational administration, but see a trend toward decentralization. Their prediction raises a question: No matter how good an idea from an educational standpoint, given that tradition and interest groups enforce a high degree of centralization in virtually all institutional settings, how likely is it that education can, in the foreseeable future, establish a different pattern?

Edward Beechert (chapter 14) argues that Hawai'i's unions historically have been a critical factor in the social, political, and economic assimilation of immigrant agricultural and shipyard workers. He also contends that unions continue to be the proper means to mainstream today's marginalized workforce, particularly those in tourism and other service industries. But are today's unions the best way for these workers to obtain social and economic standing, protect basic employment rights, and provide an increased level of control over their lives? Are unions too complacent or too corrupt to be the best way of doing this? What other vehicles might better serve these workers?

The questions we raise don't have easy answers, or even simple responses, to which everyone will agree. Our contention is that a knowledgeable and critical struggle with the issues that face Hawai'i is most likely to produce public policy which will be seen as sensible, equitable, and, ultimately, more legitimate.

# I

## THE POLICY ENVIRONMENT

# 1

# POLICY CONTROL: INSTITUTIONALIZED CENTRALIZATION IN THE FIFTIETH STATE

## Norman Meller

Hawai'i's formal government is the most centralized and its administration the most integrated of all fifty states in the union, a distinction with long historical antecedents.[1] It is within this constricted institutional frame that all public policy in Hawai'i takes shape and then is carried out. The passage of time normally sees some reformulation of both policy and implementation; less frequently this is accompanied by modifications in the matrix of governmental institutions within which it occurs, but there has been only minimal change in the characteristic concentration that has distinguished constitutional government in Hawai'i.

### History

Although only admitted into the Union in 1959, Hawai'i had known constitutional government since 1840. Before that, Kamehameha the Great (1782–1819) governed as an absolute monarch, but his successors—even Kalakaua (1874–1891) at the height of monarchial resurgence—never succeeded in reestablishing kingly powers to the extent that they were not subject to curtailment by constitutional institutions within the executive branch of the government. During the days of the Hawaiian Republic (1894–1898), the executive power was vested not in the president but in a council composed of the president and heads of four executive departments. The commission which drafted Hawai'i's Organic Act, the federal law establishing Hawai'i's territorial government in 1900, disagreed over placing the executive power of the territory in the hands of one individual, and the majority's recommendation favoring this prevailed. Nevertheless, the act did delineate the powers of some executive officers, and in these areas the scope of the governor's authority was correspondingly curtailed.

A half century later, the state constitution continued the trend of history by further strengthening the chief executive. By vesting the executive power in the governor, but failing to incorporate constitutional checks in the executive branch requiring the sharing of that power (for example, requiring gubernatorial consultation or approval by executive officials to gubernatorial acts) and by failing to make self-executing grants of authority to designated executive agencies, statehood returned a high degree of integration to the central government. Structurally, this recalled the days of Kamehameha the Great. The chief executive possessed the ability to exercise direction over the full gamut of state administration, but now was aided by modern staff agencies that facilitate control.[2]

Hawai'i first became known to the Western world as a very isolated group of petty kingdoms. By 1810, a single monarchy with archipelagic jurisdiction resulted from Kamehameha's conquest of all the islands but Kauai and Niihau, and their king's acknowledgment of him as suzerain. Kamehameha and his successors ruled directly, with the kings' appointed governors serving as their representatives in island-wide administrative districts, some spanning clusters of adjacent islands. Although attempted during the period of the Hawaiian monarchy, little success was achieved in establishing local self-government through New England–type town meetings, school districts, and road districts. At the time of annexation of the islands by the United States in 1898, the short-lived republic was the sole governmental unit in the islands. The United States Congress permitted perpetuation of this by phrasing the Organic Act, the legislation delineating the territory's structures, so as to authorize—but not mandate—the creation of "counties and town and city municipalities within the territory."[3] It took five years and some congressional prodding before territorial statute established Hawai'i's counties, whose boundaries mirrored Kamehameha's administrative groupings of Hawai'i's major islands.[4] With minor exceptions, such as the creation of soil conservation districts and replacement of the county of Oahu by the city and county of Honolulu in 1907, these counties continue to constitute the sum total of local government in Hawai'i.

The plantation system that evolved during the monarchy remained a dominant factor in Hawai'i's political life until after World War II, and this system in good part provides the explanation for

Hawai'i's limited local government and the centralization of governmental affairs. Until the decline of the plantation system, around a third to half of the islands' nonurban civilian population dwelt on Hawai'i's sugar and pineapple plantations. There was little need to erect local government for them, as the plantations attended to most of their municipal-type requirements. Only such functions as schools, supplemental roads and their policing, and judicial enforcement of the law through the lower courts, traditionally identified with local government, were not furnished by the plantations themselves. These public services could readily be rendered by the field offices of the central government. For those people not on plantations—and a good many of them resided in urban Honolulu— Hawai'i's government could directly serve their requirements. Consequently, a pattern of centralization had become institutionalized in the islands by the time the county government statute was enacted in 1905.

*Governmental Functions*

In setting up local governments, the territory hesitantly allocated some functions of municipal character to them, and the central government continued to administer the remainder as well as all those concerning the islands as a group. With growth in the scope of government, and with new activities undertaken, the same tilt toward centralization persisted; indeed, rather than implementing the counties' fiscal powers when their limited resources became overtaxed, the territorial government assumed direct performance of some responsibilities previously assigned to the counties. That the same general approach to governance continues is well evidenced by the fact that today's expanded functions in health, education, and welfare fall almost totally within the purview of state administration. The state government has preempted the judicial function. Other areas wholly within its jurisdiction are these: agriculture, forestry, and fish and game conservation; banks, commerce, and consumer protection; labor and industrial relations; prisons and corrections; and the public service enterprises encompassing airports and harbors. The state and the counties divide responsibility for the remaining functions of government, but, with the exception of those that are inherently local, such as garbage collection, state administration accounts for the major share: public housing, parks and recreation, and roads and highways serve as illustrations of central predominance.

Centralization in Hawai'i has always been distinguished more by the assumption of direct performance by the central government than the assignment of functions to the counties to be performed under territorial, and later state, administrative oversight. However, there has been no reluctance to apply the entire gamut of techniques potentially available for assuring central supervision of local performance. These range from the seemingly innocuous requirement that county officials submit periodic reports, to the extremes of removal of a county official and authorization of central government personnel to assume jurisdiction over what is normally a county activity. Hawai'i's attorney general in the past has replaced county attorneys in conducting criminal prosecutions, state monies have been withheld from local governments until they complied with specific state criteria, and the central audit of county expenditures is no novelty. Rather, given Hawai'i's limited size and with the bulk of its population residing on Oahu, the easiest course for assuring the execution of policy in the manner desired by policy makers of the state has been to continue the historic practice of placing implementation of that policy in the central bureaucracy.

## Executive

While attempting to become a state, Hawai'i faced a repetitive stalemate in Congress. Hawai'i adopted the alternative of "force action," rather than waiting for the passage of congressional legislation authorizing the drafting of a state constitution.[5] The convention delegates who assembled in Honolulu in 1950 consequently undertook a dual task, proposing an executive structure appropriate for the new state and producing a model constitution which would further Hawai'i's case for statehood. What could cloak the constitution with greater respectability than to incorporate the then-prevailing canons for state administrative reorganization? Their concentration of authority in the governor, through eliminating other elective executive officials, and reduction of the breadth of his span of control closely coincided with current practice in Hawai'i and were fully consonant with prevailing island attitudes. No matter whether this was a Machiavellian solution or a happy coincidence, the delegates applied themselves to their work buttressed with the current public administration literature and the counsel of private citizens interested in achieving "efficiency and economy" in government.[6]

Prior to statehood, Hawai'i knew no elected officer serving in the executive branch of the Hawaiian government.[7] As a territory, Hawai'i had not been allowed to name its own governor, consistent with then-existing federal policy applicable to American possessions. This the state constitution proceeded to rectify, and, in addition to a provision for popularly choosing the governor, the constitution also substituted an elected lieutenant governor for the Washington-designated territorial secretary. But there innovation stopped until later constitutional amendments tacked on an elected Board of Education and the anomalous Office of Hawaiian Affairs. At the time of drafting the state constitution, Hawai'i's short ballot was surpassed by only one state, New Jersey, and today its limited provisions for elected executive officials is still exceptional. Even the impact of electing the lieutenant governor was narrowed by failure of the constitution to confer any powers upon the office other than these: succession to the governorship, and the duty of placing on the ballot the question of whether or not to call a constitutional convention should Hawai'i's legislature neglect to put the issue on the ballot periodically. Nor has the lieutenant governor been endowed with statutory responsibilities significantly different than those of the former territorial secretary. Consequently Hawai'i's governor, like his predecessors, remains the dominant executive officer in the islands,[8] but now that power is buttressed by a range of modern staff services and an executive budget that affords him direction over state agency expenditures.[9]

At the time of statehood, the territorial administration included some twenty-eight major and thirty-five minor agencies, commissions, and advisory boards, as well as twenty-three regulatory boards. A constitutional ceiling—following the precedents of Massachusetts, New Jersey, and New York, and reinforced by the recommendations of the model state constitution—directed that all executive agencies be compressed into not more than twenty principal departments, grouped, as far as practicable, according to common purpose and related function. Only temporary commissions or special purpose agencies were to be excepted. Consolidation rapidly followed, and Hawai'i's first state legislature compacted all agencies into eighteen principal executive departments, excluding the offices of governor and lieutenant governor. Despite readjustments that have occurred subsequently, the number of eighteen departments persists when the University of Hawai'i is classed as a department.[10] To keep within this small compass, the governor's office has been used as a catch-all; today it incorporates some eight disparate programs, including the Executive Office on Aging, the Office of State Planning, and an Agriculture Coordinating Committee.

Hawai'i's constitution did not merely repeat the usual phraseology vesting the executive power of the state in the governor; it also declared that each of the principal departments is under his supervision. The governor appoints all department heads with the consent of the senate, except for the state's two educational boards; the elected school board chooses the superintendent of education for the public schools and the board of regents selects the University of Hawai'i's president. The departmental heads hold office for terms expiring with that of the governor and except for the attorney general, he may remove them at his pleasure; only in the case of the state's chief legal officer must the senate consent to the removal. Cumulatively, these powers equip the governor with capacity to play a dominant administrative role throughout his term.

The approved tenets of the administrative reorganization movement fitted like a template over all of these provisions incorporated in the state constitution. Authority and responsibility are concentrated in the governor, provision is made for a small number of integrated departments, and the use of boards and commissions for purely administrative work is disapproved.[11] (However, while Hawai'i's constitution frowns upon the use of collegial bodies as administrators, it does direct that the public management of natural resources be vested in one or more executive boards.) For full measure, the state constitution empowers the governor with an item veto, avoids the earmarking of funds, which otherwise might restrict the inclusive scope of the executive budget, and makes express provision for the postaudit function. Constitutional sequestering of funds for specific purposes would have correspondingly reduced the ability of the governor to budget them for other state functions, and accompanying the provision for postaudit is an internal audit system under gubernatorial control that keeps the governor apprised of ongoing state activities. Except that it fails to authorize executive formulation of reorganization plans (at the time of statehood this had only recently been elevated to the importance of constitutional status) Hawai'i's constitution incorporates all of the "tools of management" championed by the administrative reorganization movement. With a constitutional framework designed to facilitate the integration of state administration, Hawai'i became a state with potential for having "one of the most powerful executive officers in the United States."[12]

## Legislative

Prior to Hawai'i being admitted as a state, the legitimacy of the territorial legislature was challenged in the federal courts for disproportionately underrepresenting the people on Oahu. The fifteen-member territorial senate and thirty-member house of representatives had not been reapportioned since the passage of the Organic Act, despite the express direction of Congress to re-adjust membership with the 1910 census "and from time to time thereafter."

The delegates who drafted Hawai'i's "hope chest" constitution proposed a compromise bicameral legislature of expanded size (sen-ate—25 members, house—51 members), with house of representa-tives district lines that reflected the distribution of Hawai'i's registered voters and in which Oahu would gain a clear majority of membership. To turn the thrust of judicial inquiry, the U.S. Con-gress hurriedly amended the Organic Act to adopt the relevant por-tions of the proposed constitution, replete with enlarged chambers, revised districts, and the new apportionment formulas, deleting the old. The effect was multifold. (1) Seven years before the impact of the landmark case of *Baker* v. *Carr* swept through the mainland like a whirlwind, reapportioning state legislatures Hawai'i had experi-enced the threat of a federal court–directed redistricting. (2) Even before statehood, voters in Hawai'i enjoyed implementation of part of their proposed constitution. (3) Further court action based on the denial of equal protection was still very much in the offing, both due to the use of the registered-voter formula for apportioning legisla-tures and because the convention compromises in effect had pre-served perpetual neighbor island control of the senate.[13] A number of later judicial decisions on Hawai'i's malapportionment, including one rendered by the United States Supreme Court, resulted in a ma-terially restructured state legislature.[14] While maintaining the size of each house, representation is now allocated on an adjusted pop-ulation base, numerical dominance by the neighbor islands has been broken, and the constitutional confinement of legislative districts within county boundaries need no longer be observed. Today some members are elected from "canoe" districts comprised of parts of several counties separated by miles of open ocean.

At the time of statehood, the median number of legislators from a single district was five senators and three representatives. Multi-membered legislative districts in Hawai'i date back to the initiation of legislative government under the monarchy. This practice, too, was eventually changed by judicial redistricting. After the Federal District Court of Hawai'i ordered temporary use of single-membered districts in both houses, the state's constitutional reapportionment commission found it politically too difficult to revert back to multi-membered districts without physically displacing incumbents. It is claimed that multimembered districts encourage the holding of a broader perspective by affording political parties and individual candidates a degree of maneuverability not possible with the single-membered district. This is held particularly true in view of the long familiarity of Hawai'i's people with "plunking," where, by failing to vote for the allotted number of candidates in a multimembered district, voters give their favorite candidate both their cast vote and the indirect benefit of his fellow candidates' failure to have their tallies increased. To that extent, the legislative frame for policy formulation has been narrowed as a consequence of Hawai'i's lengthy experience with court-ordered reapportionment.

Voters in about half of the states in the union may directly propose and review legislation through initiative and referendum. Hawai'i has never permitted direct voter participation in state lawmaking other than for adoption of constitutional amendments, whether proposed by convention or legislature. Nor do state bond issues require voter consent, as in some states on the mainland. A concerted effort was launched at the last constitutional convention, in 1978, to incorporate some form of voter initiative in Hawai'i's constituent document, but this was strongly opposed. Overtly, the objection was that popular participation in lawmaking would give undue weight to organized minorities; underlying this was the fear that the initiative would threaten entrenched positions in Hawai'i. Provisions for the initiative and referendum process are included in the charters of the City and County of Honolulu and Hawai'i's counties.[15] Indignation over a recent Hawai'i Supreme Court decision which upheld a state statute on zoning controls over action taken under charter-sanctioned initiative, promises the whole subject will be reviewed in Hawai'i; for the moment, at least local initiative is assured.[16] Meanwhile the case stands as but another illustration of Hawai'i's extreme centralization.

## Judiciary

Volume 1 of the Hawai'i Reports commences with a case decided in January 1847,[17] and the same, unbroken series of cases extends to the present, spanning monarchy, republic, territory, and now state. On annexation "the courts of Hawai'i were reported to be already established and functioning in the American mode: [T]he organization and procedure of the Hawaiian courts had been patterned after courts found on the mainland [particularly the courts of Massachusetts]."[18] For the most part, the Organic Act merely extended the court system as it was, incorporating such minor changes as necessitated by territorial status, and created a federal district court mainly to enforce United States laws.[19] The territorial courts fitted into the same relative position as that occupied by the state courts on the mainland, except that both federal and territorial judges in Hawai'i owed their appointment to the president, with U.S. Senate consent. Upon statehood, federal designation of territorial judges ceased, and the former territorial supreme court was enlarged.

The metamorphosis of the judiciary did not end with statehood. The inferior district courts and, to a minor extent, the circuit courts had occupied a somewhat anomalous position during the territorial period, as the counties paid part of their cost and received some of the revenues derived from their process. Now, three decades later, there is no question but that the judicial function is solely lodged in the state government, with a single judicial system under the supervision of the chief justice aided by a constitutionally created administrative director, and funded by the state treasury. Of even greater import, by virtue of constitutional amendment, the court system has been expanded by the addition of an intermediate appellate court to relieve the state supreme court of part of its review burden, judicial tenure has been lengthened, and the political component previously inherent in the naming of justices and judges for Hawai'i's courts has been reduced.

The Jacksonian movement of the early 1800s in the United States which sought to make all public officials—including judges—democratically responsible through elections, never took root in Hawai'i. Although some attention was given to an elected judiciary when drafting Hawai'i's constitution, the majority of the delegates considered this too radical an innovation. Instead, they opted for the course of gubernatorial nomination followed by state senate confirmation. At the time, the somewhat median position of the Missouri Plan (election after a probationary period on a yes/no ballot of judges appointed by the governor from lists of nominees selected on merit) was just gaining attention. However, with the spread of the merit selection concept to the judiciary of other states, a highly pub-

licized effort reminiscent of orchestrated legislative lobbying unsuc-
cessfully sought to convince the 1968 constitutional convention to
adopt a nonpartisan means for selecting Hawai'i's judges.[20] A decade and another convention later, after a more subtle campaign
and buoyed by the range of merit selection and merit retention
plans found on the mainland, the 1978 convention agreed on a compromise for choosing justices and judges. It created the Judicial Selection Commission, composed of executive, legislative, and judicial
nominees as well as some chosen from the Hawai'i bar. The commission prepares a list of recommended persons for each judicial vacancy. For all but district courts, the governor designates one
individual from the list submitted, and submits the appointment to
the senate for consent. The chief justice similarly fills vacancies in
the district courts, but without need for senatorial confirmation.[21]
Once appointed, a judge's term may be renewed, upon commission
review and approval, without any involvement of governor or senate.
The tendency for the law profession to regard the court system as its
private preserve is partially countered by the requirement that a
majority of nonlawyers comprise the commission. However, posses-
sion of a license to practice law in the state remains an essential req-
uisite to sit on the Hawai'i bench. The result of the constitutional
creation of the Judicial Selection Commission has been to introduce
both a nonpartisan means for scrutinizing candidates' qualifica-
tions and capabilities for judicial office and a unique merit retention
system, but not to banish partisan politics from the entire appointment and confirmation process.

## State Agencies on the Brink of Semiautonomy

Various state programs rely upon the receipt of federal monies
for at least partial funding, a situation which normally entails state
compliance with federally imposed standards and conditions. One of
the effects is to narrow the parameters within which Hawai'i's executive and legislators may shape the formulation and implementation of policy. The degree of autonomy available to four agencies
within the state government similarly constricts the scope of gubernatorial and legislative management. Two of them—the University
of Hawai'i as a body corporate, and the Department of Education,
run by an elected school board—are considered in chapter 13 which
is on education. To the extent that all four agencies actually operate
outside the normal constraints raised by the governor and legisla-

ture, this introduces an element of decentralization not familiar to the islands, with potential for significant impact on governmental policy in Hawai'i.

## Hawaiian Homestead Commission

At the end of the territory's second decade, the U.S. Congress created the Hawaiian Homes Commission (HHC) for the purpose of improving the welfare of native Hawaiians through homesteading, financial aids, and other assistance related to their rehabilitation. The HHC is funded in part by income realized from lands assigned to the commission for that purpose. With the admission to statehood, Hawai'i incorporated into its constitution a compact with the federal government to further HHC activities. While the governor appoints the members of the commission who exercise direction over the operations of the Department of Hawaiian Home Lands, including its chairperson who sits in his cabinet, some of the activities of the department are beyond his or the legislature's control. As illustration, by virtue of the delimitation contained in the HHC act, specified benefits may be made available only to native Hawaiians. A "native Hawaiian" is defined as one who is at least fifty percent descended from the islands' indigenous inhabitants.

## Office of Hawaiian Affairs

Mainly as a result of dissatisfaction with the limited accomplishments of the HHC, a decade ago Hawai'i established by constitutional amendment what may become an independent branch of government—the Office of Hawaiian Affairs (OHA). Voters of Hawaiian ancestry choose a board of trustees, also of Hawaiian ancestry, at elections held simultaneously for other state officers. The trustees are charged to work for the betterment of the condition of ethnic Hawaiians, with OHA being "the principal public agency of the state responsible for the performance, development, and coordination of all programs and activities impacting on Hawaiians, with the exception of programs administered by the Hawaiian Homes Commission."[22] At the time OHA was created, a direction was also added to the state constitution that federal lands returned to Hawai'i upon statehood be held in trust "for native Hawaiians and the general public."[23] State statute determines the power to be exercised by the trustees, and also presently allots twenty percent of the income from this trust fund to OHA, limited to "native Hawaiians."[24] In addition, operating funds to benefit all Hawaiians are appropriated to OHA out of the state treasury. The political dynamics of the trustees' elective character and OHA's distinctive ethnic base portend OHA's gradual disengagement from effective state policy control other than that exerted by the nature and amount of resources made available under the state's legislative process. Some see OHA as ultimately possessing limited sovereignty analogous to Indian tribal government on the mainland.

### Post-Statehood Decentralization

Conventional wisdom in the islands attributes centralization during the territorial period to the near-monopoly of organized politics exercised by the Republican Party. This constitutes but an abridged way of referring to a combination of forces that found their collective expression in the symbolism of the Republican Party, its program and leaders. Included is the *haole* (Caucasian) oligopoly centered in Honolulu that exerted its influence on the course of governmental policy through the Republican Party, which it strongly supported with both work and money. Also encompassed is the defensive strategy followed by the neighbor islands to counter the colossus that was Honolulu: through continuing a malapportioned territorial legislature in Republican control they succeeded in obtaining a greater share of governmental funds than warranted by their proportion of the citizen population. And after the threat of the Home Rule Party was turned,[25] territorial government policy remained safely in the hands of the Republicans; even when a Democratic administration in Washington filled Hawai'i's gubernatorial seat with a Democratic nominee, this failed to make much change due to Republican dominance of the territorial legislature and government on the neighbor islands.

Although the Democratic Party in Hawai'i remained eclipsed, some candidates running at least nominally under its banner did succeed. This was particularly true in the City and County of Honolulu.[26] It was only to be expected, then, that such local government as did exist would remain anemic and be kept internally decentralized, since the counties were but creatures of the territory and subject to plenary territorial government control. To change this would require reversal of political dominance and capture of both legislative and executive branches of the central government by the Democratic Party. Meanwhile the platform of the

Democratic Party perennially pledged it to the strengthening of local government.

The signs of reversal in political party dominance began appearing after World War II, and by statehood the Democratic Party had become politically ascendant. Thereafter, the Republican Party went into near eclipse and since then has been playing a minority role in the islands, in many ways comparable to that of the Democrats previously. Despite the turnabout in political fortunes, the centralization of Hawai'i's government continues almost unmodified.

In the first flush of victory, the Democrats transferred police and liquor-control functions to the counties by eliminating gubernatorial appointment of their local boards. Instead of the legislature establishing county government by statute, constitutional provision now empowered each of the political subdivisions to draft its own self-government charter. This they quickly proceeded to act upon, and in the process began adopting highly centralized administrative systems, reflecting on the local level the form found in state government. However, the state constitution did not throw all caution to the winds, and it still allows state statute to prescribe limits and procedures on such local action, although subsequent amendment did narrow this by prohibiting any requirement for a local charter to run the gauntlet of approval by a legislative body. In addition, charter provisions regarding "executive, legislative, and administrative structure and organization" of local government are declared to take precedence over state statute.[27] But as each political subdivision may only exercise those powers that are conferred under general law, and the legislature still retains ability to allocate governmental functions, the final authority over what local governments in the islands can and cannot do resides in the state government.

Until 1978, the counties possessed no taxing powers other than those delegated to them by the legislature. Now the state constitution grants the revenues from the real property tax and exclusive control over its administration to the counties. Nevertheless, they are still dependent upon state grants to supplement property tax collections and the smaller revenues derived from license charges and user fees. By denying local government access to tax bases premised upon income or selected transactions, the state government continues to set effective boundaries beyond which the counties do not have the fiscal capacity to act. Somewhat ironically, perhaps as demonstration that turnabout is fair play, the state constitution now prohibits the legislature from transferring any new program to the counties, or mandating them to increase the level of services under any existing program, without also sharing in its cost.[28]

Belying the past, when the administration of nearly everything governmental appeared to gravitate inexorably toward the central government at the capital in Honolulu, today there is also a tendency to weigh local governments' capacity to undertake new functions. Contributing to this has been a reversal of the population movement to Oahu and a gradual shifting of the tourist income base outward from Waikiki to the neighbor islands, so these islands' seeking of protection in the state government against the City and County of Honolulu no longer seems so imperative. However, this has not yet stopped the long-term flow of functions to the state government. An example is the new State Water Management Commission, which is gradually stripping powers from local water authorities. Notwithstanding the Democratic Party's championing of home rule in Hawai'i, a Democratic state administration has, since statehood, repeatedly enacted laws and created authorities overriding the City and County of Honolulu. Abstract principle easily becomes subordinated to the political reality of partisan conflict—whether interparty or internecine—so that the centralization of Hawai'i's government continues.

## Notes

1. See Norman Meller, "Centralization in Hawai'i: Retrospect and Prospect," *American Political Science Review* 52 (1) (March 1958), p. 98.

2. Except for the unusual constitutional provision made for the Hawaiian Homes Commission, when the state constitution became effective no state executive could successfully challenge the governor's direction, as was possible under the Organic Act.

3. Hawaiian Organic Act, sec. 56, U.S., *Statutes at Large*, XXXI, 141.

4. Besides Hawai'i, Kauai, Maui, and Oahu counties, another county consisting of the Hansen's disease settlement on Molokai was later created and placed under the administrative direction of the Department of Health.

5. Seventeen states, including Alaska and Hawai'i, have joined the union without prior authorization of Congress to set up their constitutional governments. Roger Bell, *Last Among Equals* (Honolulu: University of Hawai'i Press, 1984), p. 325, n. 2. Also see Daniel W. Tuttle, " 'State' Elections prior to Admittance into the Union," report no. 1, 1951, Legislative Reference Bureau, University of Hawai'i.

6. For the mechanics of drafting Hawai'i's state constitution see Henry Wells, "Constitutional Conventions in Hawai'i, Puerto Rico, and Alaska," in W. Brooke Graves, ed., *Major Problems in State Constitutional Revision* (Chicago: Public Administration Service, 1960), p. 52. Also see Norman Meller, *"With an Understanding Heart"—Constitution Making in Hawai'i* (New York: National Municipal League, 1971).

7. Interestingly, the closest Hawai'i came to a popularly chosen chief executive was during the monarchy when it became necessary for the legislature to choose a successor to Kamehameha V after his death without an heir. A plebiscite voiced the wishes of the populace to guide the legislature. See Ralph S. Kuykendall, *The Hawaiian Kingdom, 1854–1874* (Honolulu: University of Hawai'i Press, 1953), pp. 242–44.

8. Election by statewide vote of course furnishes the lieutenant governor with a potential base for becoming a political rival of the governor.

9. Not only does the governor have an executive budget including the proposed expenditures of all state agencies, but after legislative approval he or she may withhold monies appropriated.

10. The attorney general has ruled that, as the constitution declares the regents of the university to be a body corporate, it is not one of the twenty principal departments contemplated by the constitution, and its president need not sit on the governor's cabinet.

11. See Ferrel Heady, *State Constitutions: The Structure of Administration,* no. 4 of State Constitutional Studies Project (New York: National Municipal League, 1961), pp. 16, 17; Rowland Egger, "Power is not Enough," *State Government* 13 (8) (August 1940) p. 149; A. E. Buck, *The Reorganization of State Governments in the United States* (New York: Columbia University Press, 1938), pp. 14, 15.

12. Gale Lowrie, "A Constitution for Hawai'i," *American Political Science Review* 45 (3) (September 1951), p. 771.

13. See Norman Meller and Harold S. Roberts, "Hawai'i" in Eleanore Bushnell, ed., *Impact of Reapportionment on the Thirteen Western States* (Salt Lake City: University of Utah Press, 1970), p. 117.

14. Ibid., pp. 118–27; Anne F. Lee and Peter J. Herman, "Ensuring the Right to Equal Representation: How to Prepare or Challenge Legislative Reapportionment Plans," *University of Hawai'i Law Review* 5 (1) (1983), p. 1.

15. Initiative and referendum in Hawai'i and Kauai; only initiative in Maui and the City and County of Honolulu. Matters excluded from consideration under initiative and referendum vary, as do the specified procedures to be followed.

16. *Kaiser Hawai'i–Kai Development Co.* v. *C & C of Honolulu,* vol. 70, Hawai'i Reports, 480 (1989).

17. *Wood* v. *Stark, Jr.,* vol. 1 Hawai'i Reports, 9, (1847).

18. Samuel P. King, "The Federal Courts and the Annexation of Hawai'i," *Western Legal History* 2 (1) (winter/spring 1989), p. 8.

19. The addition of a separate federal district court in Hawai'i was viewed as an aberration, as practice in other American territories was for the territorial courts also to exercise federal jurisdiction. Ibid., pp. 15, 16.

20. Meller, *"With an Understanding Heart,"* pp. 107, 108.

21. Subjecting the appointment of district court judges to senatorial consent is now being advocated.

22. Legislative Reference Bureau, "Guide to Government in Hawai'i," 9th ed. (Honolulu: 1989).

23. Hawai'i Constitution, art. 12, sec. 4.

24. Ibid., sec. 6.

25. The Home Rule Party succeeded in electing Hawai'i's first delegate to Congress and gaining a majority in each chamber of the Territorial Legislature. At the next election a Republican delegate was sent to Washington; the Home Rulers comprised only a minority in the Territorial Senate and held but half the seats in the House of Representatives. Thereafter they virtually disappeared from the political scene.

26. In the period 1905–1945, Democratic mayors outnumbered Republicans in the City and County (10–7). During the same period, elected Democrats holding the comparable post (chairman) in the neighbor islands were almost nonexistent (Hawai'i had one). Republicans predominated in the other elected positions: C & C: R—51, D—66; Hawai'i: R—152, D—37; Kauai: R—169, D—12; Maui: R—191, D—7.

27. Hawai'i Constitution, art. 8, sec. 2. Note that there is no reference to judicial structure and organization being within the scope of local government control.

28. Ibid., sec. 3.

# 2

# THE STATE ECONOMY

## David L. Hammes, Ronald A. Oliveira, and Marcia Sakai

In this chapter we give a brief economic history of the Hawaiian islands and a comparative look at the state's economic makeup. Without a feel for the composition of an economy, its important sectors and those less important, and its economic interrelations with both neighbors and the national economy, there can be no informed policy discussion.

### The Rise and Decline of Industries in Hawai'i

As a small, island economy, Hawai'i stands alone among U.S. states in its distance from neighboring states and foreign nations. Its mid-Pacific location has been both beneficial and costly, affecting Hawai'i's comparative advantage in the production and trade of goods and services.

Prior to the arrival of the British Captain James Cook in 1778, Hawai'i was a closed economy, essentially isolated from the rest of the world. Traditional accounts place the population of the time at two hundred thousand to three hundred thousand people. However, a recent reexamination of population suggests the possibility of a number closer to eight hundred thousand people.[1] While constrained by the limited amount of land with accessible water supplies, the absence of metals, and the absence of draft animals, the closed economy more than adequately supported this native population.

The economic system itself was organized around a highly structured hierarchy headed by a king followed by lesser chiefs, priests, and, finally, commoners. Providing the institutional glue for the economy was the *kapu* system, a system of rules governing behavior and relationships between members of the society. As with

29

most feudal societies, the commoners produced goods for consumption, while the priests and chiefs provided services to maintain stability of the society.

Cook's arrival and the publication of his *Voyages* ended the isolation of the islands and started a historical sequence of events which resulted in the eventual demise of traditional Hawaiian society. The agent of change was trade. Significant trade arose with the increasing number of ships stopping for provisions, first en route to the fur posts of the North American continent and later with the expansion of whaling into the Pacific. The fur trade and subsequent sandalwood trade clearly increased consumption possibilities for the economy, but the gains from trade were not distributed evenly. Indeed, the commoners paid dearly for the increased consumption of the chiefs in labor diverted from food production. Increasing Western contact also placed the *kapu* system under severe stress and weakened the established social fabric as the economy shifted from a traditional to a trade-based market economy.

One of the consequences of the whaling trade, in particular, was an increased presence of foreigners residing in the islands. Whaling had established commercial banks and a professional merchant class, and a greater Western presence increased missionary attempts to bring the native Hawaiians to Christianity. Foreign investment in mercantile and various agricultural ventures in Hawai'i was especially risky, however, because the existing land tenure system essentially reserved all lands to the king. Foreigners agitated for fee simple ownership of land, a concept eventually embodied in the Great Mahele (1848). The Mahele distributed lands to the crown, the government, the chiefs, and the commoners. Within two years, foreigners also obtained the right to fee simple ownership, and the aggregation of land parcels began soon thereafter. The risk attached to land ownership was greatly reduced.

The development of sugar as a major export commodity came with the U.S. Civil War and the decline of whaling in the Pacific. Union blockades of Southern ports prevented the flow of sugar to the North, resulting in surges in the price of sugar. At the same time, decreasing numbers of whaling ships released the capital which might otherwise have been used to finance the extensive whaling voyages. Both events generated significant interest in developing sugar production. In 1860, 722 tons of raw sugar were exported; by 1865, export increased to 7,609 tons.[2]

The Reciprocity Treaty of 1876 propelled the sugar-driven Hawaiian economy into the twentieth century. This treaty laid the foundation for the overthrow of the Hawaiian monarchy in 1893 and later annexation of the kingdom to the United States in 1898. The end of the Civil War and the return of normal relations between the Northern and Southern United States had depressed sugar prices. Hawaiian producers were competing with other foreign sugar producers in this depressed market. The treaty resulted in the negotiation of tariff removals from Hawaiian sugar (1½¢ to 4¢ on the pound), which gave Hawaiian producers a distinct market advantage. An 1887 revision of the treaty also established United States interests in Pearl Harbor as a potential naval base. Sugar production exploded. Between 1870 and 1880, production tripled from 9,000 tons to 28,000 tons and the number of plantations tripled from twenty to sixty-three. By 1890, sugar production was at 105,000 tons, with capital investment of $28 million, compared to $3 million in 1870.[3]

Over this period, the sugar industry made tremendous gains in productivity per acre with changes in the technology of production, the increased use of capital, and the organization of production. Increasing plantation size promoted and benefited from risk taking and the specialization of tasks. Agents increasingly provided the financing, transportation, insurance, and banking functions previously carried out by plantation owners, who were the growers. Fluctuations in business conditions and loan defaults eventually led to consolidation of many plantations under agent ownership. By the 1930s, five such factor companies, known as the "Big Five," controlled over ninety-six percent of the sugar crop.[4]

Sugar's contribution to the economy today is essentially determined by federal price support mechanisms which have kept the value of production between $300 million and $400 million a year since 1981.[5] Sugar production represented 1.1 percent of gross state product (GSP) in 1987.[6] Increasing pressures on the industry, brought about by relatively high costs of production, increased competition from sugar substitutes, and the uncertainty of federal policy regarding the price support system have resulted in the conversion of marginal lands into alternative crops and contraction of both acreage and employment. Nevertheless, sugar continues to be a force in state policy making.

Although the 1876 Reciprocity Treaty established United States interests in Hawai'i, a large federal presence did not occur until the years surrounding World War II. From 1941 to 1944, the state's population doubled, mostly attributable to the influx of the military. Federal government spending increased from $40 million in 1940 to

$800 million in 1944. Local recession followed the war, with federal spending plummeting to $224 million in 1946. However, military spending increased during the Korean War in the early 1950s and the Vietnam War in the late 1960s and early 1970s. Indeed, expenditures related to the Vietnam War contributed substantially to the growth of the economy during that period. Entering the 1990s, a federal military presence remains a stable element in the Hawaiian economy, contributing approximately 10 percent of the GSP.

At the threshold of statehood in 1959, visitor expenditures accounted for $109 million, sugar and pineapple together accounted for $251 million, and the federal government accounted for $316 million in export earnings.[7] In the first decade of statehood, 1960–1970, the tourist industry, measured in visitor spending, grew at a real annual rate of 13.6 percent. In contrast, real GSP grew at 5.8 percent per year over the same period.[8] Contributing to the rapid rate of growth in tourism were decreases in the relative price of air travel, growth in real income in the major markets of the U.S., and the advent of jet travel. Tourism's rate of growth has slowed from the initial highs as the industry has matured. Still, the tourist industry is the driving force behind Hawai'i's economy today, accounting for 33.4 percent of the GSP in 1987.[9]

## Trade and Interrelationships

Reliance on trade makes the Hawaiian economy highly dependent on foreign, and U.S. national, economic performance. This is especially true as small changes in the size of vast national economies may result in proportionately larger swings in the smaller Hawaiian economy. In 1988, the nominal Hawaiian GSP of $21.28 billion was slightly less than 0.5 percent of the U.S. gross national product (GNP).

Hawai'i derives a much larger percentage, relative to the nation, of its GSP from trading activity. Total exports accounted for 54 percent of the Hawaiian GSP in 1988. Nationwide export earnings in 1987 accounted for only 5.5 percent of the U.S. GNP.[10]

Not only is trade more important for Hawai'i, the pattern of Hawaiian trade differs from that of the nation as a whole. As shown in Table 2.1, which compares the national and Hawaiian exports to Japan and Asia as a whole, trade with these regions is relatively more important for Hawai'i than it is for the U.S.

### Table 2.1: Export Trade to Japan and Asia as a Percentage of Total Exports[11]

| | Japan | | Asia | |
|---|---|---|---|---|
| | 1975 | 1986 | 1975 | 1986 |
| United States | 8.9% | 12.4% | 26.2% | 29.7% |
| | 1987 | | 1987 | |
| Hawai'i | 26.8% | | 62.3% | |

Looking at trade with the U.S. mainland as well as with foreign countries, Hawai'i's direct income from the four major export industries, raw sugar and molasses, fresh and processed pineapple, defense expenditures, and visitor expenditures, rose sixfold from 1970 to 1987. During that period, the portion of the Hawai'i GSP attributable to these export industries has risen from 35 percent to 46 percent.[13]

As shown in Table 2.2, Japan and Asia are also major shippers to the United States and Hawai'i.

Within the four major export industries listed above, only visitor expenditures have grown faster than the state GSP, rising from 13.5 percent of the GSP in 1970 to 33.4 percent of the GSP in 1987. The other three industries, raw sugar and molasses, fresh and processed pineapple, and defense expenditures, taken together, have fallen from 21.8 percent of the GSP in 1970 to 12.4 percent of the GSP in 1987.[14] As the reader will see in these numbers, and will read later in chapter 11 on tourism, the tourist industry has played a major role in the size and growth of the Hawaiian economy.

Because Hawai'i derives such a large portion of its GSP from external sources, both national and international, we expect to find that its aggregate economic performance is closely related to the

### Table 2.2: Import Trade from Japan and Asia as a Percentage of Total Imports[12]

| | Japan | | Asia | |
|---|---|---|---|---|
| | 1975 | 1986 | 1975 | 1986 |
| United States | 11.8% | 22.1% | 28.1% | 41.6% |
| | 1987 | | 1987 | |
| Hawai'i | 29.8% | | 88.3% | |

economic performance of the U.S. and other large national economies. We see in Figure 2.1, which shows real gross products for the
U.S., Hawai'i, Japan, and Canada from 1970 to 1988, relative to their
values in 1970, that all four economies have grown, albeit unevenly,
over the 1970 to 1988 period.[15]

Hawai'i, the U.S., and Canada all experienced declines in their
real gross products in the 1981–1982 period. Hawaiian growth was
relatively flat between 1974 and 1977, recovering more slowly from
the shock of rising oil prices than did the U.S. and Japanese economies. Canada, as a net oil producer, was not affected negatively in
these same years.[16]

One way to measure co-movements in economies more precisely
than by eyesight is to look at the statistical correlation coefficients
between the economies. For example, if two economies moved inde-
pendently of one another, their correlation coefficient would equal
zero. If movements in the two economies were perfectly positively
correlated, that is, as one grew so did the other, the coefficient would
equal +1; and if they were perfectly negatively correlated, that is, as
one grew the other declined, the coefficient would be equal to −1.[17]

To test co-movement among the Hawaiian and other economies
over the period 1970 to 1988, we calculated correlation coefficients of
real economic activity in Hawai'i, as indicated by the Hawaiian real
GSP, with real economic activity in the U.S., Japan, and Canada,
also indicated by their real GNPs.[18] The resulting correlation coefficients over that period are +0.99 between the real GSP in Hawai'i
and the real GNP in the U.S., +0.994 between Hawai'i and Japan,
and +0.995 between Hawai'i and Canada.[19]

## Employment

One means of examining the structure of an economy is to look
at the distribution of employment across various industries. In Table 2.3, the percentage distribution of actual 1980 and 1988 Hawai'i
employment levels is shown for various industries (i.e., sectors)
within the economy. In 1988, 92 percent (or 533,915) of all jobs in the
state of Hawai'i were outside of agriculture. This amount included
56,815 resident military positions. One can see from Table 2.3 that a
large proportion of employment is concentrated in two sectors: trade
and services. The only other sector which is close in size is government, which is dominated by total federal—military and civilian—
jobs.[20] Thus, looking at employment we see Hawai'i's economy

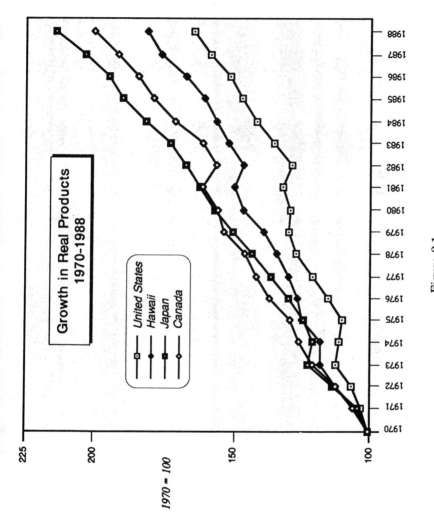

Figure 2.1

## Table 2.3: Hawai'i Statewide Employment by Industry (1980 and 1988)

| Industry | 1980 Actual | Percent[1] | 1988 Actual | Percent[1] | Growth Rate[2] |
|---|---|---|---|---|---|
| Nonagriculture, wage & salary | 462,000 | 91.4% | 533,915 | 92.0% | 1.8% |
| Contract Construction | 23,950 | 4.7% | 23,050 | 4.0% | −0.5% |
| Manufacturing | 23,350 | 4.6% | 22,300 | 3.8% | −0.6% |
| Durable goods | 4,700 | 0.9% | 4,250 | 0.7% | −1.3% |
| Nondurable goods | 18,650 | 3.7% | 18,050 | 3.1% | −0.4% |
| Food processing | 11,150 | 2.2% | 10,300 | 1.8% | −1.0% |
| Textile, apparel | 3,050 | 0.6% | 2,750 | 0.5% | −1.3% |
| Printing, publishing | 3,100 | 0.6% | 3,500 | 0.6% | 1.5% |
| Other nondurables | 1,350 | 0.3% | 1,450 | 0.2% | 0.9% |
| Transp., commun., utilities (TCU) | 31,200 | 6.2% | 38,000 | 6.5% | 2.5% |
| Transportation | 21,500 | 4.3% | 27,900 | 4.8% | 3.3% |
| Communication | 7,150 | 1.4% | 7,450 | 1.3% | 0.5% |
| Utilities | 2,550 | 0.5% | 2,650 | 0.5% | 0.5% |
| Trade | 105,250 | 20.8% | 127,600 | 22.0% | 2.4% |
| Wholesale | 18,600 | 3.7% | 20,550 | 3.5% | 1.3% |
| Retail | 86,700 | 17.1% | 107,050 | 18.4% | 2.7% |
| Finance, insur., real estate (FIRE) | 32,850 | 6.5% | 34,750 | 6.0% | 0.7% |
| Services & miscellaneous | 98,450 | 19.5% | 132,250 | 22.8% | 3.8% |
| Hotels | 24,900 | 4.9% | 34,500 | 5.9% | 4.2% |
| Other services & misc. | 73,550 | 14.5% | 97,750 | 16.8% | 3.6% |
| Government | 146,950 | 29.1% | 155,965 | 26.9% | 0.7% |
| Federal | | | | | |
| Civilian | 30,000 | 5.9% | 33,450 | 5.8% | 1.4% |
| Military | 57,900 | 11.5% | 56,815 | 9.8% | −0.2% |
| State | 45,150 | 8.9% | 52,850 | 8.9% | 1.7% |
| Local | 13,900 | 2.7% | 13,850 | 2.4% | 0.0% |
| Agriculture, wage & salary | 10,650 | 2.1% | 10,000 | 1.7% | −0.8% |
| Sugar | 4,950 | 1.0% | 3,700 | 0.6% | −3.6% |
| Pineapple | 2,500 | 0.5% | 1,750 | 0.3% | −4.4% |
| Other | 3,400 | 0.7% | 4,550 | 0.8% | 3.7% |
| Nonagric., self-employed[3] | 28,300 | 5.6% | 32,750 | 5.6% | 1.8% |
| Agric., self-employed[4] | 4,600 | 0.9% | 3,600 | 0.6% | −3.0% |
| Total Employment | 505,550 | | 580,265 | | 1.7% |

[1]Percentages shown are relative to total employment.
[2]Average annual growth rate for the period 1980–1988.
[3]Includes unpaid family workers and domestics.
[4]Includes unpaid family workers.

dominated by services, trade, and government. Moreover, the relative importance of services and trade jobs has increased from 1980 to 1988. How does this employment structure differ with that for the U.S. as a whole?

Nationally, service-oriented jobs were about 21.6 percent of total employment in 1988. This was an increase from 17.1 percent in 1980. As can be seen from Table 2.3, Hawai'i's service-oriented employment increased from 19.5 percent in 1980 to 22.8 percent in 1988. Thus, in relative terms, service employment has had a larger structural increase nationally. Although total service jobs have about the same percentage of importance for both Hawai'i and the U.S., the composition is different. Hotel employment is considerably more important in Hawai'i than the U.S. (for 1988, 5.9 percent statewide versus less than 2.0 percent nationally).

Other sectors or industries which have a higher concentration of jobs in Hawai'i compared to the U.S. economy are transportation, communication, and utilities (TCU), finance, insurance, and real estate (FIRE), trade, and government. Within TCU jobs, transportation and communication employment concentration is greater in Hawai'i relative to the rest of the U.S. The proportional mix of trade employment is also different. Hawai'i has a slightly higher proportion of trade jobs in retail firms relative to the rest of the U.S. Even if one ignores federal military employment, Hawai'i has a larger proportion of federal civilian employment, 5.9 percent, whereas in the U.S. as a whole the average is 2.5 percent.

Another difference between the Hawaiian and U.S. economies is the low percentage of manufacturing jobs, 3.8 percent in Hawai'i versus 16.4 percent nationally. For the U.S. economy, about 60 percent of all manufacturing jobs are in durable manufacturing. However, in Hawai'i the reverse is true, with over 80 percent of manufacturing jobs being in nondurable manufacturing.

Hawai'i's employment structure differs from the rest of the U.S. not only in composition but also in pattern of sectoral growth. In the last column of Table 2.3, the average annual growth rates for the period 1980 through 1988 are shown by industry. Over this period Hawai'i and U.S. total nonagricultural employment had approximately the same annual average growth rate. Average annual growth rates differed by industry however. For example, contract construction employment—which includes all types of construction activity plus mining—decreased in Hawai'i with an average annual decline of 0.5 percent. For the U.S. economy, contract construction employment increased over the same period with an annual average

growth rate of 1.1 percent. Hawai'i's contract construction employment has not only declined in absolute numbers but has also declined in relative importance. In spite of the apparent demand for
hotel construction (especially on the outer islands) total contract
construction employment declined in Hawai'i. This trend may be re-
versing, as 1989 has seen increasing employment for this industry.

Employment in TCU has shown a higher growth rate in Hawai'i
relative to the rest of the U.S. Most of this growth has been in
transportation-related employment (movement of passengers and
freight), which has almost doubled in magnitude since 1970.

FIRE employment has had a significantly faster growth rate
nationally, 3.3 percent, than in Hawai'i, 0.7 percent. Historically,
however, this industry has had a higher employment concentration
in Hawai'i relative to the rest of the U.S.

Similar to the FIRE sector, service employment has not grown
as fast in Hawai'i: 3.8 percent relative to 4.8 percent for the rest of
the U.S. It has been a major growth industry nationwide. However
in 1980, service employment in Hawai'i was already 19.5 percent of
total employment. Thus, it is possible that service employment in
Hawai'i had already reached a slower growth stage, whereas the
U.S. services sector, being of a relatively smaller concentration in
1980, was showing signs of strong growth. Currently, as shown
above, the service sector is roughly the same size in both the state
and national economies.

Total agricultural wage and salary employment in Hawai'i and
the entire U.S. has been declining. In Hawai'i this decline has been
concentrated in two subsectors of agriculture: sugar and pineapple.
Employment in production of other agricultural commodities, for example, macadamia nuts, papaya, and coffee, shows significant positive growth over the past nine years. This growth, however, has not
been large enough to offset the decline in sugar and pineapple.

## A Dual Labor Market in Hawai'i?

The nature of the Hawaiian job market changed dramatically
through the 1960s and 1970s reflecting the rise of the tourist industry. To some observers this move has been accompanied by a split of
the Hawaiian labor market into high-wage and low-wage sectors,
with little or no labor mobility between sectors. This phenomenon
has been termed a "dual" labor market.

Casual observation lends some credence to this dual labor market proposition. In Hawai'i, 62 percent of families have two or more
wage earners while the national average is 54 percent of families.

## Table 2.4: Percentage of Families in Income Classes (in 1980 constant dollars)[22]

| Percentage of families in income class | 1970 | 1975 | 1979 | 1985–1987 |
|---|---|---|---|---|
| less than $10,000 | 13.3 | 13.5 | 17 | 11.1 |
| $10,000–$19,999 | 28 | 23.2 | 25.8 | 21.2 |
| $20,000–$34,000 | 32.4 | 32.4 | 32.1 | 28.9 |
| $35,000–$49,000 | 18.6 | 12.6 | 15.9 | 18.8 |
| $50,000 and above | 7.8 | 18.4 | 9.2 | 19.8 |
| Median family income | $23,100 | $26,200 | $22,750 | $27,000 |

Women account for approximately half of the Hawaiian labor force compared to 45 percent nationally. Finally, the female participation rate is about 60 percent in Hawai'i compared to 56 percent nationally. And when we recognize that 69 percent of women work in sales, clerical, and service jobs, the case seems strong that a dual labor market may indeed exist in the state.[21]

Assessing the dualness of the labor market requires more information. Median family incomes and the distribution of low, middle, and high income families should be tracked over time if the argument for a dual labor market is to be supported. If it can be shown that the distribution of income has become more unequal, with greater percentages of families at the lower and higher ends, then the dual market hypothesis will be strengthened.

Table 2.4 shows, in 1980 dollars, the changing distribution of family income and median family income levels in Hawai'i over the period 1970–1987.

If there is one thing that is evident from Table 2.4, it is that income distributions differ considerably depending on the years chosen. Therefore, it would seem that economic conditions, recession years or boom years, matter more for the distribution of family incomes than any structural shift in the labor market.

For example, 1979, a year when political uncertainty and oil price shocks both militated against travel, Hawai'i suffered. This is evident from the distribution of family incomes and the median family income relative to the year of 1975.[23] Comparing 1979 against the annual averages from the relative boom years of 1985–1987 makes the improvement in family income distributions look even more dramatic. It is also evident that median family income has rebounded in the 1980s.

Based on this evidence we are skeptical of the claim that there is a dual labor market in Hawai'i. Obviously, in years of economic recession family incomes suffer on average, with more families falling into lower income classes; hence the middle of the distribution gets narrower. However, buoyant years see a reversal of this phenomenon, with families moving up in the distribution. Therefore, while we do not deny the possibility of a dual labor market, we do think that available evidence fails to support such a claim.

## Alternative Measures
## of Hawai'i's Economic Activity

Both employment and the GSP may be used as means of describing Hawai'i's economy and comparing it to the U.S. economy. The GSP is generally viewed as being a broader measure of economic activity, whereas, employment is seen essentially as a job count.

When these two measures are used to describe economic structure, differences may arise due to the value of products and services produced and relative wage rates. For example, in 1986, Hawai'i's service employment accounted for 23.1 percent of all employment. However in 1986, Hawai'i's GSP attributable to the service industry was 19.8 percent. The main reason for this difference in percentage importance is the relatively low wage rates for most service-oriented jobs. A reverse example is given by the FIRE sector, where a relatively small number of jobs produce a high value-added economic activity.

The percentage distribution of Hawai'i's GSP in 1986 is compared to the 1986 employment distribution in Figure 2.2.[24] Significant increases in proportional importance are seen in the GSP for high-value output sectors such as contract construction and mining, TCU, FIRE, and manufacturing. Those sectors showing significantly less importance, using GSP percentages, are those with relatively low wage rates or low-value output, which include trade, services, and state and local government.

If we compare Hawai'i's GSP distribution with an equivalent distribution for the nation, we get a description similar to that obtained with employment. Hawai'i has proportionately less economic activity in manufacturing, wholesale trade, and utilities. Sectors where Hawai'i's economy has relatively more economic activity are transportation, retail trade, hotel services, and federal government.

The comparatively greater concentration of economic activity in transportation is primarily due to location. Proportionately higher

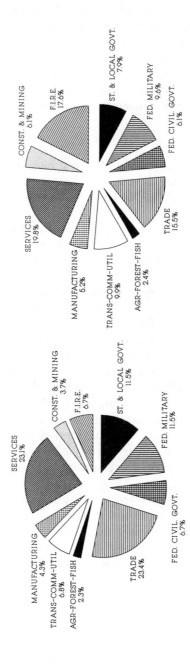

**EMPLOYMENT**

SERVICES
23.1%

MANUFACTURING
4.3%

TRANS-COMM-UTIL
6.8%

AGR-FOREST-FISH
2.3%

TRADE
23.4%

FED. CIVIL. GOVT.
6.7%

FED. MILITARY
11.5%

ST. & LOCAL GOVT.
11.5%

F.I.R.E.
6.7%

CONST. & MINING
3.7%

**GSP**

SERVICES
19.8%

MANUFACTURING
5.2%

TRANS-COMM-UTIL
9.9%

AGR-FOREST-FISH
2.4%

TRADE
15.5%

FED. CIVIL. GOVT.
6.1%

FED. MILITARY
9.6%

ST. & LOCAL GOVT.
7.9%

F.I.R.E.
17.6%

CONST. & MINING
6.1%

Figure 2.2 Distribution of Total Employment and Gross State Product in Hawai'i by Sector (1986)

activity in hotel services is explained by Hawai'i being an attractive destination for tourists. Higher concentrations of retail trade activity are due to location and tourism. Since most consumer goods are shipped into Hawai'i, wholesale trade is more concentrated; however, Hawai'i's retail trade sector is characterized by many small retailers. High tourism activity also leads to a relatively higher demand for retail establishments (especially those with higher priced goods).

### Foreign Direct Investment in Hawai'i

One area of intense recent interest has been that of foreign direct investment in the U.S. Much of this interest stems from concerns that the U.S. will lose its economic sovereignty, that opportunities for U.S. labor will decline and that the U.S. standard of living will fall as a result. The same concerns are often expressed on a state-by-state basis as well.[25] In the U.S., this type of investment has risen from $13.3 billion in 1970—1.3 percent of the GNP—to $260 billion in 1987—5.3 percent of the GNP.

Foreign direct investment in Hawai'i has risen as a percentage of the national total from approximately 0.33 percent in 1970 to about .5 percent in 1987. The volume of foreign direct investment in Hawai'i in 1987 represented approximately 6 percent of the GSP. The growth rate of foreign direct investment in Hawai'i is greater than that in the U.S. and the pattern of investment is very different between the U.S. and Hawaiian economies as well. In Hawai'i, the total of direct investment by Japan, from 1950 onward, has made up roughly 80 percent of total foreign direct investment in the state. In 1986, the Japanese share of total foreign direct investment in Hawai'i was over 96 percent. In the national economy, the Japanese share of total foreign direct investment rose from 1.7 percent in 1970 to 11.2 percent in 1986.

From 1970 to 1988, over 85 percent of Japanese direct investment in Hawai'i has been in hotels and real estate, including golf courses. Approximately 29 percent of all overnight visitor units in Hawai'i are owned by Japanese. On the island of Oahu, where Honolulu is located, the Japanese ownership of visitor units is 34 percent of the total.

### Government

As noted earlier, government (including resident military) employment plays a significantly larger role in Hawai'i's economy rel-

**Table 2.5: Per Capita Revenue, Expenditure, and Debt of State and Local Government (1986)[27]**

|  | Amount (dollars) | U.S. average (dollars) | % of U.S. average | Rank |
|---|---|---|---|---|
| General revenue | 2,873 | 2,661 | 108.0 | 13 |
| Tax revenue only | 1,780 | 1,547 | 115.1 | 8 |
| Debt outstanding | 3,193 | 2,733 | 116.8 | 16 |
| General expenditure | 2,691 | 2,504 | 107.5 | 15 |
| Capital outlay | 483 | 375 | 128.8 | 11 |

ative to the rest of the U.S. In 1988, 24.5 percent of all jobs in Hawai'i were in government. The comparable U.S. figure was 16.1 percent. The relatively larger role of federal, especially resident military, jobs in Hawai'i accounts for essentially all this difference. Hawai'i's relatively high concentration of federal government jobs is primarily due to the military bases on Oahu. A secondary explanation is that the mass of employees needed for any federal office will have a larger relative impact on a small state such as Hawai'i. It should be noted that federal pay scales are higher than those in the private sector.

The state and its four counties are also large contributors to the economy, employing 61,700 people and spending $3.2 billion on goods and services, out of a total GSP of $19.8 billion in 1987.[26] State and local government revenue generation efforts and general expenditures give some indication of the size of Hawai'i's government, relative to other states in the country (see Table 2.5).

Several factors contribute to the apparent size of government spending. First, state and local government relations are characterized by a high degree of centralization with respect to revenue and expenditure allocation authority, a direct result of the state's history of monarchy. In the relatively simple two-jurisdictional structure of state and counties, the state is dominant. Many functions typically allocated to local government elsewhere, such as education, are allocated to the state in Hawai'i. Other typically local functions performed by the State of Hawai'i include lower level courts, beach parks, airports and harbors, public health, and public housing.[28]

A major implication of the centralization of functions is greater uniformity in public service levels across jurisdictions, leading to higher levels of service for nonurban areas than might otherwise have prevailed. Higher government expenditure may be one result of this higher, uniform service level. Other contributing factors include the institutional arrangement of statewide collective bargaining for government employees and the existence of certain overlapping state and local functions.

A second factor which contributes to the size of government, especially with regard to the measures reported in Table 2.5, is the presence of a large visitor population. A comparison of the 1987 de facto population of 1.2 million, which includes visitors, with the resident population of 1.08 million indicates the relative magnitude of potential visitor demand for public services.[29]

A third factor is the cost of producing government services, relative to other states. There are no data on the relative cost for goods and services purchased by government in Hawai'i, but federal cost-of-living allowances for consumption items suggest anywhere from a twelve to twenty-two percent differential, depending on the particular location in Hawai'i.[30] For purposes of constructing price indexes, government services are usually priced at their cost of production, which is primarily wages and salaries. Therefore, if the federal government is paying a differential in wages and salaries to federal employees in Hawai'i, the cost of federal government services is higher in Hawai'i.

The existence of the Hawai'i Land-Use Commission with a statewide land-use planning function also affects county authority regarding local zoning and land-use decisions. Thus, state and local relations continue to be characterized by state dominance.

State and local government, as a proportion of total economic activity, has declined slightly over the past ten years from 18 percent to 15 percent. This followed dramatic growth in the 1960s, when employment, measured in terms of state and local employees per thousand of population, grew 47 percent over the decade. The income tax structure—which is highly responsive to economic growth—has also resulted in tax revenue growth sufficient to support increased public expenditure.[31] Thus, the government sector remains a significant proportion of the state economy.

## Constraints

In a small, open economy such as Hawai'i's, growth and change depend very heavily on what happens in the larger economies of the state's trading partners. As shown above, many of the state's key industries—most of them associated with tourism—are closely tied to movements in the national economies of the U.S., Japan, and Canada. Years when economic activity slows in these countries presage downturns in Hawai'i. This is especially so in periods when common, negative shocks hit the large national economies resulting in lower spending on Hawai'i's main exports. For example, when the international prices of oil and its derivatives—such as jet fuel—rise, Hawai'i's tourist industry is negatively affected. Given that the tourist industry is such a large part of the state economy, a decrease in the one causes a corresponding depression in the other. We saw above that the mid-1970s was such a period for the state.

To the extent that different national economies are hit by different shocks, Hawai'i is partially protected from large swings in economic activity due to its draw of visitors from diversified sources. Other states in the U.S. remain the major source of visitors to Hawai'i, though the Japanese share has been rising and the U.S. and Canadian shares falling.[32] As a result of stronger foreign business, Hawai'i's economy grew faster in the late 1970s and early 1980s than did the U.S. economy, which was relatively stagnant.[33]

The price of oil does not affect just the tourist industry in Hawai'i. Virtually all the oil used in the state for production and energy generation is imported. As a source, petroleum provides over 98 percent of the state's energy. Additionally, most manufactured goods or the material to make them must be imported from either the U.S. mainland or from abroad.[34]

This raises the cost of goods by at least the transportation costs over prices paid elsewhere. The Hawai'i market, being small relative to that necessary for achieving optimal plant size for most productive processes, does not allow for economies of scale to be reached in many agricultural or manufacturing processes. Consequently, the prices on most goods are higher in Hawai'i.

As a rough measure, consider that the price of a "market basket" of food in Honolulu has averaged twenty to thirty percent higher than the same basket of food in other U.S. cities over the 1979–1987 period. If transportation costs were nil, we would expect the prices of these foodstuffs to equalize among cities.

By the broader measure of comparative annual living costs, Honolulu residents in 1988 faced a cost of living seventeen percent higher than that of residents of the average American city. Meanwhile, per capita personal disposable income (after tax) was only two percent higher in Hawai'i than the average in the U.S. as a whole.[35]

The process of finding and following comparative advantages should allow Hawai'i, as it does any trading region, to continue to grow. Clearly, Hawai'i is constrained by transportation costs, lack of raw materials, land costs, living costs, and the size of its population from being a large-scale manufacturer of, say, automobiles. However,

Hawai'i has a comparative advantage in its year-round attractive-ness to tourists. Growth in tourism will continue to propel the state as long as international shocks do not lower economic activity in the large national economies that trade with or (as in the case of the U.S. government) transfer resources to Hawai'i.

In trade, Hawai'i has not changed from the days when Captain George Vancouver sailed to the islands. What is traded and to whom has changed, but the trading nature of the islands has not. The only constraint the state faces would be the inability to follow its com-parative advantage. That inability would come through policies shaped by interests, public or private in nature, which work to al-locate resources differently than would a market-driven mechanism. Some of these issues and policies are treated in subsequent chapters dealing with aspects of the policy process which affects the economy.

## Notes

1. Stannard, D., *Before the Horror,* SSRI (Honolulu: University of Hawai'i Press, 1989), p. 30.

2. R. Schmitt, *Historical Statistics of Hawai'i* (Honolulu: University of Hawai'i Press, 1977), p. 551.

3. Ibid.

4. J. Mak, *A Concise Economic History of the Hawaiian Islands,* mimeo, 1978. Also, Lyle E. Hendricks, J. Mak and G. Tamaribuchi, *Hawai'i's Economy,* State of Hawai'i Department of Education, 1989. The Big Five were Alexander and Baldwin, C. Brewer, American Factors, Castle and Cook, and Theo. Davies.

5. Sugar production between 1934 and 1974 was fairly stable at the quota levels set under the Sugar Act of 1934. There were, however, fluctu-ations, with unprocessed sugar cane tonnage of 8,535,000 tons in 1940, 7,889,000 tons in 1950, 9,391,000 tons in 1959, 11,258,000 tons in 1969, 8,994,000 tons in 1977 and 8,014,000 tons in 1987. Sources: State of Hawai'i, Department of Business and Economic Development (DBED), *Data Book 1974,* table 234, p. 229, and *Data Book 1988,* table 584, p. 514.

6. Gross state product is defined as the gross market value of goods and services produced in a state in a given period of time.

7. Schmitt, *Historical Statistics,* p. 165.

8. See DBED, *Data Book 1988,* p. 360.

9. In 1987, measuring direct income from major export industries rel-ative to the GSP in that year, we find that the tourist industry accounted for

33.4 percent of the GSP, while raw sugar and molasses accounted for 1.7 percent, fresh and processed pineapple 1.3 percent, and defense expenditures were 9.4 percent. See DBED, *Data Book 1988,* p. 359.

10. Data for the U.S.: Department of Commerce, *Statistical Abstract of the United States, 1989,* table 1342; data for Hawai'i: DBED, *Data Book 1988,* p. 624.

11. These figures, from tables 1346 and 1332 in *Statistical Abstract,* can be somewhat misleading as it should be noted that not all exports going through U.S. Customs in Honolulu are produced in Hawai'i; some goods are transshipped from the mainland U.S. and exported through Hawai'i. For example, in 1987, most exports, forty-three percent, going through Honolulu to Japan and Asia, were aircraft and spacecraft and related goods. Knowledge of Hawaiian manufacturing suggests that these exports are not manufactured within the state. However, the available data do not allow us to distinguish the manufacturing location of exports out of any particular U.S. Customs office.

12. *Statistical Abstract, 1989,* table 1342. Again, as per note 11, we cannot tell the size and types of these goods passing through Honolulu to the Mainland U.S. However, roughly one-half of the manufactured shipments to the U.S. going through Honolulu are metals and metal-related products, primarily integrated circuits and motor vehicles. For consumption in Hawai'i, the main imports are petroleum and natural gas products.

13. DBED, *Data Book 1988,* p. 359. It is easy to understand why income from the sale of physical commodities like sugar and pineapples sold abroad are considered export earnings. A commodity is exchanged for money. Income derived from the provision of services may also be counted as export earnings no matter whether the service is physically performed abroad by a U.S. citizen or whether people come from abroad to enjoy our services domestically. Tourism is a service, provided domestically, which generates income from individuals coming from out of the state. Therefore, those incomes derived from tourism and the tourist industry are considered export earnings for residents of the state of Hawai'i.

14. DBED, *Data Book,* p. 359. Other, smaller areas of agriculture, defined as "diversified" agriculture, have grown in recent years. Macadamia nut production, papayas, cut flowers, and coffee have all provided export earnings. Federal government defense expenditures in Hawai'i are also export earnings (relative to Hawai'i's trade with the other forty-nine U.S. states) as they represent an expenditure from an out-of-state source for services (e.g., strategic location) rendered by the state.

15. The 1970 value of real gross product is used as a base of comparison for each region. This value is divided into the real gross product of the region for each successive year. One is left with an index of growth in real gross product over time for each region. For example, in 1970, U.S. real GNP (in 1982 constant dollars) was $2,416.2 billion. This value was then divided into

itself (U.S. real GNP for 1970, the base year) and this result multiplied by 100. The initial value is then 100. The following year, 1971, U.S. real GNP was equal to $2,484.8 billion. This is a growth rate of 2.84 percent from the year before. This percentage is arrived at by the calculation: (2484.8 ÷ 2416.2) × 100 = 102.84, compared to the 1970 value of 100. This procedure was used to set all the real gross product series values at 100 for 1970. This makes the growth rates of the vastly different real gross products comparable one to the other in situations when comparing levels of real gross product would be difficult.

16. Data for Hawai'i, DBED, *Data Book 1988,* p. 360; for the U.S., Canada, and Japan: Federal Reserve Bank of St. Louis, *International Economic Conditions,* annual edition, July 1989.

17. The co-movements and correlation between any two sets of information, for example national GNPs, may be due to a causal relationship running from one set to the other, or to common influences from a third set of information that affects the first two sets similarly. For example, the growth of corn and the growth of wheat on adjacent plots of land might be highly correlated, but not causally related one to the other. Instead, rainfall levels—similar on both plots—may cause the growth in both crops. Consequently, there can be no presumption here of causality running from one set of GNPs to the other. However, once we know the structure of the Hawaiian economy, as outlined in the section on employment, pp. 00–00, it is reasonable to assume that what happens in the U.S. and other large international economies will affect Hawai'i, if only indirectly, to a much greater degree than movements in Hawai'i can be expected to affect the much larger national economies.

18. We chose these three countries for the reason that they are the major partners for most of Hawai'i's trade. For example, in 1987, 63 percent of visitors staying overnight and longer came to the state from elsewhere in the U.S., another 20 percent of those visitors were from Japan and 4 percent (the next highest total) were from Canada. In total, these three economies account for just under 90 percent of the visitors to the islands.

19. Upon breaking the Hawaiian economy into its constituent industrial sectors and computing correlation coefficients between those sectors and the three national economies, we find that the sectors of retail trade and services, which are the main components of the tourist industry, are most highly correlated with the three national economies, each having a correlation coefficient of plus 0.95 or higher over the period.

20. As a glance at Table 2.3 shows, if we compare civilian federal to state government job totals, the state provides approximately five out of every eight government (nonmilitary) jobs in Hawai'i.

21. See L. Minerbi, "Sustainability versus Growth in Hawai'i and Oahu," *Sustainable Development or Suburbanization? Cumulative Project*

*Impacts in Ewa and Central Oahu,* Spring 1989, Department of Urban and Regional Planning, University of Hawai'i. See also G. G. Y. Pai, "Long Term Changes in the Structure of the Hawaiian Economy and Their Impact on Social and Economic Welfare in Hawai'i," mimeo of an address given March 19, 1989.

22. Data from DBED, *Data Books.* 1970 from *Data Book 1974,* table 105, p. 112; 1975 from *Data Book 1978,* table 214, p. 197; data for 1979 and 1985–1987 from *Data Book 1988,* tables 417 and 418, pp. 375–76. The authors interpolated between classes to transform the nominal income classes into real (1980 dollar) income classes in order to make valid comparison of the distributions.

23. Using 1982 as a comparison, as Pai and Minerbi both do in the articles cited in note 21 above, makes the deterioration in family incomes look even more extreme. Recall that 1982 was a recent low point in both the Hawaiian and U.S. economies.

24. Economics Department of the Bank of Hawai'i, "Hawai'i Gross State Product by Industry," *Business Trends* 33 (5) (September/October 1988), p. 1–2.

25. See M. Ott, "Is America Being Sold Out?," *Review,* Federal Reserve Bank of St. Louis, 71 (2) (March/April 1989). In this article Ott makes a convincing case that foreign direct investment benefits U.S. labor and investors. Similar, but slightly weaker arguments in favor of foreign investment are made by W. J. Khaley, "F.Y.I. U.S. and Foreign Direct Investment Patterns," *Economic Review,* Federal Reserve Bank of Atlanta, 74 (6) (November/ December 1989).

26. DBED, *Data Book, 1988,* pp. 293, 361.

27. *Statistical Abstract, 1989,* pp. 274–75. *General revenue* includes tax revenues and use-related charges for government services and federal grants. *Debt outstanding* represents the principal amounts state and local governments have borrowed and that remain unpaid. *General expenditure* includes operating and maintenance spending for such government functions as education, highways, public welfare, and health. *Capital outlay* represents expenditure for infrastructure items. Note that general revenue efforts exceed the national average by about 8 percent (rank 13) and general expenditures exceed the national average by 7.5 percent (rank 15).

28. Centralization of revenue-raising authority has also accompanied the centralization of functions at the state level. The state constitution (art. 7, sec. 3) substantially circumscribes county authority: "The taxing power shall be reserved to the state except so much therefore as may be delegated by the legislature to the political subdivisions." Although the counties have lobbied for more extensive taxing authority, the only such power transferred to the counties since the framing of the constitution in 1950 is the taxation

of real property. A constitutional amendment in 1978 provided for the transfer of real property taxation authority after an eleven-year period. The transfer became fully effective in 1989.

29. DBED, *Data Book 1988,* p. 14.

30. DBED, *Data Book 1988,* p. 399.

31. Economists refer to this type of tax structure as "progressive": tax rates rise as income rises.

32. It is also true that the spending patterns of visitors from different areas differs as do their average lengths of stay. Japanese visitors spend over three times as much per day per visitor than do visitors from the U.S. mainland. In 1987 the figures were $366 for Japanese visitors versus $102 for visitors from the U.S. mainland. Consequently, in 1987, Japanese visitors accounted for thirty-one percent of total visitor expenditures. DBED, *Data Book 1988,* p. 205.

33. The value of the U.S. dollar on foreign exchange markets is also of importance here. When the U.S. dollar depreciates, foreign imports become more costly. In 1988, these accounted for sixteen percent of total state imports of goods and services (DBED, *Data Book 1988,* p. 359). However, trips to Hawai'i become relatively cheaper for foreigners and the dollar costs do not change for U.S. residents. Given the large difference in earnings from the tourist industry relative to foreign imports for consumption within the state (in 1988, the value derived from the tourist industry was over three times larger than expenditures on foreign imports), it is arguable that a depreciating U.S. dollar encourages economic activity in Hawai'i.

34. Manufactured imports account for seventy percent of total imports into Hawai'i, and the value of imports relative to the Hawaiian GSP (1988) is approximately sixty-five percent. Hawai'i, like the U.S., has had a trade deficit in the 1980s. In 1988, the trade deficit was $1,613 million, which was 7.6 percent of the GSP. See DBED, *Data Book 1988,* p. 360.

35. See DBED, *Data Book 1988,* tables 408, 435, and 437, pp. 368, 397, and 398. One disturbing trend has been the drop in Hawaiian per capita disposable income relative to the U.S. average. Over the period 1960–1970, Hawaiian per capita disposable personal income rose from 101 percent to 120 percent of the U.S. average. From 1970 to 1987 that percentage dropped back to 102 percent. See DBED, *Data Book 1988,* table 408, p. 368.

# 3

## SOCIAL DYNAMICS OF
## THE ALOHA STATE:
## THE POPULATION OF HAWAI'I

*Jeffrey L. Crane and Alton M. Okinaka*

In this chapter we will profile Hawai'i's population by presenting, and briefly discussing, some of its more sociologically interesting characteristics. It is our contention that an accurate
understanding of Hawai'i's population is a prerequisite to the formation of viable social policy and planning in the fiftieth state. It
is not enough to say that Hawai'i is a special place, and therefore it
must have different social processes. The unique social features of
Hawai'i must be empirically established and their importance understood. Such a view is by no means original. It was first expressed
by Romanzo Adams in his 1925 classic, *The Peoples of Hawai'i*.
It was also expressed by Andrew Lind in his 1938 text *An Island
Community* and again in his 1955 sequel to Adams's text, *Hawai'i's
People*.[1]

Against common sense, much contemporary public policy formation and social planning in Hawai'i is undertaken with little
more than a superficial acknowledgement of the state's ethnic diversity. If ethnic diversity were the only important demographic factor
that needed to be considered in policy issues and debates, then a
book such as the present one would be unnecessary and all claims
that Hawai'i was in some manner unique could rightfully be labeled
naive.

In this chapter we will examine a number of the important demographic characteristics and factors in Hawai'i's population, keep-
ing in mind that Hawai'i is far more than a geographical location or
a locale where numerous ethnic groups interact. It is, as Lind so correctly observed, an island community born of people with diverse social characteristics who, by living and working with one another,
have created a fascinating social world.[2]

## Population Growth and Distribution

In discussing Hawai'i's population, the most logical place to begin is with its numeric changes. Conventional wisdom maintains that prior to the arrival of Captain James Cook in 1778, somewhere between two and three hundred thousand native Hawaiians resided in Hawai'i. Recently, Professor David Stannard, in his book *Before the Horror,* has made the controversial claim that Hawai'i's precontact population was at least eight hundred thousand individuals, and that the figure should more likely be set at over a million.[3] Stannard bases his argument on the fact that prior population estimates were not based upon rigorous data collection or observational methods. In addition, according to Stannard's analysis of other locales similar to Hawai'i, the land of Hawai'i was theoretically capable of supporting a population in the million-plus range. If Stannard is correct, then Hawai'i's precontact population would have been equal to its current population.

Regardless of whether one accepts or rejects Stannard's estimates, the fact remains that Hawai'i's precontact Hawaiian population experienced a sharp, indeed catastrophic, decline due to the introduction of Western diseases and social conventions. For example, using the most conservative estimate of precontact population, two hundred thousand individuals, it would not be until over 130 years later, in 1910, that such a population size was again approximated. It should be noted, moreover, that increases in post contact Hawaiian population can be attributed almost exclusively to non-Hawaiian immigrants. The native Hawaiian population was never able to recover from its remarkable postcontact decline. Table 3.1 gives some indication of the changes in Hawai'i's population since Western contact in 1778.

Over 40 percent of the population growth in the 1980s was the result of in-migration. Immigrant arrivals in 1987 numbered 6,800 and were primarily from the Philippines. In addition, Hawai'i's military personnel and their dependents represent a sizable 11.4 percent of the whole population. Despite considerable in-migration, 64 percent of the population was born in Hawai'i, with 21 percent mainland born, and 13 percent foreign born.

While there has been steady growth in the size of Hawai'i's population since 1900, the population has never been equally distributed across the six major islands in the Hawaiian chain, nor has it been distributed proportionately to the size (i.e. land mass) of each island. Table 3.2 presents the population distribution between the

### Table 3.1: Hawai'i's Resident Population, by Selected Years (to 1987)[4]

|  | Population | % Change |
|---|---|---|
| Before 1778 | 200,000 |  |
| 1831–32 | 130,313 | −34.8 |
| 1835–36 | 108,579 | −16.7 |
| 1850 | 84,165 | −22.4 |
| 1860 | 69,800 | −17.1 |
| 1870 | n/a |  |
| 1880 | n/a |  |
| 1890 | 89,990 | +28.9 |
| 1900 | 154,001 | +71.3 |
| 1910 | 191,874 | +24.6 |
| 1920 | 255,881 | +33.3 |
| 1930 | 368,300 | +43.9 |
| 1940 | 422,770 | +14.8 |
| (1944) | (858,945) | +(103.2) |
| 1950 | 499,794 | +18.2 |
| 1960 | 632,772 | +26.6 |
| 1970 | 769,913 | +21.7 |
| 1980 | 964,691 | +25.3 |
| 1987 | 1,082,500 | +12.2 |
| 1988 | 1,096,200 | +1.3 |
| 1989 | 1,112,100 | +1.5 |

### Table 3.2: Population by Selected Island (1940–1980)[5] (population totals and percentages)

|  | 1940 | 1950 | 1960 | 1970 | 1980 |
|---|---|---|---|---|---|
| Hawai'i | 73,276 (17.3%) | 68,350 (13.7%) | 61,332 (9.7%) | 63,468 (8.2%) | 92,053 (9.5%) |
| Maui | 46,919 (11.1%) | 40,103 (8.0%) | 35,717 (5.6%) | 38,691 (5.0%) | 62,823 6.5%) |
| Oahu | 257,664 (61.0%) | 353,006 (70.6%) | 500,394 (79.1%) | 630,497 (81.9%) | 762,534 (79.0%) |
| Kauai | 35,636 (8.4%) | 29,683 (5.9%) | 27,922 (4.4%) | 29,524 (3.8%) | 38,856 (4.0%) |
| Molokai | 5,340 (1.3%) | 5,280 (1.1%) | 5,023 (0.8%) | 5,261 (0.7%) | 6,049 (0.6%) |
| Lanai | 3,720 (0.9%) | 3,136 (0.6%) | 2,115 (0.3%) | 2,204 (0.3%) | 2,119 (0.2%) |
| Total | 422,770 | 499,794 | 632,772 | 769,913 | 964,691 |

state's six major islands from 1940 to 1980. During the period between 1980 and 1989, Maui experienced the greatest increase in population (40.2 percent) followed by the islands of Hawai'i (32.9 percent), Kauai (30.5 percent), Molokai (14.1 percent), Oahu (10.4 percent), and Lanai (3.8 percent). These trends are expected to continue with the result that Maui, Hawai'i, and Kauai will continue to experience considerable growth and social change. Oahu, where approximately three-quarters of the state's entire population resides, will continue to be the center of economic activity and population concentration into the twenty-first century despite the impressive gains made by these other islands. As might be expected, social services and human support agencies are also concentrated on this island.

A complicating factor in public policy and planning is the character and frequency of intrastate migration. Job and career opportunities, as well as educational opportunities, are concentrated in urban areas, especially Honolulu, thus producing the common pattern of rural to urban migration within the State of Hawai'i. This is reflected in the steady increase in population for Oahu (Honolulu being the state's only metropolitan area), with other islands experiencing declines in population between 1940 and 1960.

Hawai'i consists of approximately 6,425 square miles of land. A census area is classified as rural on the basis of having less than 2,500 people in contiguous residence. Of Hawai'i's total land mass, 6,100 square miles are classified as rural, with the remaining 5 percent being classified urban. This indicates an extremely high population density for Hawai'i's urban areas—over fourteen hundred persons per square mile in Honolulu. Moreover, this already high density will continue to increase in future years. Population projections prepared by Hawai'i's Department of Business and Economic Development (DBED) estimate that the state's population will surpass 1.2 million by 1995. By 2010, DBED has projected a population of close to 1.5 million. It is reasonable to expect, based upon DBED's projections, that by the year 2015, Hawai'i's total resident population will be heading toward 1.7 million.

In considering the issue of population density, it must be acknowledged that geographical constraints are significant factors in the distribution of population. Narrow coastal areas constrained by surrounding mountainous terrain necessarily produce planning problems that are dissimilar to those encountered in vast open rural areas where population density is very low. Thus, for example, while transportation problems brought about by traffic congestion loom large for an area such as Honolulu, infrastructural problems such as a lack of adequate roads, emergency services, utilities, and water are the concerns in rural districts such as Puna and Ka'u on the island of Hawai'i. Public policy born of central planning that does not factor population density into its models is very likely to fail. In fact, given Hawai'i's remarkable variations in population density, and the base causes of that variation, it is reasonable to assume that centralized planning is not an altogether adequate response. Decentralized planning is a logical alternative.

## Transient Population Composition

As impressive as Hawai'i's population increases have been and are projected to be, the resident population is only a part of the total population picture. Hawai'i, more than most other states, experiences tremendous shifts in its population due to tourism and its military installations. If we define a tourist as someone who stays in Hawai'i overnight or longer, but is not a resident and does not intend to become one (albeit "intent" is often difficult to establish), then since shortly after statehood, Hawai'i's annual tourist population has exceeded its annual resident population. In fact, it has exceeded it at an increasing rate. Table 3.3 presents data on the number of visitors to Hawai'i between 1965 and 1989.

While far less impressive in terms of quantity, a large military presence also has its influence on Hawai'i's population. For example, in 1970, the resident population was 769,913, of which 55,142 individuals (7.2 percent) were in the military. And, in 1989, of the 1,112,100 residents of the state, the total number of military personnel rose to 56,400 people (5.1 percent) of the state population). These figures do not take into account the dependents of military personnel which, if considered, would increase the military population to approximately 10.5 percent of Hawai'i's total population.[7]

### Table 3.3: Visitors to Hawai'i by Selected Years (1961–1987)[6]

|      | No. of visitors | % change |
|------|-----------------|----------|
| 1965 | 686,928         |          |
| 1970 | 1,746,970       | 154.32   |
| 1975 | 2,829,105       | 61.94    |
| 1980 | 3,934,504       | 39.07    |
| 1985 | 4,884,110       | 24.14    |
| 1989 | 6,641,820       | 36.00    |

The tourist industry and the military provide Hawai'i with two important pools of temporary population members. While there are social, economic, and cultural benefits derived from these transient population sources, they also contribute to population instability.[8]

## Age and Ethnic Population Characteristics

As with many locations on the mainland and throughout the world, Hawai'i's population is experiencing an aging trend. In 1980, the median age of Hawai'i residents was 28.3 years of age (27.6 and 29.1 for men and women respectively). By 1989, estimates placed the median age at 32.3 (31.5 and 33.2 for men and women respectively).

There is a slight imbalance of about fifty-one men for every forty-nine women in the state. Men outnumber women in all age groups below 45; a common phenomenon in immigrant entry points and areas with a large military presence. While these age and gender patterns hold for the major islands, there is some variation between islands in terms of median ages, gender ratios, and percentage of the whole that each age category represents. This variation would indicate that centralized state planning initiatives which feature age and gender factors might not be as effective as more regional (i.e., island-based) initiatives.

As mentioned previously, social scientists have long recognized the importance of ethnicity on Hawai'i's social character. Table 3.4 presents data on Hawai'i's ethnic groups for the year 1988. Given Hawai'i's social history, the proportion of the population that each ethnic group represented in 1988 cannot be generalized to years much previous to that time. Moreover, it would be incorrect to assume that these proportions will remain unchanged in the years to come.

While of interest in itself, ethnic variation takes on special policy and planning significance when associated with variation in cultural practices. In Table 3.5 language practices in Hawai'i's homes are presented. What is important to notice is that approximately a quarter of Hawai'i's homes have residents aged five and above speaking a language other than English. While other areas in the U.S. have similarly high proportions of non-English speakers, each area generally has one language group (e.g., Spanish in the Southwest), not the diversity of languages one finds in Hawai'i. This has an important impact on policies which strive to include all ethnic groups.

## Table 3.4: Ethnic Background (1988)[9]

| Ethnic background | Numbers | % of total |
|---|---|---|
| Unmixed | 703,990 | 68.8 |
| Caucasian | 239,294 | 23.4 |
| Japanese | 235,207 | 23.0 |
| Chinese | 48,727 | 4.8 |
| Filipino | 115,519 | 11.3 |
| Hawaiian | 8,903 | 0.8 |
| Korean | 13,284 | 1.3 |
| Black | 23,032 | 2.3 |
| Puerto Rican | 4,279 | 0.4 |
| Samoan | 3,825 | 0.4 |
| Other/unknown | 12,729 | 1.2 |
| Mixed | 318,755 | 31.2 |
| Part-Hawaiian | 203,355 | 19.9 |
| Non-Hawiian | 115,401 | 11.3 |
| Total | 1,022,745 | 100.0 |

## Vital Statistics

An examination of Hawai'i's population would be incomplete without reference to the vital and health characteristics of the population. Birth rates and death rates, the incidence of diseases, and the quantity and availability of human/health services are all indicators of the quality of life. Hawai'i's vital statistics, in general, compare favorably to mainland and other Pacific Basin locations. For example, for those persons born in Hawai'i between 1984 and 1986, males have a life expectancy of 75.4 years and females can expect to live to nearly 81 years of age. This compares to an average of only 74.9 for both men and women on the mainland. Hawai'i's population

## Table 3.5: Language Spoken at Home in 1980
### (Speakers five years of age or older)[10]

| | Percent | Number |
|---|---|---|
| English Only | 74.21 | 658,752 |
| Japanese | 9.04 | 80,230 |
| Philippine Languages | 7.51 | 66,655 |
| Chinese | 2.26 | 20,066 |
| Spanish | 1.34 | 11,933 |
| Korean | 1.04 | 9,231 |
| All Others | 4.60 | 40,840 |
| Total | 100.00 | 887,707 |

**Table 3.6: Percent of Adult Population Affected by
Specific Health Risk Factors (1987)[11]**

| Health Risk Factor | State | Oahu | Other | Male | Female |
|---|---|---|---|---|---|
| Seatbelt non-use | 7.3 | 5.9 | 2.2 | 9.1 | 5.6 |
| Hypertension | 15.7 | 15.7 | 15.7 | 15.2 | 16.1 |
| Sedentary Lifestyle | 51.7 | 51.6 | 52.0 | 45.3 | 57.9 |
| Obesity | 18.1 | 17.5 | 20.3 | 21.3 | 15.0 |
| Smoking | 22.3 | 21.4 | 25.5 | 23.6 | 21.2 |
| Acute Drinking | 22.6 | 21.2 | 27.7 | 35.3 | 10.2 |
| Heavier Drinking | 8.9 | 7.4 | 13.9 | 15.2 | 2.7 |
| Drinking & Driving | 3.7 | 3.0 | 6.2 | 5.5 | 1.9 |

enjoys high health standards although, as one would expect, there is variation among different subgroups of the population.

Hawai'i does not differ significantly from the mainland United States in terms of the leading causes of death. While enjoying slightly greater longevity, the major causes of death are nearly identical with the causes reported in mainland epidemiological data. It should be noted, however, that the leading causes of death do vary across gender and ethnic lines. Moreover, the health risk factors, as expected, also vary by gender and ethnicity. Tables 3.6 and 3.7 present data on health risk factors as they affect different segments of Hawai'i's population. These data provide an insight into the variations which occur in the life styles of Hawai'i's residents.

## Social Inequality

A complete examination of Hawai'i's population must include a discussion of social inequality and the system of stratification existing in the state. Planning and policy initiatives disregarding these

**Table 3.7: Health Risk Factors by Ethnicity (1987)[12]**

| Health Risk Factor | Cauc. | Fili. | Haw'n | Jpnse. | Other |
|---|---|---|---|---|---|
| Seatbelt non-use | 10.5 | 6.5 | 11.9 | 2.7 | 5.8 |
| Hypertension | 13.5 | 16.3 | 16.4 | 18.1 | 14.2 |
| Sedentary Lifestyle | 42.8 | 69.5 | 45.3 | 60.2 | 42.4 |
| Obesity | 16.3 | 11.7 | 41.9 | 12.3 | 14.9 |
| Smoking | 25.0 | 23.2 | 27.8 | 17.9 | 18.5 |
| Acute Drinking | 28.3 | 17.0 | 30.4 | 18.9 | 16.3 |
| Heavier Drinking | 10.7 | 5.7 | 15.5 | 6.1 | 6.8 |
| Drinking & Driving | 4.7 | 3.4 | 7.5 | 1.9 | 1.8 |

important topics will be as likely to fail as those disregarding Hawai'i's ethnic and cultural diversity or Hawai'i's population characteristics and trends. In fact, social inequality in Hawai'i is strongly correlated with ethnicity and general population trends—especially immigration and migration. From the standpoint of social analysis and policy, the system of social inequality in Hawai'i is the single most important factor to be considered. Because of this, it will occupy the remainder of this chapter.

Hawai'i can be characterized as a region of intense social differentiation and inequality. Social class, including its influence with other factors (e.g., age, education, gender, and ethnicity), is a major feature of contemporary Hawai'i—as it has been a major feature of Hawai'i's social history since the early nineteenth century. Social inequality is an important determinant of the quality of life for most of Hawai'i's residents and there is little empirical evidence to suggest that it is abating. On the contrary, social class differences appear to be remaining stable or increasing.

Social issues such as affordable housing, transportation, medical care, food, child care, and occupational mobility are of national concern. In Hawai'i, however, these issues have taken on far more significance as the cost of living, the generally dependent character of Hawai'i's economy, and the real limitations on available land have combined to create market conditions which prevent more and more individuals and their families from participating at an acceptable level in the economy. In a recent televised debate on affordable housing in Hawai'i, for example, a city official and a developer commended one another for creating "moderate priced homes" for Oahu's residents who could not afford to buy into the existing housing market. Their definition of a "moderate priced home" was in the range of $175,000 to $275,000. If we consider the Hawai'i resident income data (see Table 3.8), what is being touted as affordable excludes over ninety percent of Hawai'i's residents—assuming of course that most individuals and families making less than $75,000 a year are incapable of fronting more than $30,000 as a down payment on a house.

The most salient indicators of social inequality in Hawai'i are those directly associated with economic factors. Table 3.8 presents data on the average annual income for households and families for the periods 1982–1984 and 1985–1987. As should be expected, there has been an increase in income during both periods. However, when Hawai'i's cost of living is factored in, the gains are not very impressive. To illustrate the point, the per capita income in 1970 was

### Table 3.8: Annual Mean Income (before taxes) of Households and Families (1982–84 and 1985–87)[14]

| Income Range | Households 1982–1984 | Households 1985–1987 | Families 1982–1984 | Families 1985–1987 |
|---|---|---|---|---|
| $0–9,999 | 16.96% | 12.54% | 11.38% | 7.60% |
| $10,000–19,999 | 21.43% | 18.95% | 19.08% | 16.20% |
| $20,000–34,999 | 27.38% | 24.64% | 29.79% | 25.49% |
| $35,000–49,999 | 19.18% | 18.15% | 22.63% | 20.17% |
| $50,000–74,999 | 11.72% | 17.81% | 13.25% | 21.29% |
| $75,000– | 3.33% | 7.91% | 3.88% | 9.24% |
| Total | 100.00% | 100.00% | 100.00% | 100.00% |
| Number | 327,405 | 349,890 | 247,521 | 266,736 |
| Median Income | $26,343 | $30,858 | $30,071 | $35,478 |

$4,944. In comparison the 1985 per capita income in Hawai'i was $11,003, which compares to $10,797 for the nation as a whole.[13] By 1987, Hawai'i's per capita income had increased to $15,679. If the 1987 figure is converted to 1970 constant dollar value, real income in 1987 was $5,581. In 1970, the per capita income of Hawai'i's residents was 122 percent of the national average. By 1987 that figure had declined to 101 percent of the national average. Even if constant dollar comparisons are not made, the fact of the matter is that Hawai'i's cost of living generally consumes significant proportions of income simply for basics—food, housing, and utilities. Thus, even at the $15,679 figure, the typical individual could anticipate spending as much as eighty percent of that pretax income on basic necessities.

In Table 3.9, data on the median income of families by ethnicity is presented. The actual dollar amounts are less significant than the relations of families in various ethnic groups to the overall median family income. Ten years later, this relationship has changed very little.

### Table 3.9: Median Family Income of Major Ethnic Groups (1980)[15]

| Ethnic group | Median family income | Percentage* |
|---|---|---|
| Chinese | $23,859 | +27.0 |
| Japanese | 23,209 | +23.5 |
| Caucasian | 20,823 | +10.8 |
| All Group Median | 18,782 | |
| Part-Hawaiian | 16,445 | −12.4 |
| Filipino | 16,361 | −12.9 |
| Hawaiian | 11,997 | −36.1 |

*Percentage difference from state median.

**Table 3.10: Poverty Status of Families and Unrelated Individuals**
**(1969–1987)[16]**

| | Families below poverty level | | | Individuals below poverty level | | |
|---|---|---|---|---|---|---|
| | Total | Number | Percent* | Total | Number | Percent* |
| 1969 | 170,729 | 13,046 | 7.6 | 55,588 | 16,833 | 33.3 |
| 1975 | 201,000 | 13,000 | 6.4 | 66,000 | 14,000 | 21.6 |
| 1979 | 227,974 | 17,700 | 7.8 | 107,787 | 24,775 | 23.0 |
| 1985 | 253,914 | 18,776 | 7.4 | 117,639 | 27,243 | 23.2 |
| 1986 | 264,689 | 23,419 | 8.8 | 122,419 | 31,828 | 26.0 |
| 1987 | 281,599 | 20,468 | 7.3 | 107,656 | 19,513 | 18.1 |
| 1988 | 272,948 | 22,805 | 8.4 | 124,501 | 27,241 | 21.9 |

*Percentage of total state population.

Another measure of social inequality in Hawai'i is the poverty status data for families and individuals. Table 3.10 presents trend data for the period 1969–1987. In reviewing these data, the reader is cautioned to keep in mind that the poverty thresholds employed in the table were developed for mainland populations. Since the cost of living in Hawai'i is higher, the data actually underestimate the family and individual poverty percentages in the state. It should be noted that Hawai'i's poverty thresholds are approximately 15 percent higher than those employed on the mainland.

Crime statistics, though with their own limitations, can be employed as another general indicator of social inequality. Table 3.11 presents data on selected crimes by ethnicity. To place the data in proper perspective, each ethnic group's proportion of the total population is also included in the presentation. Similar disproportional representation occurs in the area of incarceration rates, with Hawaiians being the most disproportionately overrepresented. Incarceration data are presented in Table 3.12.

In bringing to a close our discussion of social inequality, it is important to note that social inequality in Hawai'i is very much a product of the relationship between general population factors and the availability and use of land. In fact, if there is one factor that simply cannot be disregarded in social planning and policy formation in Hawai'i, it is this relationship between the population and the land. It is not an exaggeration to argue that much of Hawai'i's social and political history since the Great Mahele of 1846 has been the direct or indirect product of this changing relationship. Through Hawai'i's plantation era and the period when the Big Five corporations dominated Hawai'i's political economy, control of land continued to be the single most important factor in Hawai'i's system of social

### Table 3.11: Ethnic Distribution of Hawai'i's Population, Arrests, Murder Arrests, Murder Victims, and Drug Abuse Arrests (1986)[17]

|  | % of total population | % nontraffic arrests | % murder arrests | % murder victims | % drug abuse arrests |
|---|---|---|---|---|---|
| Caucasian | 33.0 | 34.5 | 13.5 | 42.2 | 45.5 |
| Japanese | 24.9 | 6.3 | 5.4 | 11.8 | 7.7 |
| Filipino | 13.9 | 12.3 | 54.0 | 13.7 | 8.6 |
| Hawaiian and part-Hawaiian | 2.0 | 23.4 | 13.5 | 15.7 | 16.9 |
| Chinese | 5.8 | 1.5 | 2.7 | 2.0 | 2.0 |
| Korean | 1.9 | 1.2 | n/a | 3.9 | 0.8 |
| Black | 1.8 | 4.0 | n/a | n/a | 6.2 |
| Samoan | 1.5 | 4.7 | 16.2 | 3.9 | 2.2 |
| Amerindian | 0.3 | 0.2 | n/a | n/a | 0.1 |
| Other | 5.0 | 11.8 | 2.7 | 7.8 | 10.0 |

inequality.[19] It is beyond dispute that much of the social power of contemporary Hawai'i is directly tied to various groups' relationship to land—ie., land ownership and control.[20]

## Conclusion

Most of the central public policy issues and debates which confront the residents of Hawai'i today feature land, the cost of living, and the dependent character of Hawai'i's economy. For example, issues pertaining to agriculture, geothermal development, tourism, the military presence, the development of a spaceport facility on the island of Hawai'i, and foreign investments are all tied directly to land use, the cost of living, and Hawai'i's dependent economy. Despite claims and hopes to the contrary, it seems unlikely that Hawai'i will

### Table 3.12: Hawai'i Adult Incarceration and Arrest Rates (1980)[18]

|  | Arrests | | Incarceration | |
|---|---|---|---|---|
|  | Number | (%) | Number | (%)[†] |
| Hawaiian/part-Haw. | 4,617 | 24 | 467 | 49 |
| Oriental* | 5,179 | 27 | 187 | 20 |
| Caucasian | 9,388 | 49 | 302 | 31 |

*Includes Filipinos and Pacific Islanders.
†Percentage of state total.

be able to break away from its economic dependence upon the various Pacific region centers of economic power. As such, Hawai'i will remain economically dependent and its economy will be forced to emphasize those activities which reflect that status: tourism, foreign investments, and a large military presence. Attempts to circumvent this reality and to develop economic independence through such activities as agriculture are going to succeed primarily in exacerbating social problems associated with land shortages. Even those attempts to reduce energy dependence via geothermal development are going to further intensify land and housing problems.

Hawai'i's demographic reality is such that public policy initiatives in the foreseeable future must attempt to balance the cultural, political, and social needs of Hawai'i's residents with the economic circumstances stemming from limited land resources, a cost of living that marginalizes many of the state's residents, and a general lack of local investment capital which results in unavoidable appeals for foreign capital. Population growth will further complicate the situation as demands for basic human services increase and an already critical housing shortage worsens. Finally, income disparities, already quite remarkable, will further widen social class differences, creating for Hawai'i a class situation that has both long-term and short-term policy implications.

## Note on Sources

Additional data on Hawai'i's population can be found in a number of important publications. For those engaged in, or students of, public policy formation and social planning, the authors recommend the following as indispensable resources: *Statistical Abstract of the United States: 1988, Historical Statistics of Hawai'i, State of Hawai'i Data Book 1990,* and the annual statistical reports of the Hawai'i Department of Health. There is also the federal publication *Vital Statistics* published annually with data at the state, county, and city level.

## Notes

1. Romanzo Adams, *The Peoples of Hawai'i* (Honolulu: Institute of Pacific Relations, 1933); Andrew Lind, *An Island Community: Ecological Succession in Hawai'i* (Chicago: University of Chicago Press, 1938); Andrew Lind, *Hawai'i's People* (Honolulu: University of Hawai'i Press, 1955).

2. Lind, *Island Community.*

3. David Stannard, *Before the Horror* (Honolulu: Social Science Research Institute, University of Hawai'i, 1989).

4. Department of Business and Economic Development (DBED), *State of Hawai'i Data Book 1988* (Honolulu: Department of Business and Economic Development, 1990), p. 13.

5. Ibid., p. 15.

6. Ibid., p. 186.

7. Ibid., p. 13.

8. The benefits from Hawai'i's tourist and military industries stem primarily from the jobs which are added to the economy and from the infusion into the state's economy of capital required to maintain the economic infrastructures of both of these industries. The authors readily acknowledge, however, that a cogent argument can be made that these benefits are somewhat marginal, since the jobs created tend to concentrate at the low end of the occupational ladder, and the infusion of capital tends to remove land from public use and further increase an already high cost of living.

9. DBED, Data Book 1990, p. 40.

10. Ibid., p. 46.

11. Ibid., p. 78.

12. Ibid., p. 76.

13. *County and City Data Book, 1988,* Bureau of the Census, U.S. Department of Commerce.

14. Ibid., p. 376.

15. Cited in *Current Facts and Figures about Hawaiians,* by George S. Kanahele, sponsored by Project WAIAHA, Honolulu, 1982.

16. DBED, Data Book 1990, p. 363.

17. Hawai'i Criminal Justice Data Center HCJDC, *Crime in Hawai'i 1986: A Review of Uniform Crime Reports* (Honolulu: Hawai'i Criminal Justice Data Center) p. 20. The differences in percentages between Table IV and XI for various ethnic categories are a product of data collection technique (ethnic categorizations, etc.) and the data being from different years.

18. HCJDC, *Crime in Hawai'i 1980, p. 18.*

19. Jeffrey Crane and Jan Mejer, "From History to the Quest for Believable Myth," *Humboldt Journal of Social Relations* 15 (1) (1988), pp. 53–78.

20. George Cooper and Gavan Daws, *Land and Power in Hawai'i* (Honolulu: Benchmark Books, 1985).

# II

## POLICY PROCESSES

# 4

## BLOOD RUNS THICK: ETHNICITY AS A FACTOR IN HAWAI'I'S POLITICS

### Dan Boylan

### Introduction

This chapter examines ethnic politics and the impact of ethnicity on elections in the islands. Although many have argued that ethnicity or race plays a small role in politics and elections in the state, there is, in fact, strong evidence that ethnicity is a major factor in Hawai'i politics.

In 1986, Hawai'i Republicans felt they had a good chance of seizing the governorship, an office that had not been theirs since 1962. The three-term incumbent, George Ariyoshi, was ineligible to succeed himself. For the Democrats it was just as well, for, according to mass analysis, there was a large bloc of voters anxious for a change—a bloc Republican strategists assumed would be theirs.

Contributing still more to GOP optimism, however, was the presence of Mayor Frank Fasi in the Honolulu City Hall. In 1984 the Republicans had recruited Fasi—a former Democratic three-term mayor, frequent gubernatorial candidate, and one of the state's most popular politicians—into their ranks and returned him to the Honolulu mayoralty after a four-year forced hiatus. The Republicans further attempted to expand their electoral base by bringing Filipino-Americans into city hall and by providing D. G. "Andy" Anderson, one of the Republicans' most attractive candidates for the past twenty years, with a forum in the managing director's office from which to demonstrate his administrative ability.

Thanks to Fasi, the Republicans entered the 1986 campaign season with what seemed to be a lock on three of Hawai'i's four largest groups: Caucasians, Hawaiians, and Filipinos. Only Japanese-Americans were expected to remain loyal to the Democratic Party,

**Table 4.1: Selected Districts: 1986 Election**

| District | Primary | | General | |
|---|---|---|---|---|
| | *Heftel* | *Waihee* | *Anderson* | *Waihee* |
| 11th | 2253 | 2177 | 3137 | 4379 |
| 36th | 1626 | 1480 | 2194 | 2950 |
| 37th | 1875 | 1491 | 2112 | 3037 |
| 38th | 1552 | 1470 | 1901 | 2825 |
| 39th | 1938 | 1347 | 2506 | 2630 |
| 45th | 1927 | 1666 | 2288 | 4034 |

which had served as their primary instrument of social mobility in the post-War years.

But the Republicans' dreams were to remain unfulfilled. For governor, the Democrats nominated John Waihee, thus giving Hawaiians and part-Hawaiians their first chance since statehood in 1959 to see one of their own in the state's highest office. For lieutenant governor, the Democrats nominated Ben Cayetano, offering a Filipino-American a chance for the first time to win any statewide office. With the continued loyalty of Japanese-Americans to the Democrats, the Republican hope was defeated. Despite a quarter century of pent-up resentment against Democratic chief executives, the Waihee-Cayetano ticket beat the Republican ticket of Andy Anderson and John Henry Felix by 13,195 votes out of approximately 335,000 cast.

The ethnic pull of the Waihee-Cayetano ticket is made startingly clear by an analysis of six representative districts in which Filipinos made up more than thirty percent of the electorate. Gubernatorial candidate Cecil Heftel, a five-term U.S. Congressmen, campaigned hard for the Filipino vote in the Democratic primary. And in each of the Filipino districts he defeated Waihee. But in the general election, with Cayetano on the ticket, all six of the Filipino districts voted Democratic—despite Fasi's support of the Anderson-Felix ticket.[1]

In contrast, John Henry Felix added nothing ethnically to the Republican ticket. Anderson was a Portuguese-American small businessman; so too was Felix. Frank Fasi, at least, understood how vitally important an ethnically balance ticket was in 1986; in the Republican primary he had endorsed the candidacy of Filipina Vicky Bunye. Unfortunately, Bunye had never previously run for elective office. Indeed, her most prominent position prior to her bid for the lieutenant governorship was as an aide to liberal Democratic councilwoman Patsy Mink. Bunye came in third in the Republican primary, behind Felix and another Caucasian candidate, lawyer Cynthia Thielen.[2]

The 1986 election provided only the most recent example of how ethnic voting has lent form and direction to island political life. Ethnic voting—more than any other factor—has defined the constituencies Hawai'i's Republican and Democratic parties since the territorial government began functioning in 1900.

## The Decline of Party Politics

Following statehood, many held out the vision of a Hawai'i in which the color of a person's skin and the place of their origin would count for nought in Hawai'i society or its politics. Three decades later we see ethnicity playing an ever larger role in the political equation.

This is for a variety of reasons. First, American history, whether written on the eastern seaboard or on a chain of islands in the Pacific ocean, has proven that democracy and ethnic voting mix well. Minorities in Hawai'i and throughout the nation have used politics as a successful route to greater social and economic status. Irish, Italians, Jews, Blacks, Hispanics—and in Hawai'i, Chinese and Japanese—have all written this tale repeatedly in different city, state, and national arenas.[3] And Hawai'i, like many parts of the nation, is experiencing a new wave of immigration, largely Southeast Asian and Pacific in origin, which is using democratic politics in the same manner as those who have gone before them. (Although, as will be seen in the concluding section of this chapter, there are factors at work which may slow the political progress of Hawai'i most recent immigrants.)

Secondly, the weak nature of Hawai'i political parties points to a renewed need for ethnic solidarity. Hawai'i's Republican Party crumbled following its failure to meet the Democrats' post-War success in forging a coalition of Japanese-Americans and labor unions. By 1962, three years after statehood, the Republicans had lost control of everything save the mayoralty of Honolulu and a U.S. Senate seat.

Hawai'i Democrats, on the other hand, fell victim to the twin slayers of party politics across the mainland—television and the political action committees of the nation's countless special interest groups. Island political rallies draw few of either partisan persuasion for any political office; folks stay home to watch television. Television, in turn, became the principal means of reaching the voters. That takes money, and political action committees had far more of it than did party organizations.[4] In lieu of political parties selecting candidates, island voters have been forced back on ethnicity—or their special interests—whichever informs better.

Mainland pollster Stanley Greenstein expressed the weakening of party politics well in commenting on similar racial voting among mainland Caucasians: "In another era, party machines would have managed the gradual process of coalition building. But now, with the machines weakened or gone, people are out there on their own, and, to some degree, they are left to their own prejudices."[5]

Finally, ethnic considerations have become, if you will, Hawai'i's most militant special interest. Within the past two decades, for example, many native Hawaiians have concluded that American democracy, Hawaiian style, has not paid off for them. They now ask for extensive land reforms and a high degree of political sovereignty over their own lives. These are demands that mainstream political parties find almost impossible to address. Parties are in the business, after all, of putting together majority coalitions. It would be difficult indeed to find fifty-one percent of the electorate in a land-poor society willing to give up political or economic rights to nineteen percent of the population—Hawaiians and part-Hawaiians.

### The Myth of Ethnic Voting? The Myth of the Melting Pot

Despite the obvious importance of ethnicity in island politics, many have been loath to acknowledge it. Two of the very few political scientists who have studied local political culture in the Islands, Professor Dan Tuttle of the University of Hawai'i, Manoa, and Professor James Wang of the University of Hawai'i, Hilo, have both, to some degree, denied the role of ethnicity in local politics. In his text on Hawai'i state government, under the subtitle "The Myth of Ethnic Bloc Voting," Wang writes:

> There is very little evidence that there is frequent or widespread ethnic bloc voting in Hawai'i, despite persistent but unwarranted charges. The proposition that a political leader can deliver a group in a local election is, and economic issues are more important in state and local politics. Ethnic groups in Hawai'i do not constitute political units. Infrequent, isolated cases can be found where a preponderance of members from one ethnic group votes for a candidate

**Table 4.2: Ethnicity and Party**

|  | 1976 | | | | 1986 | | |
|---|---|---|---|---|---|---|---|
|  | D | R | I | | D | R | I |
| Caucasian | 49 | 30 | 26 | | 33 | 43 | 24 |
| Japanese | 58 | 11 | 31 | | 68 | 9 | 23 |
| Hawaiian/pt.-Haw. | 49 | 17 | 34 | | 46 | 21 | 33 |
| Filipino | 77 | 9 | 14 | | 41 | 24 | 35 |
| Chinese | 40 | 29 | 31 | | 37 | 20 | 43 |
| Other | n/a | n/a | n/a | | 44 | 21 | 35 |
| Total | 52 | 18 | 30 | | 45 | 27 | 28 |

from their own group, but such cases usually have extenuating circumstances. They are frequently contests between two unknown candidates or between two well-known and popular candidates.[6]

The real operative myth in Hawai'i politics, of course, is not that of ethnic bloc voting, but its denial. No one knows that better than Gerry Keir who has been directing political polls for the *Honolulu Advertiser* since 1974: "Ethnicity is the single most reliable indicator of how a person will vote in Hawai'i. The second- and third-best indicators are length of residence in the islands and income level. But they lag far behind ethnicity. Nothing comes even close to ethnicity in importance."[7]

*Advertiser* polling shows that the party loyalties of various ethnic groups in Hawai'i have shifted during the past decade and a half. The chief beneficiary, except in the case of Japanese-Americans, appears to be the Republican Party[8]:

Numbers do not tell all, however. Hawai'i Caucasians, for example, have always provided the bedrock support for the Republican Party—throughout the territorial period and into the 1960s. Any GOP state party convention or fundraiser still provides abundant visual proof of that axiom. But by the mid-1970s, the Republican Party offered neither attractive statewide candidates nor access to power. Thus, many Caucasians identified themselves as Democrats or independents.

Things have changed. "In the '80s more *haoles* (Caucasians) are identifying themselves as Republicans," says Keir. "It's probably a combination of the Reagan years and Fasi's switch to the Republicans. Fasi gives a local person a prominent Republican they can vote for. As an institution, the GOP has been close to a dodo bird, but in every election lately there's been a good local Republican at the head of the ticket."[9]

Fasi's reincarnation as a Republican in 1984 largely explains movement of Filipinos toward the GOP. Fasi appointed an unprecedented number of Filipinos to city hall posts and articulated a populist rhetoric attractive to an ethnic group near the bottom of most of the state's social and economic indexes. In 1976, Filipinos were even more Democratic than Japanese-Americans; in 1986 they appeared to be an ethnic group in transition between parties.

The most cursory look at the makeup of the Hawai'i House of Representatives underscored the power of ethnicity in the state's voting patterns. In sixty percent of the state's fifty-one house districts, a candidate from the largest ethnic group resident in that district holds the seat. In twenty of the twenty-three house districts in which one ethnic group composes forty percent or more of the population, the district's voters have elected a candidate from its dominant ethnic group. What the figures demonstrate is that, when they have the chance, Caucasians vote for Caucasians, Japanese-Americans for Japanese-Americans, Filipinos for Filipinos, Hawaiians for Hawaiians, and Chinese for Chinese.[10]

*Advertiser* polls bear this out. In 1974, Caucasian voters acknowledged supporting a relatively weak, but all-white, Republican ticket for the governorship and lieutenant governorship by a margin of two to one. Japanese-Americans, on the other hand, admitted that they voted for George Ariyoshi in his first bid for the governorship by a five to one margin. Four years later in a classic face-off between Ariyoshi and Fasi, a Caucasian, in the Democratic party primary for governor, Japanese-Americans said they voted for Ariyoshi three to one, while *haoles* gave their support to Fasi five to one.[11]

Politicians, of course, understand the importance of ethnic voting in Hawai'i far better than political scientists, reporters, or pollsters. Anecdotal evidence of their awareness of ethnic voting is overwhelming. Rare is the *haole* candidate for any office who does not have a Japanese-American's name listed as his campaign treasurer on political advertising, or vise versa. Island publicists weigh carefully the mix of pictures of Caucasian, Japanese-American, Hawaiian, and Filipino supporters which go into their campaign literature. Blessed is Oahu state Senator Eloise Tungpalan who is married to a Filipino. More than forty percent of her constituents are Japanese-Americans; more than twenty-five percent Filipino. In her campaign literature, she gives equal prominence to her Japanese maiden name, Yamashita, and her constituents understand why.

And, behind closed doors, at least, local politicians speak openly of ethnic voting. In 1984, James V. Hall, a former executive director of the Hawai'i Republican Party, an unsuccessful candidate for legislative office, and, most recently, a city deputy managing director, analyzed the presidential and mayoral vote in 171 Oahu voting precincts. His twelve-page "Analysis: Honolulu County General Election (1984)" circulated throughout the Republican Party. Its "Summary Conclusions" began with the statement: "Ethnic politics are alive and well and living on Oahu!" The summary continued:

- Voters of Caucasian ancestry voted overwhelmingly for Reagan, somewhat less for Frank Fasi. In general, they also supported Republican candidates.

- Voters of Japanese ancestry voted overwhelmingly for Eileen Anderson, somewhat less for Mondale. They supported other Democrat candidates except when the Republican candidate was of Japanese ancestry.

- Voters of Filipino ancestry voted overwhelmingly for Fasi but much less for Reagan and other Republican candidates.

- Voters of Hawaiian ancestry voted overwhelmingly for Fasi and Reagan.[12]

Since World War II, Democrats, of course, have been playing ethnic politics in Hawai'i far more successfully than Republicans. Mike Tokunaga has been intimately involved in Democratic campaigns for the past forty years, and he willingly admits the centrality of ethnic considerations in local campaign strategy. "How major ethnic groups will vote is the first consideration in a major race," says Tokunaga. "I don't think we have to be apologetic about that, because wherever you go in America it's the rule. 'Birds of the same feather flock together.'"[13]

## A Psychology of Denial

Why, then, the denial of Hawai'i's ethnic politics? Such denial is not to be found in Hawai'i's early history as an American territory. Most historians of the overthrow of the Hawaiian monarchy in 1893 admit that its Caucasian instigators did so with confidence that Republican President Benjamin Harrison would reward their labors with the quick introduction and passage of a bill to annex the islands. Their timing, however, was poor. Harrison was a lame-duck president in the spring of 1893, and no congress would pass so controversial a bill before the newly elected president, Democrat Grover Cleveland, took office.

Cleveland was an anti-imperialist. He ordered an investigation of the overthrow, rebuked its perpetrators, and urged that they restore the monarchy. Instead, they formed a republic, largely disenfranchised promonarchist Hawaiians, and waited the return of an imperialist Republican to the presidency. They didn't have to wait long. In 1897, Republican William McKinley took the oath of office. Within months after McKinley's swearing in, the United States was waging an imperial war against Spain. With the annexation of the Philippines opposition to acquiring Hawai'i vanished.[14]

The Republican candidacy of Prince Jonah Kalanianaole Kuhio for delegate to congress in 1902 established the ethnic foundations of the new territory's political parties. Discriminatory legislation prohibited many Asians from naturalizing, so Hawaiians constituted the largest single ethnic voting bloc in the islands until well into the twentieth century. The territory's Caucasian oligarchy of rich sugar factors and their commercial servants seduced Kuhio into carrying the Republican banner. Kuhio's Republicanism, in turn, plus patronage jobs for Hawaiians, cemented an alliance of Caucasians and Hawaiians which assured Republican control of both houses of the territorial legislature plus the delegateship.[15]

Prior to World War II, few denied the ethnic factor in Hawai'i politics. Indeed, voters often heard ethnic slurs at island political rallies, directed at politicians from every race.

But the genesis of Hawai'i's denial of ethnic politics is to be found in the 1930s. "From the time we went to kindergarten, we were taught that we had to be good American citizens," says Mike Tokunaga. Japanese-Americans felt the seriousness of that injunction; throughout the decade, the aggression of their mother country caused the Americanism of Japanese-Americans in Hawai'i to be suspect. "You'd see the results of that training down in Moiliili in the old days," Tokunaga continues. "Moiliili was an AJA precinct. The votes were counted by hand, and the Buddhaheads would always give one of their three votes to someone of another ethnicity. I think the AJAs had a guilty conscience."[16]

Japanese-Americans in Hawai'i suffered numerous indignities during World War II. A small portion of them went to internment camps on the mainland. The military government denied a much larger portion of them its prewar jobs in areas considered vital to the war effort. Despite the overt discrimination against them (or because of it), thousands of AJA youngsters joined the 100th Battalion and the 442d Regimental Combat Team and fought in Europe to prove their patriotism. But their fear of being seen as less than totally American undoubtedly persisted—right into the voting booths of Moiliili and other Japanese-American precincts.[17]

Hawai'i's post-War struggle for statehood also muted any admission of blatantly ethnic politics. Community leaders, the majority of whom where Caucasian, began to campaign aggressively for statehood in the mid-1930s. In arguing their case for a territory whose population was eighty percent non white to an American mainland where the population was better than eighty percent white, Hawai'i statehood proponents stressed how well assimilated Hawai'i's multiethnic society had become. Like the mainland at large, they argued, Hawai'i was a melting pot, only a different mix of elements were melting.

Mainland opposition to statehood for Hawai'i came primarily from Caucasians in the Southern states. In the midst of their own rearguard action against the forced breakup of racial segregation, Southern politicians feared the entrance of a multiethnic state whose representatives would undoubtedly support integration.[18]

Finally, Hawai'i's denial of ethnic politics rests on expediency and good taste. In a society so ethnically diverse, one in which no ethnic group dominates, politicians have recognized that ethnic considerations must be limited to the back rooms where they gather to forge campaign strategy. In public, however, on the political stump and in campaign advertising, ethnic appeals have been kept subtle.

As well they must. Caucasians constitute the largest ethnic group in Hawai'i—24.5 percent of the population. Japanese-Americans make up 23.2 percent, Hawaiians and part-Hawaiians 19.9 percent; and Filipinos 11.3 percent. Chinese, Koreans, Samoans, various southeast Asians, and others make up the remaining 21.1 percent. No Hawai'i politician or political party leader schooled in the barest essentials of mathematics will indulge in public racial baiting—not if he or she wants to win elections. Building winning majorities in Hawai'i means constructing coalitions of a number of ethnic groups.[19]

Throughout the long period of Hawai'i's public denial of ethnic politics, its political leaders have flagrantly practiced them. Indeed, they've failed to do so at their own peril. In 1959, Hawai'i's first election as a state, ambitious island Democrats jumped into the party primary, beat each other up, and entered the general election with a terribly unbalanced ticket. It was made up solely of Caucasian and Japanese-American candidates: Frank Fasi and Oren Long for the two U.S. Senate seats, Daniel K. Inouye for the U.S. House of Representatives, John A. Burns for governor, and Mits Kido for lieutenant governor. The resulting imbalance allowed the Republicans, despite the ethnic imbalance of their party membership and its precipitous decline in the 1950s, to field an ethnically more balanced ticket and to put Chinese-American Hiram Fong in one of the Senate seats, Caucasian William Quinn in the governorship, and Hawaiian Jimmy Kealoha in the lieutenant governorship.

The Democrats learned their lesson. In preparation for 1962, when one U.S. Senate seat, the governorship, the lieutenant governorship, and two seats in the U.S. House were at stake, the Democrats formed a fact-finding committee whose real task was not to gather facts, but to make a slate. Chaired by freshman state representative Robert Oshiro, the committee recommended a ticket made up of AJA Inouye for the U.S. Senate, Caucasian Burns for governor, Hawaiian William Richardson for lieutenant governor, Caucasian Tom Gill for one of the U.S. House seats, and Chinese-American Herbert Lee for the other. Spark Matsunaga refused to heed the dictates of the slate-making committee, but the resultant ticket of Inouye, Burns, Richardson, Gill, and Matsunaga still contained three of the state's four largest ethnic groups. The Democrats swept all five offices and gained control of both houses of the state legislature.[20]

Similarly, twenty-four years later, in 1986, former state Senator Nadao Yoshinaga urged fellow Democrats to support a "Rainbow ticket" composed of AJA Daniel Inouye for U.S. Senate, Caucasian Neil Abercrombie and Hawaiian Dan Akaka for the U.S. House, Waihee for governor, and Cayetano, a Filipino, for lieutenant governor.

Besides his pivotal role in making the Democrats' 1962 slate, Robert Oshiro chaired the Democratic Party through most of the 1960s and ran gubernatorial campaigns for John A. Burns (1970), George Ariyoshi (1974, 1978, and 1982), and Waihee (1986). As Oshiro remarked:

> In all of the campaigns I've taken part in, I've tried to remind people what the Democratic party has meant to their ethnic group.
>
> In the mid-1960s I said publicly that ethnicity was important in Hawai'i politics. And it's playing an even greater role today. It's a

numbers game. *Haoles* and Japanese are the two dominant groups, but the balance has shifted. In the 1950s Japanese made up one-third of the electorate; today it's twenty-two percent. The Filipinos constitute the emerging group. Then there are new groups: the boat people, the Vietnamese and Cambodians, the Pacific Islanders. They'll all want their place in the sun and they'll use politics to achieve it.

Caucasians have a different problem. Unlike the plantation workers or boat people, they didn't come as a group. Most came on their own volition for various reasons. And they don't have a culture which emphasizes working as a group.[21]

### Hawai'i's Third Party—And the Uncertain Future of Ethnic Politics

Hawai'i's new ethnics will have more difficulty finding their place in the sun. They may have to look to the Republican Party for help, and they will definitely find their way blocked, at least temporarily, by a force far stronger than either of Hawai'i's political parties—money and the attendant power it lends to incumbents.

Hawai'i Republican Party chair D. G. Andy Anderson predicts that by the mid-1990s, the domination which Democrats now enjoy over Hawai'i's political life will be over. "The Republican Party is beginning to steal away Democrats and independents, particularly Democrat youngsters," he says. "The *sansei* and *yonsei* (third and fourth generation Japanese-Americans in Hawai'i) can't remember Uncle Sparky (Matsunaga) and Uncle Dan (Inouye). The old loyalties are dying. Mortgage payments, school tuition, car payments: They're all more important to them than ethnic loyalties." Anderson is convinced that new ethnic loyalties and aspirations will also help the Republican Party. "It'll be wide open because of the in-migration of Caucasians, Filipinos, Vietnamese—and support from younger Japanese-Americans," he asserts. "It'll be a brand new, healthy political Hawai'i in which Republicans enjoy political parity."[22]

Honolulu *Advertiser* editor Gerry Keir is not so certain; his figures from recent election polling show no particular drop-off among younger Japanese-Americans. Neither does Mike Tokunaga discern diminished loyalty to the Democratic party among younger AJAs. "Third-generation AJAs are not too concerned with whether a candidate is a Democrat or a Republican, but in the booth, when they have to choose, the ethnic pull is still there," say Tokunaga. "So too is pull towards the Democratic Party, because the pressure from the *nisei* is still there. It's harder to say how fourth and fifth generation AJAs would react."[23]

Indeed, fourth and fifth generation AJAs may be confused by their ethnicity as well as their party loyalties, for increasingly they, along with the rest of Hawai'i's children, are of mixed birth. The trend toward marriages outside of one's own race has accelerated in the 1980s, and that has meant more and more of Hawai'i's children are of mixed ethnicity. In 1988, for example, of the 15,233 children born to nonmilitary families in Hawai'i, 8,486 of them were of mixed parentage, 5,501 unmixed, and 1,246 uncertain. Thus, at least fifty-five percent (and probably considerably more) of all children born in the state in 1988 were of mixed ethnicity.[24] When they are of voting age, will they identify with the ethnicity of their fathers or their mothers? With their local brethren? How?

Wherever younger voters are going, one influence is definitely on the rise: the strength and stability of incumbents. It grows more rapidly than either the Republican or Democratic parties, and, at this state in Hawai'i's history, that means, in almost all legislative instances, the perpetuation of Democrats in office. Once an office is won, incumbency weighs far more heavily in Hawai'i's (and the nation's) political equation than any other single factor—ethnicity included.

Incumbents proved unstoppable in the 1988 election year. Thirty-nine percent of the incumbent state house and senate candidates ran *unopposed* for reelection to their seats. Of the remaining forty seats, eleven of the victorious incumbents garnered more than seventy percent of the vote and fourteen in excess of sixty percent of the vote.

Money explains the stranglehold Hawai'i's incumbents have on their seats. Some incumbent state representatives currently have fifty to seventy-five thousand dollars in their campaign treasuries— in preparation for reelection races in districts in which no more than seven thousand people vote, and usually a good deal less. Those sums intimidate potential opponents and insure that, by providing lunches for campaign workers, trophies for youth league teams, and contributions to community charities, incumbents can literally buy their reelections.[25]

Thus, the use of politics by emerging ethnic groups to advance themselves is thwarted by the influence of incumbency. The enormous size of an incumbent's campaign treasury stymies ethnic minorities, even in comparatively small legislative districts where they constitute the single largest ethnic group. If the incumbents' stranglehold persists, it may even sap the most powerful source of democratic energy in island life in this century—ethnic politics.

## Notes

1. All voter analyses in this paper are based on published official returns provided by the lieutenant governor's office of the State of Hawai'i. Lloyd Nekoba of the lieutenant governor's office did the analysis of the six Filipino precincts. All such analyses rely on "District and County Population and Ethnic Profiles, 1984 State of Hawai'i Election Districts" prepared by the Research and Information Processing Division of the Office of Lieutenant Governor, April 1984.

2. The Republicans' choice of John Henry Felix to run with Anderson is simply the most recent example of the party's insensitivity to ethnic politics in the post-War period. In only four of the eight gubernatorial elections since statehood have the Republicans fielded balanced tickets (i.e., the candidates for governor and lieutenant governor were of different ethnic backgrounds). The Democrats, however, have run balanced tickets in six of the eight elections since statehood.

3. The story of democratic politics as an instrument of social and economic mobility for America's various immigrant groups has been told many times, nowhere better, perhaps, than in Oscar Handlin's *The Uprooted* (New York: Grosset and Dunlap, 1951), pp. 201–26.

4. For the decline of America's political parties nationally, see David Broder, *The Party's Over: The Failure of Politics in America* (New York: Harper and Row, 1972).

5. As quoted in Larry Eichel, "Racial Voting Still a Big Factor in American Politics," *The Honolulu Star-Bulletin and Advertiser,* March 5, 1989, p. A-28.

6. Jim Wang, *Hawai'i State and Local Politics* (Hilo: James C. F. Wang, 1982), p. 83.

7. Gerry Keir, personal interview, September 1, 1989. Not all pollsters agree with Keir that ethnicity is the single most important factor in predicting how a person will vote. But all I've talked to put it near the top of their list of indicators.

8. Polling data provided by Gerry Keir from surveys by SMS Research, Inc., run for the *Honolulu Advertiser* in 1976 and 1986.

9. Keir, personal interview.

10. My analysis is based on the membership of the House of Representatives of the Fifteenth Legislature of the State of Hawai'i and on the lieutenant governor's 1984 ethnic profile of election districts.

11. Polling data provided by Gerry Keir from the *Honolulu Advertiser's* 1974 and 1978 polls.

12. Hall based his analysis on official 1984 election returns.

13. Mike Tokunaga, personal interview, September 18, 1989.

14. For a discussion of the politics of the overthrow of the Hawaiian monarchy and the politics of the republic, the best source remains William A. Russ, Jr., *The Hawaiian Revolution* (Selinsgrove, Pa.: Susquehanna University Press, 1959), and Russ's misnamed *The Hawaiian Republic* (Selingsgrove, Pa.: Susquehanna University Press, 1961).

15. For the deal struck between Prince Kuhio and the territory's Republican leaders and the strategy for Caucasian control of the islands it effected, see Lawrence H. Fuchs, *Hawai'i Pono: A Social History* (New York: Harcourt, Brace & World, 1961) pp. 153–81.

16. Tokunaga personal interview.

17. For a discussion of the travail of Hawaiian Japanese-Americans during World War II and of their military service, see Fuchs, *Hawai'i Pono*, pp. 299–307.

18. This is the entire thesis of Roger Bell's *Last Among Equals: Hawaiian Statehood and American Politics* (Honolulu: University of Hawai'i Press, 1984).

19. *State of Hawaii Data Book*. Hawai'i State Department of Planning and Economic Development, 1985.

20. Paul C. Phillips, *Hawai'i Democrats: Chasing the American Dream* (Washington: University Press of America, 1982), pp. 61–64.

21. Robert Oshiro, personal interview, July 24, 1989.

22. D. G. Anderson, personal interview, August 30, 1989.

23. Keir and Tokunaga, personal interviews.

24. From state Health Department records provided by state statistician Robert C. Schmitt in a telephone interview, October 3, 1989.

25. Fundraising data for all state and county officeholders is available at the office of the Campaign Spending Commission, 335 Merchant St., Honolulu 96813.

# 5

# POLICY IN HAWAI'I: THE BUDGET

## *Deane Neubauer*

### Introduction

As so much of the modern policy studies informs us, the budget lies at the heart of modern government. Despite all its great powers, government has limited tools with which to accomplish its objectives. The ability to develop and implement any policy depends in an important sense on where it is situated within the budget. In a simple but powerful way, what modern government does most is spend—or not spend—money. Though a crude and imperfect tool for policy, it is an indispensable one.

In Hawai'i the budgetary process is organized through the Planned Program Budgeting System (PPBS, or PPB for short). The form employed in Hawai'i and operating through the state budgetary statute, was derived from federal and other state experiences with program budgeting in the 1960s. PPB determines the form within which all budgetary allocations may be requested and granted. It also provides for a complicated system of analysis designed to enable those who operate the system to judge objectively the comparative merits of competing budgetary requests.

In this chapter I will argue that the process of budgetary action as it exists in Hawai'i does not operate as Hawai'i's basic budget law would have it. Behind the elegant statement or picture of administrative rigor is another process with its own rules and outcomes which determines who will win or lose in the budget game. Were one to equate the budget process only with what happens through the PPB process, one would miss a great deal of important content in state politics.

### The Budget Process in General

S. Kenneth Howard argues that in all states within the U.S., what he calls the "real world" of budgeting is significantly different from that commonly put forth in government textbooks. These often hold up a model of budgeting in which rational standards are rigorously employed to make the critical program decisions which the budget will support. These texts assume an equally rational, dispassionate, and depoliticized administrator making such decisions. That, Howard argues, is simply not the case:

> A state administrator, as a human being, has his own value system, his own capacities, his own biases and prejudices, and his own perceptions of the world—in short, the set of characteristics that make him peculiarly who he is.[1]

The typical state administrator frequently finds herself operating in a climate of unmanageable complexity in which demand routinely exceeds capability, in which tension and conflict are more common than peaceful calculation, and in which conflicts are rooted in value differences among the key participants in the political arena and thus beyond her control.[2] In order to act, the state administrator is likely to proceed by making small incremental changes organized around the situation as she finds it, rather than by enacting profound rational schemes of action. Faced with this complexity, the administrator struggles to simplify, by defining problems in ways that admit to solution and by taking recourse to tried and trusted solutions.[3]

Budgetary calculations become simpler as actors seek to make them predictable. For example, budget actors come to be expected to play certain roles and by doing so provide stable expectations to others in the process. One common example is the expectation that annual allocations will be fully expended. When they are not, those who authorize expenditures have a difficult time evaluating requests for the subsequent year. "If they had a surplus last year," the administrator asks himself, "why do they need the same amount or more this year?"

Those who work in the centralized budget staffs (which are usually positioned organizationally close to the direct control of the governor) are meant to be more committed to the budget process and hold a more comprehensive view of it than those who work in other (line) agencies. One implication of this role is that central staff will tend to be focused on and evaluate overall budget requests in terms of various "objective" measures of the programs executed by the line agencies. As long as both parties hold to these expectations, the overall process develops predictability. State legislatures, for their part, tend to see themselves as guardians of the purse, constraining the impulse of line agencies to grow and adopting a budget-cutting image for themselves. These role attributes, which Howard terms "contained specialization," permit individuals and agencies to accept their differing roles in taxing and spending proposals. They also help to modulate the conflicts which inevitably occur over the budget, making compromise possible.[4]

Regular participants in the budget process come to share important basic assumptions about how the state budget should work. Repeat participation in the annual or biennial cycle helps actors learn the norms of the process, one of the most important of which is that there is always a "next year." This helps avoid all-or-nothing conflicts over items in a given year's budget battles. The attitude that next year is another chance reinforces a tendency present in all state budgeting to develop the budget through small increments above or below existing allocations (what is known as "the base"). This assures that participants get much of what they want in any given year and helps to balance expectations about what is possible in the process. The difficult question of deciding what makes a good decision in various budgetary areas is, in effect, sidestepped by the making of many smaller decisions. As Howard notes:

> A policy may obtain agreement even if it is not the one that achieves some goals most effectively or has the most substantial impact on some target area or group. Differences over goals and target areas or groups are played down in an attempt to get agreement on more specific policies and actions.[5]

A key element to making the above elements work is commitment to the ideas of "fair share and base." The latter is a commitment to accepting the "current service base," what an agency is currently doing, as a suitable base for the next year's allocation. This provides all participants with a certain sense of security while at the same time simplifying decision calculations. In effect, everybody enters the budgetary cycle with the expectation that current expenditures will be continued, while conflict will be reserved for deciding on new items to be put in the budget. The idea of fair share holds that when new resources are discovered they will be shared fairly among all competing agencies. These two practices assure existing agencies that they are not being excluded from central budget decisions. With that assurance they are more likely to go along with decisions which identify some particular items as high priority, and assign special resources to these.

## Budget Practices in State Government

All states experience budgeting as a highly fragmented process. State departments, which already tend to be large organizations given to compartmentalization and specialization, are separated even more from each other by the effects of wide varieties of federal support legislation. Federal legislation affects state agencies by providing resources to some agencies but not others, and by developing activities at the state level which have not been developed through state legislation. These agencies come to view themselves more as constituents of their federal agency counterparts (from which their money flows) than the state governmental structure of which they are an organizational part. The result is a considerable degree of autonomy on the part of line agencies and the pursuit of quite common strategies on the part of central budget agencies to establish what they consider to be an appropriate measure of control.[6]

Not surprisingly, states develop relatively common budgetary strategies.

- Agencies attempt to identify and nurture a clientele to assist in establishing each agency's strategic position.

- Agencies strive to have their competence recognized by all other participants.

- Groups fragment, providing the opportunity for one fragment to play off another, including individuals, client groups, branches of government, legislative committees, and legislative chambers.

- Agencies insure that, if cuts must be made, they are often made where the agency's most effective clientele group will be affected (in order to produce the maximum clamor for restoration).

- Budgetary increases, if they are sought, are made to appear as if they come from natural or mandatory sources, thereby presenting the agencies with no apparent choice but to request the increase.

- Agencies consistently strive to capitalize on events (e.g., natural disasters, prison riots, etc.) to enhance their position through the mobilization of public opinion.

- Agency survival and growth are constant considerations in the formulation and execution of budget strategies.[7]

Finally, the distress and dismay which incoming governors and agency heads experience over the limited discretion they possess in resource allocation is common to all states. Thus, a constant feature of the budgetary process is the interaction between the elected leader and her personal staff to "free up" funds and to pull the central budgetary agency into its camp to insure the enactment or implementation of the leader's program.[8]

To some degree all these features are present within Hawai'i's budgetary system. Not surprisingly, they develop some local coloration by being set within the particular political environment of Hawai'i. It is to this that we now turn.

## Planned Program Budgeting System in Hawai'i

PPB came to Hawai'i in 1970 when the legislature adopted the Executive Budget Act of 1970 as amended, popularly known as "Act 185" (the act subsequently became Chapter 37 of the *Hawai'i Revised Statutes*). It in turn was the product of the Central Analysis Group established by Governor John Burns in 1967 for the purpose of establishing methods and procedures to enhance planning and budgeting within state government. The intellectual, or analytical, appeal of PPB is its combination of planning (what should be done) with normal budget practices (allocating and spending funds on specific projects). The system establishes an elaborate process by which elements within the budget can be compared, with the emphasis being placed on performance. The principle is that since resources are always scarce, only the best choices should be funded. In theory, PPB would provide centrality and control to the budget system. PPB was meant to provide rationality and order where before there had been simply the aggregate of years of ad hoc decision making.

To do this, Act 185 established a comprehensive system comprised of twenty-two separate activities in the areas of basic planning, budgeting and reporting. The legislation requires four basic documents from state departments: (1) a multiyear program and financial plan; (2) the executive budget, which presents two-year financial requirements for the recommendations; (3) program memoranda; and (4) the variance report, which identifies variances in actual program performance from planned program performance. A supplemental budget is required in even-numbered years to create changes in the state's program and financial plan.[9]

From the earliest efforts to establish PPB at the federal level (in the Department of Defense), those who would employ it have been overwhelmed by the enormous amount of information both generated by the system and required to operate it properly. Aaron Wildavsky, the acknowledged guru of both American and comparative budgeting, has examined the federal governmental experiences with PPB. He comments:

> Why does PPBS fail? There can be no single answer. The problem is that PPBS fails for so many different reasons that it is difficult to sort them out. . . . My own view is that PPBS fails because it cannot meet a necessary condition for its success—the human knowledge required for performing the operations it stipulates. Although it may fail for many other reasons, such as lack of political support or trained personnel, it always fails for lack of knowledge, when and if it is allowed to get that far.[10]

Wildavsky has, in another place, called PPBS a form of "Potemkin villages"—facades without any real substance behind them, a view that he gains from a comparative analysis of PPBS experiences.[11] This view is shared by some who work with the system in Hawai'i. As one long-term analyst within Hawai'i's Department of Budget and Finance (B&F) has remarked, "with respect to the analytical aspects, PPB has been a nonstarter. It has never been really tried." Compare this with a similar California comment:

> In fact the materials produced under the auspices of PABS [California PPBS] were not used in the budget-making, and their quality generally was unsatisfactory.[12]

To fully comprehend the inability of PPB to achieve its promise, it may be necessary to gain a better understanding of what it tries to do. PPB seeks to formalize and centralize the budget process while submitting individual budget requests to rigorous objective analysis, modeled after cost-benefit principles. (It is called a "program budget structure" because it establishes eleven state programs—education, economic development, employment, etc.—into which all budget requests must fit.) B&F requires from the other state departments a detailed, multiple-year expenditure plan in which each agency is supposed to make clear how all levels of expenditure within the agency (there are six) relate to each other. This vast amount of detail is meant to supply central planners with both a rationale for how the agency commits its funds and a basis on which to plan future expenditures. Since the central agency is the only one which has this information from all the line agencies, it alone is able to see the big picture and make decisions about the comparative worth (benefit) of expenditures in one part of state government versus another.

Once the central budgeting agency has reached its conclusions, these are embodied in the form of the executive budget which is then sent to the legislature for both scrutiny and its own analysis. A critical element to these reviews is the use of variance reports which detail the departures from previous statements of program promise. Variance reports are intended to provide a critical method of control by the central budget agencies and the legislature for reviewing what actually happens within agencies once money has been appropriated.

The very sophistication of PPB goes far to explain why it doesn't work in practice. While Hawai'i is hardly alone in its continued adherence to PPB (some thirty-four states employ some form of planned program budgeting), Act 185 may be one of the most comprehensive and, without question, one of the most complex in the nation. Key actors within the system have not known how to operate the system, foremost among these the legislature. Additionally, the system tends to crumble under its own weight. Prior to the adoption of reform amendments in 1974, intended to simplify various reporting features, the biennial request to B&F and the legislature produced documentation running between eight and ten thousand pages. And, while B&F personnel were highly dedicated and were given intensive training in implementing the system, throughout the program's history, staff have never been adequate to a standard of full implementation, especially within the analysis and evaluation components. As for legislative capability, it is clear that PPB documentation overwhelms the part-time staffs of a legislature committed to a sixty-day legislative period.

This may be the most important thing to say about PPB in Hawai'i: it has failed to acknowledge the realities of the structure of government, or to accommodate a stronger underlying politics of the state. This politics has in effect subverted PPB. Yet it persists, in part because it has adapted itself to a more primary politics of both budgeting and the policy process. It is to this primary politics that we can now turn to sketch the dynamics of a politics of the budgetary process far broader than its ostensible control mechanism, PPB.

## The Politics of the Budgetary Process

The politics of the budgetary process in Hawai'i is composed of: (1) those activities through which budgets are assembled within the state agencies; (2) the efforts made within B&F to present agency

requests to the legislature; (3) the legislative budget process; and
(4) the executive's powers of discretionary allocations. An additional
element is provided by the creation of revenue estimates.

One way to understand PPB's continued role in the budget process is to see it as a form within which budget requests must be presented. Because of their complexity the forms of PPB operate like a
code. If those actors within the agencies do not employ the forms of
PPB in presenting their requests, these will simply not be honored
in the process. In this sense, PPB is a necessary but not sufficient
condition for budgetary requests. Knowledge of this code is important because scarcity always insures that those who oversee budget
requests are looking to cut something. An agency not knowing the
ins and outs of the budget process is vulnerable. PPB therefore gives
a certain power to those who use and maintain the code.

Considerable discretion is also exercised at the point of budget
assembly within departments. Especially within large budgetary
units such as the Department of Education or the University of Hawai'i, the process of gaining requests from lower levels is very extensive, involving literally hundreds of people and thousands of hours of
work. The requests work their way up the organizational hierarchy
and at some point are aggregated by higher level offices. Often the
criteria by which this assembly or prioritization of the budget takes
place are not widely shared within the organization. In other words,
the extremely important process by which an organization priori-
tizes its substantive requests and thereby positions them for funding often relies more on the pattern of internal organizational
politics than on the presumed rationale of the budget criteria established throughout the state budget process. It is not unusual within
departments for arbitrary decisions to be made in assigning priorities, and then rationalized in terms of the overall budget objectives,
with which they may have an imperfect fit. (As one university dean
was heard to remark upon reading for the first time a list of budget
priorities to be recommended by the president, "This looks as if it
were done by a randomizing computer program.")

Contrary to its assumptions, little if any analysis of the form envisioned by Act 185 goes on within line agencies. Rather, the language of priority, program promise, and effectiveness becomes an
overall language of justification for the department. It decides what
it wants to request from the central administration and gives that
request the form of PPB. Because agency requests are framed and
limited by restrictions (caps) established by B&F for overall agency
requests, the process operates in effect like the familiar "base plus

increment" budget (in which departments are provided support for their current service budget plus given an increment) which PPB was meant to replace through its devices of analytical categories of comparison.

Inside B&F, agency (departmental) budget requests compete with those programs and items desired by the governor and his staff. There is thus a politics outside the agency budgetary process in which access, deciding who gets on the agenda, is the key. Edwin Hargrove, commenting on the implementation process, has pointed out that one reason new programs crowd out older, stable programs on implementation agendas is the need of elected officials to make their careers on programs bearing their imprint.[13] This is equally true of the budget process where executives are constantly searching for a piece of the budget with which to develop their own programs or to satisfy an important constituency. Older, more established programs must constantly struggle to maintain the political constituencies which will support them in bureaucratic and legislative competition with newer and perhaps more glitzy proposals.

While those individuals within the B&F staff who are committed to the kind of rigorous analysis stipulated by Act 185 are doing their best to weed through the more important agency requests and determine some criteria of value for their programs, they are frequently outflanked by this larger budgetary game. How much this occurs will depend on the personality of the sitting governor, his faith in the central budget agency, and his own preferences with respect to the financial tensions of the overall expenditure picture. Within B&F a sense exists that action on the budget occurs mainly in the interplay between its analysts and higher levels of the administration. Former governor George Ariyoshi apparently regarded this exchange as a fruitful vehicle for providing the executive with a means to compare competing agency requests in a climate of scarce resources. Governor Waihee is perceived to have a stronger agenda in which relatively more big-ticket items strongly advocated by his own staff are off limits to B&F inquiry.

These observations raise questions concerning the value of the enormous amounts of information generated by the budget assembly process. Interviews with B&F members suggest that much of this information is simply not employed in actual decision making. One veteran of the process goes so far as to term much of this information mass as "garbage." The reason is clear: for many purposes PPB is an impediment to what central stakeholders in the budget process hope to accomplish. Each agency has its own agenda, be it housing, a large Department of Educational building-maintenance program, a commitment to spend a certain amount of money to support higher education, or whatever. These decisions are made at a higher policy level, essentially outside the budget process, which is in effect tailored to accommodate these expenditures. The A+ program of after-school care initiated by Lieutenant Governor Cayetano is an example of a program which was initiated by the executive with little legislative consultation and apparently entirely outside the PPB framework. When examining the effect of PPB, another B&F analyst remarks that it is no accident that the analysis activities of PPB under B&F have not been fully developed:

> PPB was set up to look across budgets, to do studies as well as review. The analysis branch has never been used because real studies are anathema to the political process. So they get excluded—cast out from the overall process.[14]

### Legislative Role in
### The Hawai'i Budgetary Process

A similar logic applies within the legislative budgetary process, complicated by the fact that PPB as a system is simply too complex for the limited staff capabilities of the legislature. The budgetary process within the legislature is dominated by a few experienced players, those who know intimately a system to which others are often strangers, a phenomenon intensified in recent years by the relative youth of the Hawai'i state legislature. These key actors dominate access to critical informational flows and details of the budget. Of these, committee chairs are the most important.

As is the case with other state legislatures, the money committees tend to dominate the subject matter committees. The latter are the most likely to have staff least experienced in dealing with constituency pressure or bargaining within the overall budgetary process. Having little familiarity with the PPB system, the committees make do by largely ignoring it, transforming the budget in effect back into a line-item form. And, moreover, they are likely to satisfy their own anxieties within the process by creating information bundles *de novo*, bombarding agencies with requests for information all the way down to the lowest level departmental programs. Within this context, any overall controlling rationale which PPB is meant to provide the system is totally lost.

The Hawai'i legislature functions in its budgetary politics much like any other state legislature. A general system of accommodation is established between the governor and the legislature, in which the governor gets much of what he wants (within the overall constraint of the forecast revenue limits, and/or constitutional spending limitations) with some money left over for projects in which the legislature has a special interest. In the past, the Capital Improvements Budget, financed almost exclusively by bonding authority, was organized to provide each state senator and representative an amount which could be designated for improvements within her district. Even when the amount designated exceeded the funding available, this system provided a win/win situation for both legislature and executive. Each legislator could return to her district with the proud announcement that she had "secured" a project for the district. The governor could then not release funding for various projects, thereby projecting the image of fiscal prudence. This system is practiced less universally in the current legislature, but to a limited degree still exists. Other kinds of legislative bargains made within the budget reflect the influence patterns characteristic of the legislature. What one somewhat disenchanted local observer has characterized as a form of "henchman politics" built around this particular influence pattern, other experienced observers of state legislatures (and, indeed, the U.S. Congress) would be inclined to describe as business as usual.[15]

The Hawai'i legislature shares with many others a kind of craziness associated with its critical calendar points, most particularly crossover (when bills must be sent from one house to the other) and the end-of-session scramble to achieve a budget (inevitably the last major piece of legislation to be decided upon). These last-minute efforts can thwart any amount of careful consideration given budgetary requests in earlier legislative stages, and often serve to rescue politically unpalatable bits of legislation (such as executive pay raises and small-scale pieces of special interest legislation) which may gain passage under the camouflage of last-minute histrionics. Needless to say, these activities are not factored into the careful considerations of PPB.

## The Governor and the Budget Process

The executive plays two distinct and important roles within the budget process which are outside the scope of the PPB formalities.

One is the already-mentioned capability of creating special projects which can escape the scrutiny given normal agency requests. The other, perhaps of far greater significance, is the governor's control over budgetary allocations. Formal control is vested in the line-item veto, no insignificant administrative tool. In addition, however, the governor has the broad authority to restrict appropriated funds by not releasing them to designated agencies. This broad power carries with it significant implications for how agencies actually experience their budgetary realities. Former governor Ariyoshi developed the practice of across-the-board restrictions designed as "efficiency savings" meant to encourage agencies to be judicious in their spending, a practice continued by Governor Waihee.

The logic of such restrictions lies in the assumption that agencies have monies available to them which they can afford not to spend without significantly affecting agency performance. This may or may not be true, but no systematic study appears to have been done of just how such restrictions affect agency performance. What such restrictions accomplish for the governor and his staff is to create a certain amount of control over the budget, while also creating a revenue source they can use later in the year on the basis of their preferences. It illustrates Howard's point that executives, especially incoming executives, are constantly on the watch for revenues that they can control for use in their own programs. Other, lesser forms of budget control have been used in the past, such as restrictions on out-of-state travel which must be approved by the centralized budgetary authority, or forcing departments heads to negotiate with the governor for the restoration of funds cut from their budgets.

These restrictions can also have the effect of completely thwarting legislative intent. In some cases, the governor may not release the funding required for implementing a legislative initiative. Alternatively, faced with across-the-board cuts, agencies may be driven to withhold funding from those legislative initiatives which were not part of their original budget requests.

Within highly labor-intensive agencies (such as the Department of Human Services, DHS, or the University of Hawai'i), executive restrictions on funding can often be met only by allowing positions to remain vacant (e.g. caseworkers in DHS). This has the paradoxical effect of stimulating requests for more positions in the next budget cycle to fulfill unmet work needs. When agencies meet restrictions in this way, they work strongly against the value of providing maximal organizational efficiency; as a result they will be forced to cut corners in service delivery, thereby defeating efforts on the part of central budget analysts to gain an understanding of the level of resources really necessary for the agency to conduct and preserve its current service base.

The dislocations of departmental activity by gubernatorial restriction can reach extraordinary proportions during times of budgetary crisis. During the period 1971–1974 and again during 1983–1985, the state budget experienced various crises. Each was caused in some way by revenue shortfall or predictions of shortfalls generated by the revenue estimation authority. (The 1978 constitutional convention created a Council on Revenues which provides official estimates of state income. Prior to that time various bodies, public and private, provided estimates.) During both periods Governors Burns and Ariyoshi responded by imposing various restrictions, including hiring freezes on existing positions and prohibitions against the addition of new positions. During the Ariyoshi crisis, in which a shortfall of predicted revenues was compounded by the loss of routinely expected liquor tax revenues, agencies were asked repeatedly to create budget scenarios based on different estimates of the size of restrictions to be imposed. The initial requests took place within budget years for which long-term personnel commitments had already been made. The result was to destroy any sense of rational allocation or planning within agencies as they scrambled to find monies from any available source to meet already existing commitments.

Each of these crises was followed by a period of budgetary surplus, generating suspicion that, in addition to whatever reality the crisis possessed—defined as a shortfall of revenues over projections—crisis also served as the pretext for enlarging central budgetary control and restricting the growth potential of various state agencies, most especially the Department of Education and the University of Hawai'i. Revenue forecasting has played a critical role in determining how budgetary politics will go forth in both the executive and legislative arenas. If revenues are underforecast (and for a variety of reasons the estimations tend to be conservative), this can have the effect of strengthening the relative power of those who determine what funds agencies will receive.

An illustration of the extent to which executive restriction has become a conventional policy is the current policy of the Waihee administration. The 1989 surplus was in excess of $500 million; something in excess of $250 million is predicted for 1990. Despite these large surpluses, the governor's 1990 budget execution policies continue to impose restrictions on agencies.

As of June 1, 1989, the constitutionally mandated Council on Revenues officially projected relatively favorable economic conditions over the upcoming fiscal biennium, which should allow the State to proceed with a reasonable degree of optimism. At the same time, appropriations just authorized by the legislature have been substantial, as well as programmatically ambitious and extensive.[16]

The instructions go on to list categories of expenditure which are to be restricted, leading to overall restrictions of between two and four percent, depending on the agency's expenditure pattern. Whatever the rationale for these forced savings, they have three predictable consequences within the budget process. One, they dramatize that PPB no longer has a controlling effect on the budget process. Two, they emphasize the politics of control by which the executive center relates to the agency or departmental periphery. Three, they create a learning process within governmental departments in which these agencies come to anticipate such restrictions and accommodate them in future requests—new budgets come to be inflated to make up for the losses such restrictions entail. Whatever efficiencies were meant to be accomplished by the restrictions tend to be lost.

## Conclusion

Given the current politics of the budget process, what explains why PPB is sustained as a basic budget instrument in the face of extensive evidence that, at best, it creates a poor approximation of its intended results? And, if PPB does not explain how budgets are created and executed in Hawai'i, what does?

In answer to the first question, the existence of PPB is an enormously important symbolic device, an instance of what Murray Edelman calls symbolic politics.[17] It provides a rationale for the varied activities which go on within the budgetary process. It provides a set of techniques, behaviors, personnel, and actions which are carried on in its name. It stands as if it were, in fact, objectively determining budgetary outcomes. That it partially works, that agencies continue to employ its language in their requests, and utilize its forms to gird their substance, grants a legitimacy to the whole of the process. When outsiders ask how the budgetary process works, they are referred to an extensive description of the process which is consistent with Chapter 37.[18]

These formalisms mask many actual practices of the budgetary process, practices which privilege some actors over others. One respondent, for example, has emphasized that most of the information created by the process is simply ignored. B&F, he asserts, goes through the formality of complying with the law but the documents (e.g., variance reports) are not used in actual decision making. Many of these activities, he maintains, are a waste of time, negative productivity. Their importance is that they shift the gaze away from one set of activities onto another. Lest we be too surprised by this contention, let us recall that Aaron Wildavsky has argued that one of the most common errors of the policy process is to confuse information systems, such as PPB, with control systems.[19]

What of the political process which underlies this formal, symbolic budgetary process? To what extent is it a politics of the budget peculiar to Hawai'i? As our frequent references to Wildavsky and Howard should make clear, many aspects of budgeting in Hawai'i are easily found in other states and within the federal budget. Among these are a constant tension between the centralized budgetary agency and the various state departments; the politics within large departments; the expertise relationship between the executive and the legislature over the budget (which led Congress to create its own Legislative Budget Office in 1974); the supremacy of money committees over subject-matter committees in legislatures; and the desire of executives to establish programs outside those already managed by their executive departments.

What is unique to Hawai'i is the way in which some of these tensions are resolved and the ways that its political coloration blends itself into the budgetary process. One aspect of this is the high degree of centralization characteristic of the state. As Norman Meller argues in chapter 1 of this volume, this tendency arises in part from Hawai'i's unique past political history as a kingdom and its subsequent experience of having been closely controlled by a cohesive plantation oligarchy. This history also explains the enduring pattern of state domination over local government. Centralization is also highly evident in the extraordinary constitutional powers provided the governor. The overall tendency in such a system is for the center to control its various peripheries. The budget process faithfully reflects these tendencies.

Another special characteristic of Hawai'i budgetary politics is what might be characterized as an overall politics of control evident throughout Hawai'i politics.[20] One contributor to this outcome has been the overall weakness of the two-party system during the statehood period. As V. O. Key has wonderfully illustrated in his classic study of the American South during its period of one-party dominance, the absence of effective legislative competition forces all the interests of the state to bargain within the dominant party.[21] One effect of this bargaining is the creation of factional struggle in which various party leaders develop followings which then become distributed throughout the appointive (and often the civil service) bureaucracy. The dynamics of one-party factional rule focus on gaining and retaining control over aspects of governmental operations. Policy tends to be subordinated to the goal of self-perpetuation for which the preferred tactic comes to be an effort to create and exercise control. For such activity the budgetary process is the crucial medium of exchange.

These dynamics have been attenuated by the breakdown of party organization within Hawai'i (and the rest of the U.S. as well). Where centralized party organizations once were able to exercise marginal control over elected party members, they are now but a pale shadow of influence, as each legislative member has his own electoral organizations, and election is due far more to the personality characteristics of the individual than to either party identification or stands on issues. As centralized party control wanes, the relative influence of factions and personality-related networks grows in response. The remaining importance of party identification lies in the access it provides for spoils which are still distributed through that organizing principle, such as control of the legislature. These tendencies explain why several legislators recently have switched their identifications from Republican to Democratic without apparent electoral consequences. Their electoral constituencies are oriented toward them personally rather than through party labels.

Few electoral issues arise which separate parties qua parties. This is especially true at the gubernatorial level, where competition within the party is mostly organized by faction identification. Faction members may be motivated by identification with particular issues (e.g., slow growth versus fast growth), but those issues are peculiar to the politics of individuals within the Democratic party, and usually have little to do with what might be called "ideological issues," for example, questions of social class.

Competition between factions can come to take a form which V. O. Key termed "Throw the Rascals Out," a call for a "new brush" which will sweep the courthouse clean, bringing in a new cast of characters to run government. This seems to have been the force behind the candidacy of Tom Gill and, later, Jean King, both of whom had served as lieutenant governors to long-serving governors and whose claims were based on the need for new faces and fresh ideas in government. The delicacy of this strategy laid in the desire to replace representatives of the long-dominant faction initially forged by Governor Burns which relied on AJA voting power and membership (and which Ariyoshi came to lead), without at the same time alienating its electoral supporters. John Waihee experienced similar problems in steering his "palaka power" coalition into office, as he was required to make overtures to various parts of the historical Burns/Ariyoshi coalition.

These factional politics are all folded into the budgetary process in Hawai'i as the winning coalition uses its years in office, especially its first term, to develop policies and programs which will perpetuate its factional loyalties while enlarging its base. In a small state like Hawai'i, where governmental employment is a significant part of the work force and where state expenditures are a very large part of the action, control exercised through the budgetary process is a major vehicle of daily political life.

## Notes

1. S. Kenneth Howard, "The Real World of State Budgeting," in Robert T. Golembiewski and Jack Rabin, eds., *Public Budgeting and Finance: Behavioral, Theoretical, and Technical Perspectives* (New York: Marcel Dekker, 1983), p. 103.

2. Ibid., p. 104.

3. Ibid., p. 106.

4. Ibid., p. 108.

5. Ibid., p. 109

6. Ibid., p. 111.

7. Ibid., p. 112

8. Ibid., p. 113.

9. Hawai'i State Department of Budget and Finance, *An Introduction to the State of Hawai'i's Executive Budget System* (Honolulu, March 1976), pp. 17–20.

10. Aaron Wildavsky, *Budgeting: A Comparative Theory of the Budgetary Process* (Boston: Little, Brown and Co., 1975), pp. 353–54.

11. Ibid., p. 335.

12. Ibid., p. 343.

13. Edwin Hargrove, *The Missing Link: The Study of Implementation of Social Policy* (Washington, D.C.: Urban Institute, 1975), pp. 111–119.

14. Personal interview with B&F analyst on July 9, 1989 who declined to speak on record.

15. Lewis A. Froman, Jr., *The Congressional Process: Strategies, Rules and Procedures* (Boston: Little, Brown and Co., 1967), p.

16. Governor's Budget Preparation Policy and Instruction, July 17, 1989.

17. Murray Edelman, *The Symbolic Uses of Politics* (Urbana: University of Illinois Press, 1964), p.

18. They are, for example, shown a copy of *An Introduction to the State of Hawai'i's Executive Budget System.*

19. Aaron Wildavsky, *Speaking Truth to Power: The Art and Craft of Policy Analysis* (Boston: Little, Brown and Co., 1979), pp. 27–39.

20. Deane Neubauer and Samuel Pooley, "An Alternative Political Economy for Hawai'i," Occasional Papers, Department of Political Science, University of Hawai'i, 1983, p. and "The Politics of Hawai'i's Economy in the 1980s," paper presented to the 9th Regional Science Conference, Western Regional Science Association, Molokai, Hawai'i, August, 1985. p.

21. V. O. Key, Jr., *Southern Politics* (New York, Knopf, 1950).

# 6

# RESOLVING POLICY CONFLICTS IN HAWAI'I THROUGH MEDIATION

## *Peter S. Adler*

Conflict is inherent to human nature. All organized societies from time immemorial have generated conflict and have likewise devised methods for preventing, managing, or resolving conflict. In America, the traditional way of doing this is through formal litigation, involving the prosecution and defense of lawsuits. The foundations that underpin this time-tested system lie in adversarial truth seeking and the assurance of due process. Through litigation, parties to a dispute are able to advance their proofs before a judge or jury, cross-examine assertions, present their testimonies, and end up with a final and binding resolution to their differences.

In recent decades America's legal system, particularly with regard to noncriminal matters, has been a source of increased citizen dissatisfaction. Each year more than sixteen million civil cases, ranging in size from ordinary contract disputes and fender-benders to class-action toxic torts, are filed in the nation's state courts alone. The estimated cost of handling these cases, excluding actual amounts paid out in settlements and judgements, is between twenty and thirty billion dollars—more than 1½ percent of America's GNP. A typical lawsuit involving procedural skirmishes over documents, interrogatories, and depositions, for example, can easily cost a hundred thousand dollars in legal fees and take five years to come to trial.[1]

Generally speaking, policy makers in the United States have sought to address the problems with America's civil justice system in three related ways. First, there have been concerted attempts, with many notable successes, to streamline outdated laws, statutes, and court rules. Second, modern administrative techniques, including the use of computerized information management methods, have been installed to increase efficiency and productivity. Third, courts, legislatures, and regulatory agencies have developed various types of alternative dispute resolution (ADR) systems such as mediation and arbitration. The general aim of these systems is to facilitate in-court and out-of-court settlements without having to engage in the traditional expenses, delays, and animosities of formal adversarial litigation.

Hawai'i has anticipated, and in some ways led, the changes that are taking place in this third area, the use of ADR. Hawai'i has, in fact, been in the forefront of the mediation movement and, in addition to extending its use to various criminal, civil, and family matters, has developed specialized applications for complex, multiparty conflicts that affect the public interest. Hawai'i's experience, in this regard, includes a recent effort that helped break a long-standing impasse over the enactment of Hawai'i's water code.

## Alternative Dispute Resolution in Hawai'i

Generally speaking, the acronym *ADR* is a catch-all expression that describes voluntarily solicited interventions by arbitrators, mediators, and fact finders. In the past decade, however, ADR has also come to include a variety of applications that would embody, but not be limited to, fact finding, mandated mediation, contractual arbitration, court-ordered arbitration, "med/arb" (in which a third party first mediates and then, if necessary, arbitrates), the use of special masters appointed by administrative and law judges, and various types of minitrials and summary jury trials in which disputants negotiate settlements after abbreviated arguments by lawyers.[2] Most often, however, the term *ADR* is used to describe forms of voluntary mediation in which an individual (or team of individuals) considered to be impartial and trustworthy is agreed to by the disputants and helps those disputants to communicate, negotiate, and reach consensual—as opposed to coerced—outcomes.

The idea of mediating disputes is not new, of course. Many Asian and Pacific cultures have long-standing traditions of informal mediative dispute resolution and, even in Western countries, mediation and arbitration have been used for centuries in the maritime industries and in various specialized trades and professions. In general, the institutionalized use of ADR in the United States goes back to the onset of collective bargaining and the formation of the Federal Mediation and Conciliation Service (FMCS), constituted after the turn of the century to mediate labor-management disputes. Only in the past decade, however, has the use of ADR expanded to new areas. In great part this can be attributed to America's growing disenchantment with lawyers, courts, and litigation, and with a kind of collective hunger for more efficient, satisfying, and less costly ways of managing conflict.

In this context, voluntary mediation has become an attractive alternative and the procedural centerpiece of the ADR movement. Mediation actualizes a less confrontational philosophy of conflict. Unlike traditional litigation, mediators do not treat disputes as aberrations that need to be investigated, controlled, regulated, and eventually decided by an authoritative figure. Quite the opposite. The worldview of mediation tends to regard conflict as normal, as a potential vehicle for social, political, and personal change, and as one of the ways that ongoing relationships can be created or positively restructured.[3]

One of the primary tenets of mediation is the notion of voluntarism. In mediation any decision to continue or end the dispute remains in the hands of the disputants. Disputants are neither coerced nor directed into agreements. Instead, they are encouraged to become the architects of their own futures. Mediators may carefully raise ideas to be considered and make soft proposals, but the power to accept or reject those ideas stays with the parties. This principle of personal empowerment and voluntary decision making is one of the driving forces of the mediation movement.

In contrast to adjudicatory processes, mediation also does not rely on formal rules of evidence or on the crossfire of adversarial fact finding. Instead, the emphasis is on maximizing the use of communication, negotiation, diplomacy, and persuasion. Through these means, mediators seek to assist parties in developing common information, clarifying their interests and needs, and finding mutually prescriptive outcomes to the conflict. At its very best, mediation seeks to help parties to establish a level playing field on which to fight fair and, on that basis, to forge agreements that the parties themselves find just, efficient, durable, and wise.

Mediation is not without its critics. Nationally, various scholars and legal practitioners (on the political left and right) have stepped forward to voice concerns, doubts, and occasional hostility about the use of mediation for many types of disputes. Perhaps the sharpest attacks have come from legal fundamentalists, like Yale law professor Owen Fiss, who believe that negotiation and settlement in the context of civil lawsuits nullifies of many of the important protections afforded by formal adjudication.[4] Others believe that ADR, in its current form at least, is only dealing with minor disputes, with idiosyncratic conflicts, and with the relatively unimportant irritants of daily life.[5]

Despite these worries, mediation and other ADR methods have been readily adopted in Hawai'i. Hawai'i's emerging use of mediation cuts across courts, communities, and corporations.[6] More than thirty-five intermediate and high schools around the state have developed in-school mediation systems aimed at amicably resolving conflicts that would otherwise require the interventions of principals or police. In the state's judicial system, court-annexed arbitration, family mediation, and settlement programs for small claims cases have been adopted and integrated into case management strategies. Hawai'i is also one of five states (along with Massachusetts, Minnesota, New Jersey, and Ohio) to have established an official state office of mediation—the Center for Alternative Dispute Resolution—specializing in public interest and environmental disputes.

Mediation is also flourishing in the private sector. Each year the Neighborhood Justice Center of Honolulu and its counterpart agencies on Maui, Kauai, Molokai, and Hawai'i routinely help settle thousands of interpersonal and domestic conflicts that might other wise escalate into violence or needless litigation. In the business sector, the American Arbitration Association, the Honolulu Board of Realtors, and the Better Business Bureau provide a range of ADR services for people involved in commercial, construction, and marketplace disputes. Even more recently established is Hawai'i's Center for International Commercial Dispute Resolution, which seeks to make Hawai'i the Geneva of the Pacific with regard to the settlement of disagreements involving business entities from various Asian and Pacific rim countries.

## Mediating Public Disputes

In Hawai'i', as elsewhere, conflicts over the siting of public facilities, over the allocation of public costs and benefits, and over the formulation of public policies and standards are a daily occurrence. Consider the following situations:

> • To protect itself from fluctuations in the supply and pricing of fossil fuels, the state of Hawai'i embarks on an ambitious campaign to develop local energy resources. It proposes to drill a large number of geothermal wells on the Big Island, make that island energy self-sufficient, and cable surplus energy to Oahu. The state

runs into massive resistance and finds itself embroiled in prolonged policy and permit fights that turn the renewable energy development process into a ten-year battle.

- A private nonprofit group on Oahu tries to secure a conditional use permit that would allow it to operate a special care home for persons with physical and mental disabilities in a middle-class community. Neighbors of the proposed facility hear about the project and hire legal and public relations experts to fight the proposal. Tempers flare and the care home permit issue escalates into a public fight, with both sides lobbying against each other in the daily newspapers and the city council.

- A statewide public interest watchdog organization concerned about water pollution publicizes the maintenance and malfunction problems in a privately owned sewage treatment facility on Oahu. After a spill, the developer is fined by the state and forced to correct sewage treatment facility. The conservation group, believing that the state's fines are not strong enough, launches its own public interest lawsuit seeking damages. The case receives considerable public attention and trial seems inevitable.

Public disputes such as these represent unique challenges. In Hawai'i, as in other parts of the United States, the larger economic and political contexts in which these types of clashes take place are a constantly shifting landscape. Development policies at both the state and county levels are a routine battleground for different ideological and economic interests. Government encourages and discourages various types of development. Business interests seek to engage in profitmaking ventures. Citizens' groups routinely monitor the activities of government agencies and developers, and then advocate for or against particular projects. Government, in turn, never has all of the time and resources it needs to air public issues, to build consensus, and to then conduct monitoring, compliance, and enforcement activities after decisions have been executed.

The existence of these conflicts does not imply that Hawai'i has lagged in reforms aimed at improving the management of public controversies. Elaborate planning and permitting systems, the creation of mandatory public hearing procedures, and an expanded use of litigation have all increased public participation and allowed sunshine into public decision-making processes. At the same time, these reforms have not lessened the amount or intensity of public conflict. In fact, they have probably heightened it, since the power to affect public decisions is now increasingly shared among many vociferous interest groups.

Unlike most purely private disagreements, public disputes are challenging because of their political complexity, their technical and scientific uncertainty, and their potential impacts on future generations. Once a development has been permitted, it is virtually impossible to undevelop it. Inevitably, such cases involve multiple parties from the private and public sectors that vary significantly in their degree and style of organization. Across and within these constituencies, money, authority, decision-making power, technical expertise, access to information, access to the media, and internal and external communication styles vary considerably. Such disputes are highly charged and changeable. New stakeholders emerge as a conflict gets articulated. A dispute may, in fact, start out involving two parties—a community group and a developer, for example—and then be transformed into a conflict involving dozens of community and environmental groups, a variety of government agencies and state and federal regulators, the news media, lawyers, courts, legislative bodies, and, eventually, the entire voting public. Everyone, of course, claims to be speaking for and in the public interest.

## The Water Code Roundtable

Hawai'i is blessed with abundant and high-quality freshwater resources. As in many other Western states, the ownership and use of these waters—particularly surface and stream waters—has been a source of conflict for more than a century. Ancient Hawaiians held that water belonged to all of the people; its stewardship was organized into land and stream management districts controlled by the chiefs, and a system of ecologically sensitive customs and laws. With the advent of Western contact and the rise of plantation agricultural systems, certain customary uses by Hawaiian landowners were preserved but general water use and water rights conflicts intensified. Primarily at issue was the ownership of water and the ability to treat it as property, i.e., to transport it, use it, or buy and sell it at will. These conflicts were dominated by a trail of complex and long-running lawsuits (for example, *Territory* v. *Gay*; *McBryde Sugar Co.* v. *Robinson*; *Robinson* v. *Ariyoshi*; and *Reppun* v. *Board of Water Supply*) some of which are still not fully resolved today.[7]

During the 1960s and 1970s, water concerns, along with many other environmental issues, came to the political fore. The specters of periodic drought, chemical contamination, runoff pollution, chloride intrusion into the basal lens, and overconsumption and draw-down all raised new types of questions about water management, water quality, and the control and disposition of bulk resources. In 1978, cognizant of these emerging concerns, the Hawai'i state constitutional convention proposed several significant changes to the state constitution. Among other concerns, it affirmed the state's obligation to protect, control, and regulate the use of Hawai'i's waters, and directed the state to create a water agency that would set overall water policies and establish criteria for water use priorities. These constitutional additions were approved by the electorate and the matter was turned over to the state legislature.

Over the next eight years, various versions of a state water code were proposed and argued by advisory commissions, study groups, and lobbyists. These discussions, conducted in the context of several landmark lawsuits and the heat of highly positioned legislative testimonies from competitive interest groups, pitted developers against environmentalists, large landowners against Hawaiian rights groups and small farmers, and, on a variety of home rule issues, the counties against the state. Inevitably, each of the annual legislative water code wars ended in stalemate.

In the summer of 1986 the Judiciary's Center for Alternative Dispute Resolution, a newly formed state office of mediation, was approached by JoAnn Yukimura, a legislator from the county of Kauai.[8] Yukimura, on behalf of lawmakers from several counties, requested that the center help organize, convene, and mediate an informal and voluntary policy dialogue centering on some of the issues involved in the water code impasse. The center agreed to assist, assembled a team of mediators, and put together a general mediation strategy.

One of the most critical steps in dispute mediation is the identification of actual and potential stakeholders to a conflict, and the conversion of large numbers of stakeholders into meaningful negotiation teams. To initiate the water code discussions, the mediators first set in motion a process that identified major sectors that stood to be affected by any new water laws. These included, among others, various federal, state, and county agencies involved in water regulation; groups representing large and small farmers; county legislators; local planning departments; environmental and conservation groups; private developers and large landowners; and native Hawaiian groups. Also identified were the names of more specific stakeholding groups within those sectors (Sierra Club; Department of Land and Natural Resources; and Hawai'i Sugar Planter's Association, for example) and, following this, the names of particular individuals who could speak knowledgeably about the issues. Using a "snowball" interviewing technique of comparing names that appeared more than once, a list of names of credible potential participants was generated and invitations to an initial exploratory meeting were sent out.

Next, the mediators drafted a brief concept paper called "Towards a Water Code Roundtable." This document, focusing largely on procedural matters, suggested the creation of a neutral, ad hoc mediation forum that would allow ample opportunities for discussion and joint problem solving. Distributed to all prospective participants and to anyone else interested, it included the following statement:

> The idea of putting together a "Water Code Roundtable" is based on several assumptions: (1) That some kind of state water code is inevitable; (2) that the normal legislative and political process is a necessary but insufficient method of talking about various water code issues, concerns, and viewpoints; (3) that exchanging meaningful information, debating the issues calmly, and exploring alternatives in an orderly and neutrally facilitated manner may have both short and long term value. In the short term, it clarifies positions and reduces misunderstandings. In the long term it may bring all parties closer to agreement.[9]

In essence, the mediators recommended that a safe haven of discussion be created for people who normally take strident and opposing positions with each other before the legislature on water issues. The document, stamped "draft," was circulated to the various individuals who had been identified as prospective participants, along with an invitation to a first meeting.

The roundtable's initial session, held in a conference room of the supreme court building in July, 1986, produced an agreement to proceed with substantive, mediated discussions. All decision making within the roundtable would be by consensus. Consensus was operationally defined as "no objections." It was further agreed that the process would continue only so long as all individuals were willing to meet. Additional prospective roundtable participants were then identified, and general ground rules for participation adopted. Of particular importance was a proviso that allowed roundtable members to speak in their personal capacities, rather than as official representatives of their constituencies. In effect, this agreement permitted everyone at the table to enter into no-risk and more position-free discussions.

Moving from procedure to substance, the roundtable next concentrated on identifying and improving the definition of various water code issues. One central philosophical and legal question had to do with two competing doctrines of water ownership: the right of prior appropriation (private ownership) versus water as a public trust (the water belongs to everyone). Fierce but reasoned debate on this issue ultimately produced the roundtable's first breakthrough. While disagreements over ownership remained, all parties acknowledged that, regardless of who owned Hawai'i's various ground and stream waters, fresh water in Hawai'i needed to be regulated. The question now shifted to how such regulation should occur.

Discussions continued and the roundtable's agenda focused on three critical questions.

1. *What type of code?* To what extent should Hawai'i's new water law be a comprehensive and anticipatory planning code as opposed to a more narrowly conceived crisis code that would be triggered in the face of specific quality or quantity problems?

2. *What types of permits?* What kinds of rights and uses should be covered by permits and how should the mechanics of such permits be handled?

3. *Who should manage the system?* How should the various authorities and responsibilities for regulating Hawai'i's waters be divided between the state and the counties?

While the legislature was in session between July and December of 1986 the Water Code Roundtable held more than twenty-five group working sessions, both large and small. As the start of the 1987 legislature drew closer, the group's efforts intensified. In January, the roundtable was able to draw up an agreement in principle that covered many of the major water code issues, issues that had been sticking points in prior legislative sessions. By consensus, this agreement was forwarded to key committee chairs and to other public and private groups for consideration. Among its other features, the agreement called for:

• An independent state water commission.

• A statewide water permitting system with delineated conditions governing rights, transferability, and duration.

• The assurance of existing riparian uses for streamside water users and appurtenant rights for those with water claims attaching to lands in taro cultivation at the time of the Great Mahele.

- The development of individual county water plans consistent with local land-use policies all of which would collectively become part of the overall state water plan.

- The creation of an administrative dispute resolution system for various water matters.

Between January and April 1987, the roundtable's water code proposals were discussed and debated in various public hearings. Further compromises, tradeoffs, and modifications occurred and, in the final hours of the legislative session, a water code embracing many of the roundtable's key consensus proposals passed both the senate and house of representatives. On May 30, 1987, after nearly ten years of debate, Governor John Waihee signed Hawai'i's new water code into law and the code became a part of Hawai'i's Revised Statutes.

### Hawai'i's Embrace of Mediation

More than many other states, Hawai'i has been in the vanguard of the mediation movement. It has, over the last ten years, become a veritable hotbed of progressive experimentation and expanded ADR practice, theory building, and research. In part, this can be explained by the needs of government institutions for more efficient forms of conflict management, by the interest of leaders in all three branches of state government, especially by Hawai'i's chief justice, and by the willingness of Hawai'i's business, legal, and political communities to champion new ideas. There are probably, however, other unique forces at work as well.

First, the style and manner in which disputes are aired and decisions made in the fiftieth state—especially with regard to public policy matters—had become increasingly complex in the last ten years. The erosion of the loyalty system in party politics, the development of more independent and robust county governments, and the emergence of better organized and more articulate community and public interest groups, has led to greater attention to public issues and to stronger quarrels. In fact, Hawai'i at the start of the 1990s is more pluralistic than at any other time in its history. This makes legal stalemates, political impasses, and social dissensus more routine.

Second, people in Hawai'i may be more predisposed to mediate. Hawai'i is ethnically dominated by people of Asian and Pacific Island extraction. Combined demographically, Japanese, Filipinos,

Hawaiians, Chinese, and Samoans make up nearly seventy percent of the state's population. Avoiding direct public confrontations and open displays of anger are important aspects of various Eastern and Oceanic cultural traditions. In fact, indigenous dispute resolution methods such as *ho'oponopono* and *fono* are still practiced by some Hawaiians and Samoans. With its emphasis on communication, deliberation, and negotiation, mediation in many ways echoes, if not parallels, these traditions and traits.

Third, the very nature of living on an island probably mitigates toward settling differences in a more amicable manner than might occur otherwise. In Hawai'i, social, political, and business relationships tend to intertwine. Because the state is small, relationships are more likely to be long term and recurrent. In Hawai'i, perhaps more so than in other places, reputations count. This fishbowl effect may impel people to exercise more sensitivity in their transactions and to take greater care in insuring that relationships don't unnecessarily turn sour. Nowhere is the expression "what goes around, comes around" more true than on an island.

The future of mediation in general, and the use of mediation for public disputes in Hawai'i in particular, seems bright. Nonetheless, proponents of mediation (who sometimes sound like they have found "the cure") must be careful not to oversell the process and its potential. In Hawai'i, mediation can be—and is in fact—a valuable complement to the existing decision-making systems of government. Calling it an alternative, however, is a misnomer.

While one of the lessons of the 1980s is that mediation and consensus building have a strong role to play in the resolution of public disputes, mediation cannot be a panacea for all of the ills that plague our island society. Even in Hawai'i, where mediation is more culturally comfortable, it cannot aspire to handle every contentious debate, and somehow chill or sidetrack important public and private controversies. Rather, it is an option that should be made more broadly available and encouraged where it seems needed and appropriate. The challenge today is to move beyond the pilot-project stage and make mediation available for everyday use. In this area, Hawai'i will very likely continue to be a pioneer.

## Notes

1. Solomon, Stephen D., "Contempt of Court: How to Avoid Litigation, Cut Legal Costs, and Get on with Your Business," in *Inc.*, October, 1989, pp. 106–14.

2. See S. Goldberg, E. Green and F. Sander, *Dispute Resolution* (Boston: Little, Brown and Co., 1985) for a full taxonomy of ADR methods and techniques.

3. For a step-by-step outline of the mediation process, see J. Folberg and A. Taylor, *Mediation: A Comprehensive Guide to Resolving Disputes without Litigation* (San Francisco: Jossey-Bass, 1987) or C. Moore, *The Mediation Process: Practical Strategies for Resolving Conflict* (San Francisco: Jossey-Bass, 1986).

4. O. Fiss, "Against Settlement," *Yale Law Journal* 93 (1973).

5. R. Abel, ed., *The Politics of Informal Justice*, vol. 2 (New York: Academic Press, 1982).

6. For a complete list and description of mediation and arbitration programs in Hawai'i, see *Alternatives to Trial: Dispute Resolution Options in the State of Hawai'i* (Honolulu: The Judiciary, 1989).

7. For a brief review and summary of some of the litigation history of these and other related water issues see Jennifer C. Clark, "Hawai'i Surface Water Law: An Analysis of *Robinson* v. *Ariyoshi*," *University of Hawai'i Law Review* 8 (1986), p. 603, and R. Takemoto, "Groundwater Rights in Hawai'i: Status and Suggested Change" by *University of Hawai'i Law Review* 8 (1986), p. 513.

8. See "Statewide Offices of Mediation: Experiments in Public Policy" in *Dispute Resolution FORUM*, National Institute for Dispute Resolution, December 1987, p. 6.

9. From "Towards a Water Code Roundtable," a working paper of the Judiciary Program on Alternative Dispute Resolution, State of Hawai'i, 1986. For additional discussions and evaluations of the roundtable, see also "Hawai'i's Water Wars: A Pacific Paradise Settles a Hellish Dispute over a Scarce Resource" in *CONSENSUS*, Public Disputes Network, November 1988 and G. K. Lowry, "Mediation of Complex and Public Interest Cases: An Evaluation Report to the Judiciary," Department of Urban and Regional Planning, University of Hawai'i, 1989.

# III

## POLICY ISSUES

# 7

## ENVIRONMENTAL QUALITY IN AMERICA'S TROPICAL PARADISE

### Richard J. Tobin and Dean Higuchi

Hawai'i's resplendent natural beauty lures millions of visitors each year. No other state is as economically dependent on tourism as is Hawai'i, so its major attraction, the quality of its environment, is crucial to the state's continued prosperity. Not only is this environment alluring, but it is also unique and fragile. Separated by thousands of miles from continental land masses, the state's flora and fauna offer hundreds of species found nowhere else in the world. These traits create potentially conflicting goals: a desire to increase or maintain economic growth and tourism, while preserving and protecting an appealing but highly vulnerable environment.

### The Environmental Consequences of Immigration

Hawai'i's first settlers discovered a land rich in natural resources and with an abundance of clean air and water. Indeed, when the first Polynesian settlers arrived, the islands could easily have been described as paradise. Recognizing their good fortune, these early inhabitants lived wisely and protected their environment. They used what they needed from the land and wasted or misused little of their treasured ecological bounty. Many of their gods and religious ceremonies revolved around the land and its resources.

When the first Europeans arrived in Hawai'i, they too found the natural environment to be in excellent condition. At first these settlers also made good use of the land, but their lifestyles, cultural heritage, and economic goals were much different from those of the Polynesians. The result was an eventual change in the quality and use of the islands' environment. As these new settlers soon discovered, Hawai'i's soils and tropical climate provide ideal conditions for the widespread growth of pineapple and sugar cane. As agriculture boomed, more rapid immigration and development followed. New urban centers took the place of small farming communities, and pressures on the environment likewise increased.

As the people of Hawai'i now move to the brink of the next century, they find that their population is taxing many of the state's resources, and these people are facing environmental problems that the first settlers never envisaged (or had the technology to create). The millions of transient visitors who arrive each year likewise impose enormous burdens on the resources that serve to attract these tourists to Hawai'i. In short, potential conflicts exist between, on the one hand, the need to continue the development of an infrastructure to accommodate residents and visitors and, on the other hand, the desire to accommodate massive tourism with a clean and healthy environment. How Hawai'i addresses these issues will determine its ecological fate.

## The Institutional Setting for Environmental Decision Making

The national government has established the Environmental Protection Agency (EPA) and approved many environmental laws and regulations. Under the American system of federalism, however, individual states retain much of the responsibility for managing and protecting their resources and environmental quality. Federal laws normally establish minimum national goals (such as for air and water quality), but states are charged with implementing the relevant regulations and emissions standards necessary to achieve these or their own, more stringent goals that have been established by state laws or regulations.

Within Hawai'i the 'lead' agency for most environmental concerns is the Department of Health's Environmental Protection and Health Division, which has sections with responsibility for hazardous wastes, environmental planning, environmental permits, and pollution enforcement and investigation. In addition to implementing most of Hawai'i's environmental laws, the EPA has also delegated to these sections authority to implement federal programs covering drinking water, air and water pollution, and solid and hazardous wastes. Federal funds are provided to the Department of Health in order to help it meet the obligations that federal laws impose on the state.

Another state agency, the Department of Agriculture, is responsible for regulating all matters affecting the inspection, enforcement, registration, and use of pesticides. It too receives federal funds, in this instance to carry out and enforce the Federal Insecticide, Fungicide, and Rodenticide Act.

Still other departments in the state play a role in environmental policy. The Department of Land and Natural Resources (DLNR) oversees land use and the protection of endangered species. The Office of Environmental Quality is responsible for reviewing state-mandated environmental impact assessments, but the office also provides information to the public on environmental issues. Finally, for a few environmental problems, such as the removal of asbestos and the control of polychlorinated biphenyls, the state does not have its own programs, and it is dependent on assistance from officials in the EPA.

## Key Environmental Concerns

As the only island state, many of Hawai'i's environmental problems are unique. As an illustration, natural conditions impose limits on the state's population and the growth. Land area is obviously limited to the size of each island, and this imposes restrictions on the development of commercial, residential, and agricultural areas. With population increases and economic growth that normally exceed the national average, there are often intense pressures to convert land to more profitable uses. Thus, much agricultural land is being converted into commercial and residential developments. This squeeze on land often requires the state government to make compromises to reconcile a rising population, exceptionally high housing costs, agricultural opportunities, and a desire to preserve the appeal and attractiveness of Hawai'i's natural environment. As might be expected, these compromises do not always benefit environmental quality.

In addition, as a result of a growing population, the state's limited natural resources begin to be taxed. Of primary concern is the availability of fresh water for human use and consumption. As tourism booms, the transient population needs to make use of the same water resources that serve residents. Along with a potential water crisis, which looms if plans are not made for the future availability of water, it is common to expect summer dry spells that lead to shortages and perhaps even to enforced conservation. With frequent storms, water is unlikely to become scarce, but the people of Hawai'i can ill afford to neglect the overall availability of clean water and its protection from contamination.

A limited land area also compounds the problems associated with the disposal of solid and hazardous wastes. Land fills across the state are rapidly filling to capacity, and the safe disposal of garbage will become a far more important topic as appropriate disposal sites become fewer and more difficult to locate. As industry develops in the state and as more hazardous wastes are generated, their proper disposal also becomes an issue.

Finally, probably no other state is as economically dependent on the quality of its environment as is Hawai'i. For Hawai'i's economic success to continue, the state must insure the protection of the beaches, coastlines, swimming areas, and natural vegetation that do so much to attract tourism.

All of these concerns play an important role in influencing the actions that policy makers take. At the same time, however, these concerns similarly affect other groups who have a stake in the state's future. Such groups include the Sierra Club, as well as those who represent business, industry, agriculture, tourism, and housing developers.

Having described briefly some of the natural limits that Hawai'i faces, it is now useful to provide some more detail about environmental issues that are already, or soon will be, of major concern. The first among these is water quality.

*Water Quality*

The first link in the water supply chain is groundwater, which is the available supply of fresh water that is pumped from under the ground for drinking and irrigation. Hawai'i is somewhat unusual in that much of its groundwater is located in large aquifers. In the case of Oahu, the main source of fresh water for the entire island is the Pearl Harbor aquifer. During a typical day, well over 250 million gallons of water are pumped from the aquifer. A major concern is that demand for this water will exceed its availability. A possible consequence may be the need to limit development or to establish an effective program to conserve water.[1]

The time for such a program may soon be near. In a review of Oahu's fresh water resources in 1989, DLNR and the Commission on Water Resource Management concluded that demand for fresh water from the Pearl Harbor aquifer could exceed supply by 1993.[2] If correct, this finding could easily disrupt the state's plans for a new urban hub in west-central Oahu.[3] Previous projections had forecast that demand for the aquifer's water would not exceed sustainable yields until 2010. This sustainable yield, which is the amount of water that can be removed without eventually exhausting the source, was estimated in 1979 to be about 225 million gallons per day. As a result of their recent review, the DLNR and the Commission on Water Resource Management changed the sustainable-yield figure to 195 million gallons per day and attempted to reduce water allocations to the military, the sugar companies, and the Board of Water Supply.

Fears that Oahu will soon exhaust its supplies of fresh water are probably unwarranted. State officials recognize that alternatives to the Pearl Harbor aquifer must be explored and developed. The Board of Water Supply intends to tap new water sources in the leeward and windward parts of Oahu by 1998. Such an action could eventually reduce the demand on the Pearl Harbor aquifer by as much as ten to twenty million gallons per day. Other potential alternatives include a desalinization plant in Ewa that should provide an alternative source of fresh water.[4] The goal is to produce enough water for about seventeen hundred homes in the area by the early 1990s.

The Department of Health monitors the quality of Hawai'i's drinking water. The problems the Department faces in doing so are common throughout the United States. Lead in drinking water is an important concern and is subject to regulation under the federal Lead Contamination Control Act of 1988. One rather unusual problem involves acidic rain due to volcanic eruptions on the island of Hawai'i. Residents of the Big Island occasionally find high levels of lead in their water catchment systems because acidic rain leaches lead from nails, roofing materials, and catchment pipes.[5] Hawai'i also needs to monitor pesticide residues in water, especially in places where wells are near agricultural areas.

Concern for the availability of clean water reinforces the need to protect the quality of existing groundwater resources. Fortunately, Hawai'i's Ground Water Use Act of 1959 affords some protection to the state's most important aquifers. Under authority granted by the act, the Department of Land and Natural Resources has designated, as critical, the Pearl Harbor aquifer and two adjacent groundwater basins. Such designation allows the board to regulate drilling and groundwater development for other than domestic uses.[6] The EPA has similarly designated the Pearl Harbor aquifer as a sole-source aquifer. The result of this decision is that possible sources of contamination are monitored closely. Environmental impact assessments are also required for development projects that might affect the aquifer. More generally, the EPA has issued nationally applicable guidelines and started a program to assist states in developing their own groundwater protection strategies. Hawai'i began the development of a comprehensive water resources protection plan in 1987, and it was completed in mid-1991. The plan's prospects for success remain uncertain. On the one hand, commercial interests heavily dependent on the availability of water are sure to oppose efforts to restrict or curtail withdrawals from groundwater supplies. On the other hand, some observers criticize the plan because it assumes that fresh, clean water will be available to accommodate whatever growth occurs. They argue further that the public's interest will be subordinated to the preferences of private developers.[7]

In addition to developing a state wide policy for water use, the state has restricted the installation of new cesspools in near-shore areas in most parts of the state to protect groundwater and drinking and coastal waters.[8] The policy prohibits the use of most cesspools where they would be above underground water supplies or affect coastal areas. The Department of Health hopes that by the end of the decade no untreated sewage will be dumped into Hawai'i's waters. At first glance this preference is commendable. In contrast, however, one must realize that much of Hawai'i's sewage treatment capacity is underutilized largely because sewer hook-ups have not been required for many residential developments.

The federal Clean Water Act of 1972 mandated that all municipalities provide at least secondary treatment for their sewage by 1977. Subsequent amendments to the act extended the deadline, first to 1983, then to mid-1988. Although many municipalities did not achieve the deadlines, the legislation has forced many state and local officials to consider how to upgrade older and less efficient primary treatment facilities (which remove about sixty percent of the solids and biological organisms from wastewater) to the more efficient but more costly secondary systems (which remove about eighty five percent of solids and biological organisms).

In spite of the secondary requirement, Congress was responsive to claims that it should also consider the capacity of the receiving waters to handle treated discharges. If a municipality can demonstrate that primary treatment is sufficient for the area in which the wastewater is disposed, Congress has said that a waiver can be granted. This would avoid the need to upgrade existing primary-treatment facilities. From Hawai'i's perspective, its off-shore currents adequately disperse sewage and avoid harmful concentrations of pollution. Using this logic, the state has often requested waivers from the EPA.[9]

Some of these requests have been approved, but the prospects for future requests and approvals are uncertain. In order to receive a waiver, public hearings are required, and there is some evidence to suggest that the public opposes further waivers. When the state requested a waiver for the Kailua wastewater treatment plant, for example, the action motivated nearly fifteen hundred local residents to oppose the waiver application at the public hearing.[10] This unprecedented protest eventually led Honolulu's mayor, Frank Fasi, to withdraw the application and to call for the upgrading of all the county's treatment plants. Perhaps in response to the tide of public opinion, Governor John Waihee also called for a policy that would insure clean water for Hawai'i.

These preferences have yet to be reflected in improved treatment facilities, but when they are, the costs of upgrading all plants to secondary treatment will require each household to pay an extra thirty to forty dollars per month in fees.[11] Not everyone favors such an increase, and critics argue that existing primary treatment facilities are already adequate for many areas of the state. These people further contend that it may be both foolish and costly to require secondary treatment when primary treatment adequately protects water quality. It will be interesting to see whether these critics attract additional supporters, particularly when all property owners must start paying for the preferences of their vocal neighbors. Housing developers are also concerned about the capacity of presently available waste water treatment facilities. Although these developers may wish to build more houses, a lack of adequate capacity will surely hinder their efforts.

### Pesticides

Hawai'i's lush greenery is composed of more than just tropical rain forests and abundant natural vegetation. Agriculture has long been important to the state; much of its vegetation is in the form of sugar cane, pineapple, and other crops. These crops, and Hawai'i's tropical climate, create an ideal environment for many pests, and a typical response to them is the widespread use of pesticides. However necessary these pesticides may be, they create potential problems of contamination to food, soil, and groundwater.

This potential became a reality when the Department of Health detected unacceptably high levels of heptachlor epoxide in milk sold to the public in early 1982. The EPA had restricted the use of heptachlor in the 1970s, but had given the state of Hawai'i an exemption for its use after the ban took effect elsewhere in the United States. The pesticide is used to control ants and mealy bug infestation in pineapple fields. Once the pineapples were harvested, byproducts such as leaves and stems were turned into a cattle feed known as "green chop." Although the chop was allegedly not fed to cattle until at least twelve months after being collected from the fields, heptachlor residues still persisted on the byproducts. When the leaves and stems were fed to Oahu's dairy cattle, it led to the contamination of their milk. Two months after the unacceptable levels of heptachlor were detected (and after considerable internal debate about what to do), the Department of Health conducted eleven recalls, involving nearly all dairy products on Oahu.[12] After the recalls and the discontinued use of green chop, the situation appeared to be resolved, and dairy products were again available throughout Oahu, the only island affected. Hawai'i's unfortunate experience with heptachlor prompted the EPA to rescind its exemption for the pesticide in late 1982, and it is no longer available for use in pineapple fields.

Another episode involving pesticide-related contamination occurred in 1984, when wells providing water to Waipahu and Mililani in central Oahu were found to contain residues of ethylene dibromide (EDB) and DBCP. Although there are no regulations specifying acceptable levels of these residues, the levels detected caused the wells to be closed.[13] A temporary water shortage resulted. Alternate wells were soon drilled and the water supply restored. The contaminated wells underwent a process of filtration and cleaning, and all water from them is now filtered before use.

These two cases illustrate how vulnerable Hawai'i's natural resources are to pesticide contamination. Completely eliminating the use of pesticides in Hawai'i is unlikely and perhaps undesirable, so it is imperative to insure their proper use and to be aware of how they might affect the environment. The state's Department of Agriculture regulates the kinds of pesticides that can be used, and it attempts to effectively monitor pesticide residues in feed and food products. It is not unusual for a state's agriculture department to monitor the use of pesticides.

Some people believe, however, that such departments find it difficult to balance their obligation to encourage agricultural productivity with the need to regulate pesticides properly. This concern was one reason that regulation of pesticides at the federal level was transferred to the EPA from the U.S. Department of Agriculture upon creation of the EPA in 1970.

For Hawai'i, the proper use of pesticides is likely to remain an important issue so long as pineapple and sugar cane are widely grown. Growers of these crops consider pesticides to be essential to economic success. Similarly, as long as pressures exist to provide more locally grown fruits and vegetables, one can expect a parallel increase in the use of pesticides. The danger here is that the increased use of pesticides could jeopardize the quality of existing ground water supplies. The increased use of pesticides on golf courses and at recreational resorts could also jeopardize the quality of these supplies. One should remember, however, that even a total ban on pesticides would not soon eliminate their potential ill effects. The residues of some pesticides can be detected in groundwater for as long as forty years after their use.

## Solid and Hazardous Wastes

Disposal of solid and hazardous wastes is a critical issue throughout the United States. It is not at all unusual to read about garbage barges searching for ports to unload their unwanted cargo or to watch protesters rallying against efforts to locate new disposal sites close to their homes. The amount of waste generated seems to increase each year, and landfills across the nation are filled faster than new ones can be opened. Hawai'i shares these problems. By the end of the century Honolulu is expected to discard about one million tons of waste each year. At current fill rates, for example, most of the state's landfills will have to be closed by the turn of the century unless viable alternatives quickly appear.

In response to this impending problem Hawai'i is pursuing an alternative that is becoming increasingly popular in the United States, the incineration of solid waste. The so-called H-Power garbage-to-energy project, which started operation in 1990, could reduce disposal needs in the state by as much as ninety percent and extend the period for which existing landfills can be used.[14] Of the 750,000 tons of trash generated annually on Oahu, it is anticipated that H-Power will handle about three-quarter. One advantage of the scheme is that incineration transforms garbage into electricity— the H-Power facility will generate about fifty megawatts of electricity, enough energy for as many as fifty-thousand homes. In contrast to the benefits, the costs of the project are much higher than originally estimated, and incineration does not solve completely the waste problem. Incineration of some materials can put toxic chemicals into the air, and after burning the "trash" it is still necessary to dispose of nearly 600 tons of waste residue from the facility every day in an environmentally sound manner.

Large-scale recycling is often a cleaner and lower cost alternative to waste disposal. In some areas local residents are fairly conscientious—they recycle about seventy-five percent of all aluminum cans used in the state, thus saving tremendous amounts of energy and raw materials. Despite this success, there are still far more opportunities for additional recycling. Of all the solid waste now generated on Oahu, less than five percent (by weight) is recycled. The rest is either buried (about eighty five percent) or burned.

State officials hope that recycling will eventually be used for about twenty percent of all the state's wastes, but as much as 75% in Honolulu. To achieve this goal the state is studying how recycling can be increased. This interest notwithstanding, the state government has not sponsored any large-scale projects of this sort. Companies or private individuals are now responsible for virtually all the recycling that occurs. Should the state wish to become a more active participant in these areas, it might want to copy Japan's efforts. Japanese households are required to separate their trash into different groups—metals, paper and cardboard, and glass and plastics. This scheme facilitates recycling, but it also requires substantial cooperation from the people who generate the waste. Many people on Oahu will soon have an opportunity to demonstrate their support of such a scheme. The state government has initiated a pilot program that will require homeowners in selected communities to separate their garbage to facilitate the recycling of glass, metals, plastics, and paper. If the pilot project is a success, the expectation is that all of Oahu and, possibly, all of the state, will find itself subject to strict recycling requirements.

As for hazardous wastes, Hawai'i does not have any approved disposal sites or treatment facilities. This lack does not mean that such wastes are ignored. Many private companies collect, store, transport, and arrange for the disposal of Hawai'i's hazardous wastes on the mainland. A number of these companies also operate solvent-recycling systems that allow cleaning solvents to be reused.

Of all the hazardous waste products in Hawai'i, waste oil probably causes the most problems. The EPA does not consider waste oil to be hazardous, but this does not negate the need for its proper disposal. Hawai'i generates large amounts, and some of it is used to fuel power plant generators. The problem stems from a lack of collection points. Many gasoline stations do not want to accept waste oil for fear that it contains other hazardous materials, such as brake fluid or other solvents. If people cannot find a proper place to take their waste oil, the most convenient alternative may be the sewer or storm drains. Fortunately, all of the companies in the state that dispose of hazardous wastes are willing to accept small amounts of waste oil free of charge. The Hawai'i Gasoline Dealers Association has also established a telephone hotline that informs the public of those service stations willing to accept waste oil.

Hawai'i has succeeded so far in exporting most of its hazardous wastes, but the continued generation of these wastes may soon exceed the willingness of other states to accept them. States already facing their own problems with abandoned or improperly operated disposal sites for hazardous wastes are not likely to respond enthusiastically to requests that they accept someone else's wastes (and problems,). This means that some day people in Hawai'i may have to consider where on their islands they will dispose of their hazardous wastes. Any volunteers?

## Ocean Pollution

Hawai'i is famous throughout the world for its clean and beautiful beaches, but these beaches and their popularity also face a high vulnerability to environmental catastrophe. The state's largest oil spill to date occurred in January 1987, when forty-two thousand gallons of crude oil accidentally escaped from a barge on its way to Kahului. The resulting oil slick, which was over twelve miles long, affected every beach on Oahu's North Shore, from Hanauma Bay to Waimea Beach. In comparison to "notorious" spills elsewhere in the world, this spill was small. It underscores, however, the state's good fortune in having avoided even larger spills. Hawai'i is especially vulnerable in this regard because of its dependence on tankers importing oil for motor vehicles, commercial aviation, oil-fired power plants, and military operations. As an illustration, Hawai'ians imported about 1.7 trillion gallons of crude oil in 1988, and this amount does not even include the petroleum imported for military operations.[15]

If we consider that the average oil tanker unloading oil in Hawai'i has a capacity of nearly thirty million gallons, the possibility of a huge spill cannot be ignored. As one environmental expert has suggested, if a supertanker should break apart in Hawai'i's waters, valuable "wetland areas, irreplaceable marine sanctuaries, miles of beaches and dozens of tourist resorts would be hit by wave after wave of oil."[16] Clean-up operations would last at least a year.

In addition to oil and sewage, Hawai'i's beachcombers occasionally encounter medical and other wastes. In an effort to curb some of these intrusions, the state government has approved legislation that bans the use of plastic beverage-container rings unless they are biodegradable. Hawai'i also benefits in protecting its shoreline from the strong ocean currents that surround the islands. These currents manage to keep most beaches and adjacent waters relatively clean, except during and after heavy rain storms when streams deposit tremendous amounts of silt and other debris into the ocean. Despite the advantages these currents provide, the state's extraordinary dependence on tourism suggests that it may be in the best interest of property owners and those in the tourist industry to support more stringent water quality standards for Hawai'i's ocean areas.

## *Endangered Species*[17]

The premature loss of any species is undesirable, but it is particularly so for Hawai'i's native species. Many of these species evolved in and became dependent on highly specialized habitats. As one scientist has observed, "Isolation, time, and habitat diversity have produced a most distinctive land biota. More than 97% of Hawai'i's native flowering plants, nonmigratory land birds, insects, and land snails occur naturally nowhere else on earth."[18] Isolation provided an evolutionary advantage, but it also created a high vulnerability to disruption. Islands typically offer protections from predators, but when goats, sheep, dogs, cats, and mongooses are introduced (and when habitats are destroyed or irreparably altered), island species are limited in where they can go and how rapidly they can develop defense mechanisms. All these factors suggest that Hawai'i has a special responsibility to preserve its globally unique plant and animal resources.

However important this responsibility, it has not been well served. Among all American states, for example, none has as many species on the edge of extinction as does Hawai'i, and no other state can claim as many recent extinctions.[19] Since the Europeans' arrival in Hawai'i, about one-third of the state's endemic bird species have disappeared. Of the remaining forty-four avian species found only in Hawai'i, the U.S. Fish and Wildlife Service (FWS) classifies twenty-nine as endangered. The state's only native mammals, the Hawaiian hoary bat and the Hawaiian monk seal, are likewise in danger of imminent extinction.

Hawai'i's plant life is in similar jeopardy. No other state has experienced as many plant extinctions, and no other state has as many plants on the brink of extirpation. When the Smithsonian Institution issued a report in the mid-1970s on vascular plant species it considered to be endangered, threatened, or already possibly extinct in the United States, more than forty-five percent of the thirty-two hundred species identified were Hawaiian.[20] The FWS's assessment of the state's plant life is much the same. The agency once noted that it had enough information either to justify the listing or suggest the appropriateness of listing as endangered nearly eight hundred Hawaiian plants.[21] Of the eight hundred, about sixteen-percent were believed to be extinct. The FWS further identified fifty-one native plants for which it has "persuasive evidence of extinction"; all but six of these had once been found only in Hawai'i.

The state's Endangered Species Act is intended to provide the means to preserve these species, but more effective laws and actions are vital to the survival of Hawai'i's endangered plants and animals. Reorganization of the state's efforts to protect vulnerable species may also be desirable. The DLNR is charged with implementing the act, but it has a mixed constituency that includes not only conservationists, but also hunters, commercial fishermen, and land developers. When the preferences of the latter groups conflict with the needs for preservation and protection, endangered species are not always the victors. Unless the advocates for species achieve more victories, however, Hawai'i will suffer the further loss of irreplaceable resources of inestimable value.

This brief catalogue of environmental problems is not meant to be exhaustive. Other problems, such as air pollution or the environmental consequences of geothermal power, could have been discussed, but the topics included have given a flavor to some of the more important issues now facing the state's inhabitants. Before considering the future of Hawai'i's environment it is first useful to put the state's environmental management into some comparative perspective.

## Hawai'i in Comparative Perspective

How well does Hawai'i address its environmental problems in comparison with other states? The severity of each state's problems and its capacity to deal with them vary, so direct comparison is difficult. Nonetheless, several efforts have been made to assess state environmental programs. One of the most common measures of effort (although not of outcomes) is the amount of money a state spends on environmental management. Hawai'i's small size explains why it spent less on environmental management than any but one other state (Nevada) in 1986, the year for which the most recent comparative data are available.[22] On a per capita basis, however, Hawai'i's ranking improves considerably. For every resident, the state spent slightly more than nineteen dollars for environmental activities in that year. This amount was far less than the national average of thirty seven dollars, but enough to rank Hawai'i twenty-eighth among all fifty states in per capita expenditures.

Another way to compare expenditures is to consider a state's relative priorities—what proportion of its overall budget is devoted to environmental management? For its budget in 1986, as an illustration, Hawai'i devoted much less than half of the national average of 1.85 percent. In contrast, forty-five states spent a higher proportion of their budgets on these activities than did Hawai'i (.72 percent of total state budget).

Other researchers have attempted to rank the states' relative commitment to environmental programs. One such ranking scheme assigns a number from one to ten for different environmental programs within each state. The higher the number, the greater the commitment and effectiveness of the program, at least according to the researcher.[23] Using this scheme, Wisconsin, California, and New Jersey were said to have the best (and Mississippi and West Virginia the worst) overall environmental programs in 1987. Hawai'i's composite score for six different environmental programs ranked the state as the fortieth most effective, a rank consistent with its overall expenditures for environmental management as a proportion of total state expenditures. Hawai'i's scores for several programs as well as the average score for all other states are shown in Table 7.1.

It is immediately evident that Hawai'i's commitment to environmental quality is below average, at least if one accepts the merits of this ranking scheme. The more important issue is whether the state's relative commitment to protection insures the level of environmental quality that most residents and their incessant visitors expect and take for granted.

## The Future of Hawai'i's Environmental Quality

Hawai'i is fortunate that its environmental problems have not reached the severity of those encountered in many other states. Ha-

### Table 7.1: Relative Commitment of States
### to Environmental Protection

|  | Ground-water | Hazardous wastes | Solid waste | Drinking water |
|---|---|---|---|---|
| Score for Hawai'i | 3 | 2 | 2 | 5 |
| Average score for all other states | 5.5 | 5.6 | 4.6 | 4.4 |

Note: The higher the score the greater the commitment to environmental protection. The range of possible scores is 1 to 10.

wai'i thus has the opportunity to learn from these states' experiences and to prevent environmental problems from becoming environmental crises. Despite this assessment, Hawai'i is not immune from environmental catastrophe. A massive oil spill or the further extirpation of Hawai'i's rare plant and animal life are but two distinct possibilities. Though such events cannot be predicted with any certainty, much can be done to prevent these and other environmental nightmares.

Increased public awareness about environmental issues is no doubt disirable, but one must also recognize the intense pressures for rapid development that now plague much of Hawai'i. Whereas the environmental consequences of most developments were once slight and readily manageable, more recent growth may be exceeding the capacity of policy makers to respond.[25] Traffic jams are increasingly common, major roads are in need of frequent repair, the shortages of moderately priced housing is acute, and some sewage and water supply systems are beginning to reflect the strains of excessive demand. Where most public officials once encouraged long-term growth, some now believe it is time to slow or even halt further expansion.

Such decisions will not be made easily or without acrimonious debate. In a state so dependent on visitors, a no- or slow-growth strategy could jeopardize employment opportunities and retail businesses that thrive on tourism. In contrast, unchecked growth could easily threaten the environmental amenities that attract visitors to Hawai'i.

In sum, Hawai'i, its people, and its policy makers are now at the crossroads to the future. Thoughtful policies need to be enacted to guarantee that the islands avoid the path to environmental disaster so well travelled elsewhere. Other areas have been less fortunate and now struggle to remedy avoidable mistakes associated with policies that once looked attractive. As the next century nears, people in Hawai'i still have the enviable opportunity to assess their lifestyles and to determine whether they will take the easy path to environmental disgrace or the more demanding trail that provides a sustainable and environmentally enjoyable future.

## Notes

1. Andy Yamaguchi, "Review of Oahu Water Supply May Wash Out Second City,'" *Honolulu Advertiser*, April 17, 1989. For a useful nontechnical introduction to groundwater-related issues in Hawai'i, see Zachary A. Smith, *Groundwater in the West* (New York: Academic Press, 1989), pp. 83–93.

2. Lucy Young, "Crisis Spurs Search for More Water," *Honolulu Star Bulletin*, April 20, 1989. For a thorough discussion of the Commission's activities, see Environment Hawai'i 1 (August 1990), pp. 1–8. This monthly newsletter, which began publication in July 1990, is an excellent source of current information on environmental issues in the state.

3. Yamaguchi, "Review of Oahu Water Supply."

4. James Kumagai, "Ewa Plains Desalting Plant," speech presented to the 15th Annual Hawai'i Section, American Water Works Association Conference, Honolulu, May 1989.

5. Bruce Anderson, Hawai'i Department of Health, "Survey of Hawai'i Water Catchment Systems," speech presented to the 15th Annual Hawai'i Section, American Water Works Association Conference, Honolulu, May 1989.

6. Smith, *Groundwater in the West*, p. 89.

7. "Why Conserve Water? Or, Let Them Drink Perrier," *Environment Hawai'i* 1 (August 1990), p. 3.

8. "No New Cesspools? Like No New Taxes," *Environment Hawai'i* 1 (November 1990), p. 6.

9. Hawai'i Department of Health, "Sand Island 301(h) Waiver Application," 1986.

10. EPA and Hawai'i Department of Health, "Kailua Wastewater Treatment Plant 301(h) Waiver Public Hearing Transcript," 1988.

11. EPA and Hawai'i Department of Health, "Honolulu Wastewater Treatment Plant Public Hearing Notes," November 29, 1988.

12. For an excellent discussion of the heptachlor episode, see Richard Pratt, "The Great Hawaiian Milk Crisis: Science, Policy and Economic Interest," *Social Process in Hawai'i* 31 (1984), 50–76.

13. In *Groundwater in the West*, Smith reports that concentrations of EDB in Oahu's drinking water have reached three hundred parts per billion. This is about ten times the levels measured in California, the state with the next highest levels.

14. William Kresnek, "Council Ready to Fuel Restart of H-Power Construction," *Honolulu Advertiser*, January 10, 1988. For a lively critique of the H-Power facility's costs and environmental impacts, see "Turning Trash into Ash and Dollars into Cinders," *Environment Hawai'i* 1 (October 1990), pp. 1, 6.

15. "Ship Oil, and Court Disaster," *Environment Hawai'i* 1 (December 1990), p. 6.

16. "The Coast Guard's Nightmare: A 'Worse-Case Scenario,'" *Environment Hawai'i* 1 (December 1990), pp. 7–8.

17. This discussion is from Richard J. Tobin, *The Expendable Future: U.S. Politics and the Protection of Biological Diversity* (Durham, NC: Duke University Press, 1990).

18. Alan D. Hart, "The Onslaught against Hawai'i's Tree Snails," *Natural History*, 46 (December 1978), p. 46.

19. Andrew J. Berger, "Hawai'i's Dubious Distinction," *Defenders*, 50 (December 1975), p. 491. See also Wayne C. Gagne, "Conservation Priorities in Hawaiian Natural Systems," *BioScience* 38 (April 1988), pp. 264–71. Several other articles in the same issue of *BioScience* also discuss the plight of Hawai'i's endemic species.

20. Smithsonian Institution, *Endangered and Threatened Plants of the United States*, reprinted as U.S. House of Representatives' Document no. 94–51, 94th Cong., 1st sess., 1975.

21. *Federal Register*, 45 (December 15, 1980), pp. 82480–569.

22. R. Steven Brown and Edward Garner, *Resource Guide to State Environmental Management* (Lexington, KY: The Council of State Governments, 1988.)

23. Scott Ridley, *The State of the States, 1987* (Washington, D.C.: Fund for Renewable Energy and the Environment, 1987), p. 32.

24. Ibid., p. 5 for the 1987 rankings for groundwater and hazardous wastes. Renew America, *The States of the States, 1989* (Washington, D.C.: Renew America, 1989), pp. 40–41 for the comparable 1989 rankings for solid waste and drinking water.

25. A useful discussion of these issues can be found in Rod Thompson, "Special Report: Growing Pains," parts 1 to 4, *Honolulu Star Bulletin*, May 15–18, 1989.

# 8

## DEALING WITH SCARCITY: LAND USE AND PLANNING

### David L. Callies

#### Introduction: Hawai'i Land-Use Policy and the State Land-Use Law

There are few matters of public policy in Hawai'i that do not include planning for the use of land. Hawai'i has the most sophisticated and complete system of land-use planning and control in the United States—and perhaps the world.[1] This is not because the state has a limited supply of land, though, of course, it does. What scarcity there is results from the fact that major population centers—primarily Honolulu—are located away from the largest land area in the state: the Big Island of Hawai'i. The Big Island is larger than the rest of the state combined, yet it contains less than a tenth of its population. Stringent state land-use planning controls, which result in ninety-five percent of the state's land area being restricted to agricultural and conservation uses, combined with a lack of public facilities (roads, water, sewer) to support development in many parts of Hawai'i, produce a scarcity of land available for urban uses in the areas where people most want to live.

This chapter addresses the history, and elements of, the land-use planning and regulatory system in Hawai'i; the theory behind the state's "open space" zones, the legal limits to maintaining such zones, and new techniques for providing public facilities to support development (impact fees and development agreements), together with their policy implications and legal limits. The chapter closes with a discussion of citizen participation in the land-planning and regulatory process and the frustrations that have led to increased use of the initiative and referendum measures which, in turn, have immense capacity for frustrating public policy making.

## Historical Basis for State Control
## of Planning and Land Development

Hawai'i is unique among the fifty states in providing for state-wide regulation of land.[2] The rational basis for this state-centered land-use control is probably the historically central nature of government in Hawai'i. This is also reflected in the dearth of local governments. There are no cities, villages, towns, or special districts, but only the four counties of Honolulu, Hawai'i, Kauai, and Maui.

Hawai'i is kingdom, territory, and state has been principally governed by a king, territorial and state legislatures, and a governor. The land policy in the Hawaiian kingdom emanated from the King, who distributed large parcels of land in classic feudal fashion to nobles, or *alii*, who held that land only so long as the King permitted.[3] After the Great Mahele, which divided the land of the state into three groups (royal, chieftain, and government), the land was still controlled by a central government. Annexation of Hawai'i by the United States in 1898 did little to change this central focus. Rather than disperse the land through homesteading, the federal government was ceded about half the land area in the state. The territorial government replaced the king, and at statehood in 1959 the duly elected governor replaced the territorial governor.[4]

In all of this, local government languished. No units of government were formed except for the four counties. Their planning and zoning powers, even in relatively populous Honolulu, were rudimentary at best. It is therefore no surprise that the state took the lead in passing Hawai'i's Land Use Law in 1961,[5] only two years after statehood. Land policy in Hawai'i is comprehensible only against the backdrop of that law, to which we now turn.

## Act 187, the Land Use Law: The System in Brief

Passed by a Democratic legislature, the Land Use Law primarily represented an attempt to preserve prime agricultural land from increasing urbanization in a state that still regarded agriculture as its economic mainstay.[6] Another principal factor was the burgeoning state plan movement (culminating twenty years later in Act 100—Hawai'i's state plan).[7]

Essentially, the Land Use Law divides all the land in the state into four classifications, or distinct types: agriculture; conservation; urban; and rural. The descriptive names of the districts describe what uses are permitted in each.[8] Most of the state's four million acres is classified as either agriculture or conservation, with measurably more in the former. The amount of land in the rural districts is statistically insignificant. Approximately four percent of the state's land area is classified urban. Only in this last district—urban—do the counties control land development.[9] The state controls the rest, first by deciding what land gets urbanized and, second, by regulating the use of land in the two largest districts (agriculture and conservation), which account for ninety-five percent of the land area of the state.[10]

The state decides what land will be placed in the county-controlled urban districts (urbanized) by the process of district boundary review. This process is the province of a nine-member Land Use Commission (LUC) appointed by the governor. During most of the past thirty years, the LUC has approved boundary amendments pursuant either to a five-year boundary review (required by state law) or, more frequently, by means of landowner applications for boundary amendments (reclassification from agriculture or conservation to urban).[11]

Effective control of the use of land in the conservation and agricultural districts lies with the Department of Land and Natural Resources (DLNR) and the LUC, respectively. In the conservation district, the power of DLNR is absolute. It can, for example, grant or deny a permit to develop a golf course. In the agriculture district, counties may approve limited housing on large lots on land areas smaller than fifteen acres. The LUC controls other uses, including limited nonagricultural uses by special permit upon recommendation of a county planning commission. Again, golf courses are often approved in this way.[12]

### The Development-Free Zones: Can the State Preserve Ninety-five Percent?

There are major policy implications for county control and home rule if the state continues to hold ninety-five percent of its land area in essentially development-free agriculture and conservation zones. However, before considering such questions, we will examine the constitutionality of land-use planning and the regulation of private land.

*Regulatory Takings and the Fifth Amendment*

Since 1922, a law regulating the private use of land—like Hawai'i's land use law—could be construed as a taking of property, either without compensation or without due process of law, if it went too far.[13] This "takings" doctrine has presented local and state governments with something of a dilemma in exercising their land use control powers through local zoning and development regulations. How far can land use regulations go before they become a taking of property? The U.S. Supreme Court first held zoning legal in 1926 but in 1928 found a particular zoning ordinance illegal, then the court retired from the field, leaving it to state courts for half a century.[15] During that fifty years, state takings jurisprudence evolved to the point that, so long as there was some economic use of the land left, and the regulation was truly necessary to protect public health, safety, and welfare, there was no taking of property.

*The Takings Trilogy of 1987: The Big Chill*

In 1987 the U.S. Supreme Court decided three cases which dealt with critical questions concerning regulatory takings. The first held that a regulation must take all economic use of an owner's property to be a regulatory taking; the second declared that once such a taking occurs, the landowner is entitled to compensation, a requirement of the U.S. Constitution when private property is taken for a public use; the third permits government to require a landowner to help fix problems his development may cause the community before proceeding with that development—build a public viewing platform, for example, if the owner's new beach house would block a beach view.[15]

In the first case, *Keystone Bituminous Coal Co.* v. *DeBenedictis*,[16] the court held that a Pennsylvania law requiring coal companies to leave a percentage of coal in the ground in order to prevent subsidence was a valid health and safety regulation and that it left the owners with enough economic use of their land that there was no taking. The court even suggested that if the regulation were for health, the environment, or the fiscal integrity of the people, perhaps all economic use could be taken. This, then, is the present standard for a regulatory taking.

However, once having found a taking, a court may require the government to pay compensation, even if that taking is temporary. In *First English Evangelical Lutheran Church of Glendale* v. *Los Angeles*, the court so held, carefully avoiding deciding whether a Los Angeles ordinance forbidding rebuilding a church camp which had just been washed away by a flood was a taking in the first place.[17] (The third case is relevant primarily to development exactions and impact fees, and so is dealt with on pages 141–142).

*Preserving Agricultural Land
and Open Space in Hawai'i: A Rational Basis*

From the foregoing court cases it is clear that, whether the state is protecting agriculture through an agricultural zone, or preventing development through a conservation or agriculture zone, it must leave the landowner some economic use of the property. While there are hints in the *Bituminous Coal* case that if the safety requirement is high enough—if the regulation is based on health and safety rather than such welfare concepts as aesthetics, historic preservation, or economic well being—a regulation may take away *all* economic use. However, it would be hard to make health and safety arguments for preserving agricultural land, particularly if there were a surplus of agriculturally restricted land in the state. The same is true if conservation zones leave a landowner with no economic uses. Neither zone appears principally based upon public health or safety, but rather on economic welfare and aesthetics.

Despite this, the forty-plus percent of Hawai'i's land that the LUC classifies as conservation is probably safe enough from legal challenge. First, the state—or some government—owns much of this land, and can therefore be expected to raise few objections to how it classifies its own land. Second, most of the land in the conservation district is mountainous and/or watershed. Strong public health and safety arguments can be made for leaving it development-free.[18]

However, agricultural land is another matter entirely. It has been clear at least since the draft report of the Land Evaluation and Site Assessment Commission that the state has classified far more land for agricultural purposes than it presently needs.[19] It is also clear that much of Hawai'i's plantation agriculture (especially sugar production) is in serious economic trouble. Thus, unless land classified as agriculture can be put to some economic use, the classification is legally indefensible at its present magnitude. Among the arguably economic uses permitted in state agricultural zones are golf courses (both of right and by special permit) and other open space recreational uses. So long as the market for these uses, together with the viability of agricultural acreage, more or less equals the totality of the land in the state classified for agricultural purposes, the classification is defensible. To the extent that more land is classified than can be so used, it is not.

This has led the state to consider creating a fifth zone, an "open space" zone, based neither on a shrinking agricultural base nor a resource or site-limited conservation base. Such an open space zone would permit a limited number of low-intensity economic uses such as golf courses, cemeteries, campgrounds, and other outdoor recreational uses. The basis for the land use controls in such a zone would be the need to preserve open space for various public welfare reasons, come as simple as the desire to preserve views.[20] The state's Office of State Planning has proposed such an LUC-administered classification to complement the agricultural and conservation districts, with the addition that the counties could share some of the power over the uses permitted there.[21] Whether this will eventually take the legal heat off the agricultural district, in light of the decline of Hawai'i's agricultural activity below sufficient levels to support so classifying half the land in the state, remains to be seen.

## Who Pays for Development in Hawai'i: Impact Fees and Development Agreements

### Development and Capital Improvements

It is difficult to develop land without public facilities such as water, sewer, roads, and solid waste disposal sites, and unwise to do so without schools and parks as well. While so-called public utilities provide some of these, the vast majority have traditionally been viewed as the responsibility of government, both to provide and to maintain.[22] Not so today. Between revolts against the principal source of local government revenue—the real property tax—and the increasing withdrawal of federal funds for highways and wastewater treatment plants, local governments have barely sufficient funds to operate and maintain what they have, with precious little left over to pay for facilities necessary for new land development.[23] This has led to efforts to shift much of the burden for such new facilities to the land developer. For the past dozen years, the most popular method of shifting that burden has been to charge the landowner for the projected new facilities which the proposed development will require. These charges take the form of dedication or free provision of onsite facilities, fees in lieu of such dedication, and impact fees and public/private development agreements for offsite facilities which may be used by others. These last—impact fees and development agreements—are topics of considerable interest to Hawai'i's four counties, most of which have bills for ordinances proposing their use.[24]

### Impact Fees

The impact fee is a charge on development levied primarily for the purpose of allocating the costs of offsite capital facilities among landowners whose proposed developments generate the need for that facility.[25] It is different from, and has advantages over, the traditional subdivision dedication, or fee charged in lieu of such dedication. First, it can be used to finance facilities not normally subject to subdivision dedications and exactions, such as waste treatment facilities and public schools. Second, it can be used to finance offsite improvements. Third, it can be applied to commercial, industrial, and residential development (like apartments and townhouses) other than single-family subdivisions. Fourth, it can be collected at various stages in the land development process.[26]

The validity of such fees depends upon the meeting of a nexus test between the facility to be paid for and the land development which is being, in whole or in part, charged for its construction. There must be a close relationship between the development and the required improvement. This is sound policy, because if the development charged does not need public facilities or at least does not need the facility for which it is being charged, then the reason for the impact fee disappears and it ought not to be collected. This is the basis for the most prominent of legal tests by which such fees are judged, called the "rational nexus" test.[27] If an impact fee fails the test, then it is a county tax, for which very specific state enabling legislation is required. The State of Hawai'i does not give its counties such taxing power.

The U.S. Supreme Court recently applied such a test in the last of the 1987 trilogy cases discussed on pp. 138–139.[28] There, the court decided that the California Coastal Commission could not require a landowner to dedicate a portion of his rear yard, which happened to be adjacent to a public beach, to the public as a condition for rebuilding his beach house: "The condition would be constitutional even if it consisted of the requirement that the Nollans provide a viewing spot on their property for passersby with whose sighting of the beach their new house would interfere."[29] However, even assuming that the protection of public views was a valid purpose for restricting development, the lateral beach access which the Commission required of the Nollans would not reduce obstacles to viewing the beach created by the rebuilt house. It lacked, said the court, "essential" nexus.

The decision has been widely interpreted as knocking both the legal and policy ground out from under so-called linkage programs: the exacting of a fee from a developer—albeit for a public purpose such as affordable housing—solely because the developer needs a governmental permit to proceed with that development.[30] Indeed, several courts have recently so held.[31] This is of considerable importance in jurisdictions like Hawai'i, in which affordable housing is often made a condition for land development approvals and permits. While it is not too difficult to find a nexus between the building of a major commercial or resort facility and the need for nearby affordable housing for employees, the levying of an affordable housing fee is less defensible when imposed upon a (more expensive) housing development. It is difficult to argue that building market-priced housing generates a need for affordable housing. Nevertheless, courts in New Jersey have accepted such an argument when it appears that the market housing development is so large that it takes up all the available residentially zoned land in the region.[32] This, of course, raises once again the issue of why so little land is classified in Hawai'i's urban district, which is the only one permitting housing developments of any consequence.

### Development Agreements

Of course, if a developer voluntarily *agrees* to provide such housing, or any other fee or exaction in the public interest, in return for certainty of development rules and plans or some such, then there is no need for a rational nexus. This is the heart of the rationale for development agreements, whereby government undertakes to freeze certain development plans and regulations in exchange for developer contributions beyond what government can legally extract through impact fees and the like.[33] However, courts have traditionally taken a dim view of such bargaining away of public regulatory power. It is for this reason that several states have passed development agreement statutes setting out public policy reasons for entering into such agreements: certainty of development, better plan implementation, and so forth.[34] So far, there is not a single reported case dealing with development agreements, despite their widespread use in California, Florida, Colorado, and Arizona. Most commentators agree that they are probably legal, provided there is a statute backing them up.[35]

The principal issue is whether the development agreement effectively bargains away the local regulatory (police) power, illegally binding future governments.[36] May an existing legislature bind a future legislature by guaranteeing that land-use regulations and plans pertaining to a particular parcel shall remain the same for, say, twenty years? The answer is probably yes if, in the case of a local government, the guarantee or freeze is for a limited time, pursuant to statute and for public-purpose contributions. What has troubled courts in the past are more or less permanent guarantees without benefit of statute and/or in exchange for improper landowner contributions (political campaign contributions, for example).[37] Moreover, there are a few cases which have upheld analogous annexation agreements.[38]

A policy question raised in the debate on the use of development agreements is the extent to which they do away with planning. However, as development agreements lock in existing plans, it is more likely they will help, rather than hinder, planning. If the public sector is truly unable to decide that its plans and regulations, publicly debated, heard, and made, are good for a few years at a time, then the problem is with the planning process and not the development agreement process.

## Citizen Participation
## in the Land-Development Process:
## Initiative and Referendum in Hawai'i

Initiative is the submission of a new measure, most often a proposed law, to the people for a vote, usually at a general election. The referendum is the referral of a measure, also usually a law, already passed by a local or state legislature, to the people for such a vote. Both have been used recently in attempts to affect the use of land in Hawai'i.[39]

### Public Participation and Public Land Policy

The use of the initiative and referendum in land-use planning is a type of public decision making. Therein lies a potential public policy problem. As two planning and law experts have pungently noted, "Participation [by citizens] is not a substitute for planning or for regular government, since it often leads to non-planning and semi-anarchic government."[40]

This is not to say that there is no place for public participation in the land-planning and regulatory process. There is, and Hawai'i has plenty of it in the form of notice, hearings, and public testimony built into the system at virtually every level, from the state plan through LUC boundary amendments, local development plans, permits, and zoning changes.[41] But when it comes to the initiative and referendum, what the public wants is not participation but final decision making, and that is quite a different matter. It is one thing for the public to demand and obtain a voice in the planning and regulatory process through public hearings and the like. It is quite another for the public to demand a veto over a carefully wrought land planning and regulatory decision relating to single owner and a single parcel.

## The Initiative and Referendum In Hawai'i

In three well-reported cases, the public participated in the land use decision-making process in Hawai'i by overturning county land use plans and decisions. All resulted in litigation which ultimately made its way to the state's highest court. The first, Nukolii, involved the referendum, The next two, Date Laau and Sandy Beach, involved the initiative.

There are important differences between referendums and initiatives from a planning policy perspective. While both the initiative and referendum represent raw voting vetoes of governmental planning policy, the referendum submits to the electorate a decision which at least has had the benefit of thorough planning review and debate as well as public hearing. The initiative, on the other hand, presents as law a majority poll which has had none of these benefits and is devoid of planning and administrative review.

In the Nukolii case, the court decided that a referendum was the last discretionary permit needed by resort developers on Kauai before they were entitled to construct a hotel and condominium.[42] The court held that the *results* of a referendum (taking away the zoning) meant the developer could not rely even on his building permit once a previous referendum petition was filed, but must await the voters' pleasure. Ironically, another referendum the following year restored the commercial zoning, and the resort project was completed. The court later claimed that it did not consider whether either initiatives or referenda were legal ways to rezone land.

The Date-Laau dispute was over an initiative changing Honolulu land use map designations from high-density residential to low-density residential, stopping highrise development in a low-density, multifamily residential area in Moiliili.[43] The landowners sued to restore the high-density zoning. But the Honolulu City Council passed an ordinance shortly after the election doing precisely what the initiative ordinance had done: zone the property back down to low-density residential. Therefore, the Hawai'i Supreme Court sidestepped the question of the appropriateness of initiative in making zoning decisions in Hawai'i because the matter was now moot. Courts only decide actual cases and controversies.

This set the stage for the Sandy Beach initiative.[44] The Save Sandy Beach Coalition objected to the building of 150 homes next to a golf course and across the Kalanianaole Highway from Sandy Beach Park. Although the property had been zoned for such use for many years, the initiative measure passed, zoning the property down from residential to preservation. This time the council passed no conforming ordinance until after the court rendered its decision that the state enabling act and the emphasis on plans and planning process prohibited the use of initiative to rezone land. The court did not decide (because it did not reach) the constitutional issue of whether the initiative violates the rights of the property owner to due process of law, or whether rezoning and replanning is primarily legislative and therefore subject to the initiative or referendum or quasi-judicial in nature (and therefore referendum-proof).

*Policy Implications*

What we definitely know in Hawai'i after the *Sandy Beach* case is that neither the statutory scheme nor our commitment to land use changes by means of plans and planning permit local land use decisions through the initiative. The first is easy to correct legislatively. The second is not. Our statutory and charter provisions—particularly in Honolulu—are filled with references to planning as a necessary precedent to zoning. This is as it should be. It has always been a rubric of land use policy that planning should precede such changes. The initiative and referendum render such planning superfluous, irrelevant, or, as one judge noted, convert zoning to a "gallup poll."[45] Even if one were to tamper with such planning, it would take a series of complex statutory amendments to do so.

Even so, such legislative amendments would solve neither the constitutional nor the legislative–quasi-judicial question. The latter is perhaps the most troublesome: is the reclassification of land a basic policy determination by a legislative body (and so referendable),[46] or is it more akin to the implementation of policy (set out in plans and the text of a zoning ordinance) affecting mainly a landowner and his neighbors rather than the general public (not referendable)? It is fair enough to decide by initiative to prohibit, for example, the manufacture and sale of alcoholic beverages, but would it be fair—or legal—to target a single brewery? The Hawai'i Supreme Court has already decided that the LUC boundary amendment process—local zoning writ large—is quasi-judicial (and so not referendable). Roughly half the states that have considered the question in court have decided that zoning is legislative and therefore referendable. In all of these states, the initiative and referendum are reserved for the people in the state constitution. Hawai'i has no such clause in its constitution. The other states have decided that zoning is not legislative, and therefore not referendable.[47]

## Conclusion

Hawai'i has the statewide mechanisms to deal with scarcity in developable urban land while preserving both agricultural land and open space. However, it must pursue these goals with an eye toward the Constitution, which prohibits taking all economic use of private land without paying for it. The same constitutional safeguards affect how we go about providing affordable housing. Planning is a requirement with respect to the use of these tools. The kind of public participation that extends to absolute public decision making erodes, if not destroys, the planning process.

## Notes

1. D. Callies, *Regulating Paradise: Land Use Controls in Hawai'i* (1984); D. Mandelker, *Environmental and Land Controls Legislation* (1976), chap. 7.

2. F. Bosselman and D. Callies, *The Quiet Revolution in Land Use Control* (1971), Chap. 1; P. Myers, *Zoning Hawai'i* (1976).

3. Callies, *Regulating Paradise: Land Use Controls in Hawai'i* (1984), Ch. 1; J. Chinen, *Original Land Titles in Hawai'i*.

4. Ibid.

5. Hawai'i Revised Statutes, chap. 205.

6. Bosselman and Callies, *Quiet Revolution*; Callies, *Regulating Paradise*, chap. 2.

7. Callies, *Regulating Paradise*, chap. 2.; H.R.S. ch. 226.

8. H.R.S. chap. 205.

9. Callies, *Regulating Paradise*, chap. 2.

10. Ibid.

11. Callies, *Regulating Paradise*, chap. 2; Mandelker, *Environmental and Land Legislation*, chap. 7; Bosselman and Callies, *Quiet Revolution*, chap. 1.

12. See, for example, *Board of Supervisors* v. *Carver City Board of Comm.*, 225 N.W. 2d 815 (1975).

13. *Pennsylvania Coal Co.* v. *Mahon*, 260 U.S. 395 (1922).

14. *Village of Euclid* v. *Ambler Realty Corp.*, 272 U.S. 365 (1926); *Nectow* v. *City of Cambridge*, 277 U.S. 183 (1928).

15. *Keystone Bituminous Coal Assn.* v. *DeBenedictis*, 107 S. Ct. 1232 (1987); *First English Evang. Luth. Church of Glendale* v. *L.A.*, 107 S Ct. 2378 (1987); *Nollan* v. *Calif. Coastal Comm.* 107 S. Ct. 3141 (1987).

16. *Keystone* v. *DeBenedictis*.

17. *First English* v. *L.A.* These are not the only hurdles a landowner must surmount in order to obtain compensation for a regulatory taking. Among the most daunting (especially in a multipermit state like Hawai'i) is proving to the satisfaction of a court that all potential avenues for regulatory relief have been exhausted, so that a court can determine the amount of economic damage which denial of development approval or permission has caused, and then see if a taking by regulation has occurred. *Williamson County Reg. Plan. Comm.* v. *Hamilton Bank of Williamson Co.*, 473 U.S. 172 (1985).

18. P. Myers, Zoning Hawai'i; Mandelker, Environmental and Land Legislation; Bosselman and Callies, *Quiet Revolution*.

19. Report of the Land Evaluation and Site Assessment Commission to the State Legislature, February 1986.

20. See *Eldridge* v. *City of Palo Alto*, 129 Cal. Rptr. 575 (1976).

21. Senate Bill no. 448, House Bill no. 26, both submitted to the 1989 Hawai'i legislature.

22. See Bosselman and Stroud, "Pariah to Paragon: Developer Exactions in Florida 1975–1985," *Stetson Law Review* 14 (527) (1985).

23. Snyder and Stegman, *Paying For Growth* (ULI 1986).

24. Davidson and Usagawa, eds., *Paying for Growth in Hawai'i: An Analysis of Impact Fees and Housing Exaction Programs* (1988).

25. D. Callies, "Impact Fees, Exactions, and Paying for Growth in Hawai'i" University of Hawai'i Law Review 11 (295) (1989), p. 344.

26. Ibid. "Pariah to Paragon."

27. Bosselman and Stroud, "Pariah"; J. Nicholas, *The Calculation of Proportionate-Share Impact Fees*, APA PAS Report #408 (1988).

28. *Nollan* v. *Calif. Coastal Comm.*, 107 S. Ct. 3141 (1987).

29. Ibid at 3147.

30. R. Alterman, *Evaluating Linkage and Beyond* (1989); Callies, "Impact Fees;" Davidson and Usagawa, *Paying for Growth.*

31. For example, *Holmdel Builders Assoc.* v. *Twp. of Holmdel*, 556 A.2d 1236 (N.J. 1989).

32. The New Jersey courts did so in *In Re Egg Harbor Associates*, 464 A.2d 1115 (1983) but it is worth noting that a right to housing is guaranteed by the New Jersey Constitution—a provision lacking either in the Hawai'i State or the Federal Constitution.

33. Kramer, "Development Agreements: To What Extent Are They Enforcible?" Real Estate Law Journal 10 (29) (1981).

34. For example, Florida, Arizona, California, Colorado, and Nevada.

35. Kramer, "Development Agreements." In California alone, nearly five hundred such agreements are in effect or being negotiatied in over 150 cities and counties. Cowart., et al." "Development Agreements," Center for Real Estate and Urban Economics, University of California, Berkeley, 1986:4. Wegner, "Moving Toward the Bargaining Table: Contract Zoning Development Agreements, and the Theoretical Foundations of Government Land Use Deals." 65 *No. Car. L. Rev.* 957 (1987).

36. Kessler, "The Developmand Agreement and Its Use in Resolving Large Scale, Multi-party Development Problems," *Journal of Land Use and Int'l Law* (451) (1985). Griffith, "Local Government Contracts: Escaping from the Government/Proprietary Maze" 75 Iowa L. Rev. 286 (1990).

37. Ibid.

38. *Meeghan* v. *Village of Tinley Park*, 288 N.E. 2d 423 (1972) and *Morrison Homes Corp.* v. *City of Pleasanton* 130 Cal. Rptr. 196 (1976).

39. Callies, Neuffer, and Caliboso, *Ballot Box Zoning: Initiative, Referendum and the Law*, 39 J. Urb. and Contemp. L. 53 (1991).

40. Fogg, at 265, paraphrasing Sandercork, *Town Planning Review* 52 (265) (1981).

41. Callies, Neuffer Caliboso, Ballot Box Zoning: Initiative, Referendum and the Law, n. 53.

42. *County of Kauai* v. *Pacific Standard Life Insurance*, 653 P.2d 815 (1982).

43. *Lum Yip Kee, Limited* v. *City and County of Honolulu* 767 P.2d 815 (1989).

44. *Kaiser-Hawai'i Kai Development Co.* v. *City and County of Honolulu*, 777 P.2d 244 (1989).

45. *Udell* v. *Haas*, 235 N.E. 2d 897 (1968).

# 9

# THE POLITICS OF HOUSING IN HAWAI'I

## *Kem Lowry*

### Introduction

In mid-September 1989, model homes were opened for Kumu Iki, a subdivision in the Ewa area about fifteen miles west of Honolulu, where 312 "affordable" and 207 market-priced homes will be constructed as part of what the state government expects eventually to be a 5,000-unit project.[1] People assembled more than fourteen hours before the model homes were opened, but eventually dispersed when informed that, since the units would be sold by lottery, there was no need to line up. More than five thousand applications for the affordable-home lottery and three thousand for the market-priced units were distributed the following day.[2]

The lines and lotteries at Kumu Iki are symptomatic of the housing situation in Hawai'i. Hawai'i ranks at or near the top in median prices for new homes and resales, rents, and rates of increase in housing costs. In part, these indicators are a reflection of simple economic conditions: the gap between housing supply and demand. From 1980–1988 there was a 20 percent increase in households in Hawai'i, but only a 12.9 percent increase in resident housing units. The gap was even more dramatic on the neighbor islands.

Superficially, the solution to Hawai'i's housing problem appears simple: increase the supply. The supply of housing could be increased by direct government production or, indirectly, by facilitating housing construction by the private sector. In practice, Hawai'i's housing dilemma is much more complex. Policy makers are concerned not just with the aggregate amount of housing that is constructed, but with a host of related concerns as well. How much rental housing is needed? How should the construction of rental housing be encouraged? How can affordable homes be encouraged? Where will new housing be located in relation to existing or planned employment centers? How can housing be located so as to minimize the costs of highways, sewers, schools, and other infrastructure? Should the construction of short-term housing for nonresidents be discouraged? What weight should the loss of prime agricultural lands have in the tradeoffs in locating new housing? What should be done about providing shelter to the homeless? How should neighborhood concerns about crowding, traffic, or loss of views be incorporated into decisions about locating new housing?

These and similar questions bedevil all those concerned with housing as a public policy issue. Yet, despite the complexity of issues surrounding housing for a small, rapidly growing state like Hawai'i, a central issue is how the state's limited land resources should be allocated among many uses, of which housing is just one. This chapter outlines some of the policies and programs designed to deal with housing, focusing primarily on the interaction of land policy and housing. However, before turning to government efforts to deal with housing we first survey the economic—and psychological—aspects of the housing market in Hawai'i.

## Housing for Whom?

For those who can afford it, home ownership in Hawai'i is a sound financial investment particularly in Honolulu, where single-family homes appreciated eighty-five percent between 1980 and 1989.[3] Although the financial benefits of home ownership are substantial, they are not sufficient to account for the importance of owning a home as a social and political issue in Hawai'i. Owning a home carries important psychic benefits as well; benefits that cause people to sacrifice more financially, endure longer commutes to work, and tolerate more crowding and discomfort than can be explained in terms of net economic return on investment.

Perhaps because of its insularity, the long distances from Asia or the U.S. mainland, and the perceptions of limited space, home ownership provides those living in Hawai'i with a sense of social and economic security, of belonging, and of permanence. Belonging is an important part of the social fabric of Hawai'i. Everyday discourse is replete with distinctions and identifiers that differentiate between insider and outsider, local and transient, oldtimer and newcomer, real Hawaiian and poseur. In spite of being based purely on the ability to pay, home ownership is important to many as a sign of belonging, of being less a transient. Home ownership is also a sort of rite of passage. Parents worry about their children's ability to afford a home. The ability of a young couple to purchase a home thus becomes an indication of financial (and social) maturity.

The politics of home ownership are simple: as long as home ownership seems to be a realistic possibility for most wage earners, housing will not be a volatile political issue. As long as a young employed couple (to pick the most politically visible segment of the housing market) can expect to purchase a home by virtue of two incomes—and perhaps a little assistance from their parents with the down payment—lack of suitable housing is perceived primarily as a personal problem to be overcome by working more hours or adding a second job. However, if home ownership is perceived by most as becoming impossible, housing in Hawai'i could become the sort of pivotal issue that alters the politics of the state.

The grim facts are that it seems that the possibility of home ownership is becoming more remote for most nonowners. In 1989, the mean sales price for a new single-family home sold by private developers in Honolulu was just over $202,000; for a condominium it was $119,630 (for all single family homes the average price was just over $400,000 and for condominiums it was $185,000).[4] This was an increase of 19.9 percent for single-family homes and 5.2 percent for condominiums over the median prices in 1988.[5] Moreover, new single-family homes at these prices are frequently located fifteen to twenty miles from central Honolulu. Based on the standard formulas used to calculate a family's ability to finance a conventional mortgage (a ten percent down payment and interest rates of about ten percent) only about thirty percent of the households in Honolulu could have afforded the average priced homes in Honolulu in 1987–1988.[6]

For renters the situation is even worse. Renters occupy over 58 percent of the total housing inventory.[7] This is significantly higher than on the mainland where renters occupy only about 35 percent of all housing units.[7] Moreover, low-income households—those earning less than 80 percent of median income—represent 70 percent of all rental households.[9] And rents are high. On Oahu the average monthly rental rate for a single-family home was about $1,502 in 1991; condominium rental was $1,131.[10] Over the last five years, rental rates have increased 6 percent per year for single-family homes and 10 percent per year for multifamily units. Finally, the supply of rental housing in Hawai'i is extremely limited. Although a five percent vacancy rate in rental housing is considered normal, Honolulu's current vacancy rate is estimated at one to two percent.[11]

A further complication in Hawai'i's tight housing market is the increasing presence of transient rentals. An increasing number of condominium units are being built or converted for use by tourists. Some of these units are time-share operations in which twenty to twenty-five families share ownership of a condo unit for the purpose of an annual two-week vacation in Hawai'i. Other units are purely short-term rentals to tourists. In 1977, nonresident rental units constituted 1.6 percent of the total number of housing units in the state.[12] In 1989, the proportion of nonresident rental units had jumped to 5 percent of the total market. On Kauai, the proportion of nonresident rentals was 15 percent and on Maui it was 17 percent.[13]

## Government and Housing

About ninety-five percent of all housing in the state is produced by private developers. Although government agencies actually produce relatively few units of housing, government influence in the housing market is pervasive—some would say suffocating. Government regulatory programs determine where housing can be constructed, the density of development, building heights, maximum amounts of house lots that can be covered, appropriate construction materials and techniques, distance houses must be set back from roads and adjoining houses, widths of sidewalks, and a myriad of other housing details, including the material used for sewage pipes. Government agencies provide incentives to some developers to build affordable housing and require others to do so as a precondition for approval of zoning changes.

Generally, government activities that influence the market can be categorized in one of three ways: programs that increase the *supply* of housing; programs that provide *subsidies* to certain actors in the market; and *regulatory programs* that influence the location, timing, density and quality of housing production.

Actual government construction of housing is one obvious way to increase the housing supply. As of 1989, there were 393,354 housing units in Hawai'i.[14] Of these, almost 26,700 or about seven percent were government owned (federal and state) rental units.[15] The Housing Finance and Development Corporation (HFDC) is the major state agency responsible for housing production. The HFDC, created in 1987, cooperates with private and nonprofit entities, or with other government agencies. It has broad development and financial powers that give it substantial flexibility in planning and developing homes. Financing of HFDC's programs is provided by the Dwelling Unit Revolving Fund (DURF) and the Homes Revolving Fund (HRF). The sale of $125 million in general obligation bonds was used to capitalize DURF, while proceeds from the sale of units produced by HFDC replenish it. The Homes Revolving Fund was created by the legislature in 1988 to provide financing for the development and construction of offsite and onsite infrastructure improvements for housing on large tracts of land. It is capitalized at $120 million. Prior to establishing the HFDC, the old Hawai'i Housing Authority constructed 1,227 units in 1975, 743 in 1980, and only 355 units in 1987. HFDC constructed 327 units in 1988, but has begun to plan and develop several large tracts of land on all islands. Construction has already begun on an 830 acre site, Kapolei Village, in the Ewa area of Oahu. Kapolei Village will eventually consist of about 5,000 units. On the Big Island, work has begun on the 1,500-acre Kealakehe master-planned community.

Each of the counties also has housing development programs. Recent production figures are summarized in Table 9.1.

Subsidies constitute a second important category of government activities influencing the housing market. By far the most important subsidy is not a housing program at all but the federal and state income tax laws that allow homeowners to deduct all interest payments on home mortgages from their gross income. Mortgages are constructed so that payments for the first few years are about ninety percent interest on the loan and ten percent payment on principal. This arrangement serves the interests of the bank, which is paid the rent for its money up front. Making large interest payments also serves the short-term financial interests of the typical home-buying couple. They are able to deduct money paid in interest on their mortgage from their gross income on both federal and state

### Table 9.1: County Government Assisted Housing Production (1975–1988)[16]

|           | 1975 | 1980 | 1987 | 1988  |
|-----------|------|------|------|-------|
| Honolulu* | 14   | 824  | 942  | 2,323 |
| Kauai**   | 74   | 159  | 204  | 13    |
| Maui      | 0    | 137  | 295  | 0     |
| Hawai'i** | 182  | 137  | 30   | 224   |

*includes for-sale and rental units constructed, acquired or under development.
**includes joint state-county projects.

returns. They can also deduct real property taxes paid on the property. The availability of this deduction constitutes a subsidy to homeowners with mortgages. It also encourages home buyers to purchase more expensive homes than they might otherwise, further fueling the demand for homes and inflating prices more, particularly in some segments of the market.

There are other, more conventional housing subsidies. The State Rental Assistance Program provides rental subsidies to owners of projects who are required to set aside a minimum of twenty percent of their units for tenants whose incomes do not exceed eighty percent of the median income of the area. Although agreements have been reached with owners of four projects totaling 366 units, only one complete project is receiving subsidies.[17] To date it has been difficult to encourage landlord participation in the project. Other subsidy programs, such as Hawai'i Housing Authority's (HHA's) rent supplement program, provide subsidies to tenants.

The third and most controversial set of activities affecting the housing market is government regulations. Federal, state, and county regulations govern every phase of the housing production process, from the identification of potential development sites to the writing of mortgages for individual home owners.

## Housing and Zoning

The major regulatory program affecting housing supply is zoning. Zoning emerged in the early twentieth century as the key regulatory mechanism for influencing the physical design of cities. The establishment of multiple land-use zones, with each zone reserved for a specific land use or class of uses, was originally proposed as a means of separating potentially incompatible uses. Zoning could be justified to keep slaughterhouses or taverns out of residential neighborhoods, but it was also used to insure that Chinese laundries in San Francisco could not be located in non-Chinese neighborhoods.

Although zoning provided the legal means to regulate land uses, it was regulation without a vision or philosophy. Those who had promoted zoning as a regulatory device saw it as a means to implement a city plan. The city plan was to provide the context and rationale for which zoning was to provide the means. The U.S. Department of Commerce published a standard zoning enabling act in 1922 which states could use to authorize cities to adopt zoning ordinances. The Commerce Department draft noted that zoning regulations "must be in accordance with a comprehensive plan." The department did not get around to publishing a Standard City Planning Enabling Act until 1929 and even then was vague about the optimal content of city plans.

Honolulu was one of many cities in which the relationship between zoning and planning was vague. Honolulu's first zoning ordinance was passed in 1922, but the allocation of uses among zones was not based on substantial research of community development trends. Eventually, general plans were developed, but they were adopted by the board of supervisors (later the city council) by resolution rather than by ordinance. Zoning and infrastructure decisions did not necessarily follow the general plan.[18] Hence, planning was advisory, while zoning had the force of law.

The legal relationship between planning and zoning changed in 1969 when the Hawai'i Supreme Court ruled that rezoning decisions had to conform to long-term comprehensive general plan objectives as provided by the Honolulu City Charter.[19] The court held that the updating of the 1964 general plan had to be based on comprehensive studies of changing condition and trends—planning studies, in short. A new Oahu general plan was finally adopted in 1977 and updated in 1982 and 1985. Meanwhile, changes in the city charter adopted in 1973 mandated the preparation of regional development plans on Oahu. It further mandated that zoning be consistent with these. The initial development plans were finally adopted in 1982. In addition to zoning by the counties, Hawai'i has had what amounts to state zoning since 1961, when Hawai'i's pioneering land-use law was enacted to preserve prime agricultural land and prevent scattered urban subdivisions.[20] (For a more detailed discussion of state land use planning, see chapter 8.)

Zoning at the state level has been the regulatory key to determining where and when new urban development will occur. At the county level it has determined the location and density of new housing within urban areas. Zoning is therefore the critical element in determining land values.

Other land-use regulations also add to the cost of housing. Subdivision ordinances require streets of specific width, sidewalks, underground utilities, and other amenities. Grading and grubbing ordinances specify site-preparation practices that will minimize runoff from the site and subsequent sedimentation of coastal waters. The park dedication ordinance requires developers to dedicate park space or pay a fee in lieu of providing land. Off-site infrastructure costs—sewer and waster line extensions, connector roads to main highways, traffic signals and the like—are also frequently required and result in increased costs which are likely to be passed on to the home buyer in a new subdivision. Other requirements can also add substantially to costs. Both the state and the counties negotiate with large developers to provide additional community facilities and services, and even affordable housing, as a precondition to development approval. The time that it takes to get all these regulatory approvals—as much as seventy-three months for land units in an agricultural district—is also a regulatory cost. Developers claim that the total effect of these regulations is to add greatly to the costs of housing in Hawai'i.

At the center of the land-use regulatory dispute is the effect of state and county land policies on housing supply, location, and cost. Government land policy is frequently cited as the primary villain in Hawai'i's housing costs. The charge is that state and county zoning practices underallocate land needed for urban uses, such as housing. Such zoning practices, it is sometimes argued, stifle competition and drive up prices.

## Land Policy and Housing

In the mid-1970s a number of fast-growing U.S. communities, located primarily in the sunbelt, sought to impose controls over the pace, location, quality, and density of housing development. Overloaded schools, highways, water supplies, and increasing public costs of infrastructure were part of the justification for controls on growth, as were loss of wetlands, agricultural lands, and other environmental resources. Growth management became an issue that spawned thousands of planning and legal workshops, seminars, reports, and articles in which Ramapo, Boca Raton, and Petaluma were familiar names.

Hawai'i was part of the growth management movement. Governor Ariyoshi made it a campaign theme and repeated it in his 1977 State of the State address:

> Hawai'i is a national treasure, but it is a very fragile treasure, one which can be easily destroyed by over-population and excessive demands on its resources.
>
> . . . . . . . . . . . . . . . . . . . . . . . . .
>
> There is no reason why we must endure what an uncontrolled and unregulated future holds for us. We must shape our own future, not have it thrust upon us by forces over which we have little or no control.[21]

Although the growth management problem was initially stated in terms of over population, and solutions were offered that included limiting in-migration from the U.S. mainland as well as immigration from the Philippines and elsewhere, eventually more sophisticated (and constitutional) measures were suggested.

The growth management issue led to the adoption of the Hawai'i state plan law and subsequent planning efforts.[22] It also led the state constitutional convention meeting in 1978 to recommend extending constitutional protection to agricultural land at a time when agriculture was declining in importance to the overall state economy. Perhaps its primary importance, however, was to focus attention on the dynamics of land use—and land-use control—as the key variable in the growth equation.

Land-use regulations in general, and the allocation of land by the State Land Use Commission, came to be viewed as the key state mechanism for guiding growth. Although the process for making these allocations has been changed several times in the last twenty-five years, the salient features have remained constant: private landowners or developers propose changes in the district designation of their land; the professional staff at both the state and county level review the applications and make recommendations; and the commission votes to approve or deny the petition. More than ninety percent of the petitions proposed to the commission have involved additions to the urban district. More than forty-eight thousand acres have been added to the urban district since 1964, but the urban district still accounts for only four percent of the land in the state (twenty-four percent on Oahu).

In theory, the allocation of land among the four districts (agriculture, conservation, urban, and rural) gives the Land Use Commission the ability to guide the expansion of Hawai'i's urban areas and, in doing so, to achieve many of the objectives central to most growth management programs. In practice, the commission has been only partially successful in guiding urban development and balancing urban and other land uses in a consistent manner. The commission's effectiveness as an instrument of growth management has been undermined by three factors in particular. First, since petitions for boundary changes are initiated by the private sector, the land units that are proposed for addition to the urban district are not necessarily those that contribute to an orderly, cost-effective pattern of urban expansion. Second, ownership of land in Hawai'i is highly concentrated. The six largest landowners in the state own thirty-seven percent of all privately owned land in the state.[23] The

size and location of some of their land holdings makes some of the
owners extremely influential in determining the timing and direction of urban expansion. Because some of these owners also have
major agricultural operations, real or implied threats to scale down
or close sugar or pineapple operations increase their political influence with state officials eager to preserve some semblance of diversity in an economy so heavily dominated by tourism. This influence
is used both directly in bargaining about land-use district boundary
amendments and more subtly in shaping public discourse about
land policy in the state. Finally, the decline in plantation agriculture in relative importance to the state's economy and the continuing pressures for more housing make it increasingly difficult for the
commission to justify protecting prime agricultural land, particularly if the issue is framed as agriculture versus affordable housing.

The expansion of Honolulu into central Oahu and the Ewa plain
in west Honolulu is a case study in the complications of articulating
and defending a coherent growth management strategy. Geography
is a constraining factor in the expansion of Honolulu. The old urban
area occupies the south shore between Diamond Head and Honolulu
Harbor. Hemmed in by steep ridges and the ocean, the city has expanded east toward Hawai'i Kai and across the Pali to the windward
side. More recently it has pushed west, past Pearl Harbor toward
the Ewa plain and central Oahu. The relatively flat terrain makes
much of this area cheap to develop, but it is also prime agricultural
land. Indeed, at one time half the state's prime agricultural land
was identified as being in the rich plain sloping down toward Pearl
Harbor. Ownership is concentrated: Campbell Estate, Bishop Estate, Castle and Cooke, and the Robinson trust are among the largest landowners.

In the late 1960s, a proposal by Oceanic Properties, a subsid-
iary of Castle and Cooke, to convert a portion of the agricultural
land in central Oahu was the first real test of the land-use law. The
Land Use Commission was persuaded by the developer's promise to
build affordable homes, and the first increment of what is now Mililani Town was authorized by the commission and later the Honolulu City Council.

The Mililani Town proposal was followed by three other proposals to the Land Use Commission to convert productive agricultural
land to urban uses. Concerned about the potential loss of prime agricultural land, the potential environmental impacts, and public
service costs of such conversions, the State Department of Planning
and Economic Development initiated a study in 1971 to determine
whether incremental additions to the housing stock were needed

and where they should be placed, if approved. Four development scenarios were constructed to accommodate the projected fifty-five thousand additional housing units needed by 1990, including one scenario that allowed developers to convert all land being considered by the Commission for Urban Designation. Based on the available vacant land, the projected infrastructure costs associated with sprawl and the potential environmental impacts, the report concluded and recommended that no new lands in central Oahu be redesignated.[24]

At about the same time, the city and county of Honolulu undertook a series of planning studies related to housing and land policy. The initial study, *Elements of a Residential Policy,* set the tone by criticizing land policy as being formulated "with an inadequate understanding of the nature of housing needs and how those needs can be feasibly met."[25] It argued for a broader perspective in which land-use policy and housing objectives were combined. In a subsequent report, *An Evaluation of Alternative Residential Development Policies,* four basic land policies were evaluated: (1) intensive development—staying within current boundaries; (2) directed growth—use of agricultural land for urban purposes, both residential and employment, if significant community objectives were met; (3) private sector initiatives—full implementation of all private proposals; and (4) moderate expansion—residential expansion outside of current urban boundaries to provide for specific requirements for moderately priced housing.[26] The report contains a number of recommendations for improving the conditions for affordable housing but made it clear that the city should not expand into both Ewa *and* central Oahu.[27]

A revised city charter adopted in 1973 changed the framework for city land-use planning and regulation. The city was required to divide the island into areas for which development plans would be created and adopted by ordinance. The amount of land designated for development would be determined by the amount of population targeted by the city for the area.[28] Although the first development plans were not completed until the early 1980s, the population goals were written into the 1977 general plan. Growth was directed toward Ewa-Makakilo—a second city. This area was designated to include 10 percent of the island's population by the year 2000 (up from 3.1 percent in 1975). Growth rates in other urban fringe areas such as central Oahu would be maintained at current low levels.

The 1982 revision of the general plan continued to designate Ewa as a second city, but the population ceiling for central Oahu was increased to 12.8–14.2 percent of the island's total by the year

2000.[29] Hence, although the city continued to maintain that the second city on Campbell lands was the preferred growth pattern, urban sprawl into central Oahu was allowed. A 1985 report made this trend explicit. In *Residential Development Implications for Development Plans,* the city explicitly shifted from an emphasis on directing growth to one of responding to market demand:

> This demand [for growth in central Oahu] is expected because Central Oahu has substantial acreage designated and available for housing. . . . In light of this market trend, and the future expectations of the area, it may be appropriate to re-examine the General Plan's population policy for Central Oahu.[30]

The 1989 general plan goes even further. Central Oahu was allocated 16.5 percent of the island's population—double the amount recommended in 1974—while Ewa was allowed 13.3 percent of the total. In defending this allocation, the city's chief planning officer indicated that the opening up of central Oahu was to provide competition for the projects in Ewa, although he acknowledged that major developers in both areas are the same: Gentry, Horita, and Oceanic Properties.[31]

These changes can be viewed as a gradual relaxation of city growth policy based on directing growth toward Ewa. They can also be viewed as an evolution toward a market-driven housing policy, a policy of letting the private sector deal with the housing problem by insuring that sufficient land is available for private developers to build houses. Indeed, a constant refrain from the development community—developers, banks, and the real estate industry—has been that Hawai'i's housing shortage and high prices are due to restrictive land supply policies on the part of the city and state.

The evolution of city policy has not been smooth. While the administrations of Mayor Frank Fasi (1968–1980, 1984–present) have generally supported a more laissez-faire approach to directing growth, some members of the city council, which must approve development plan amendments and zoning changes, have fought to maintain some sort of directed growth strategy.

During the 1980s, there was a change in the public discourse about the housing issue. Although it is difficult to demarcate a precise moment when the change occurred, the publication of an article in *Forbes* magazine characterizing state government in Hawai'i's as "antibusiness" seems to have been a pivotal event. The article, which compared Hawai'i's political leaders with Soviet bureaucrats in "their rigid regulation of every facet in the island's economic life," interpreted state land-use controls as efforts to force agricultural companies to stay in agriculture.[32] This was not a new theme—the same point was often made by local business executives. Indeed, a group of developers and real estate professionals calling themselves the "Housing Coalition" had earlier launched a media blitz in which they argued that Hawai'i's extensive system of land-use and environmental controls was responsible for driving up the cost of housing. While many aspects of the land-use regulatory system were criticized, it was perceived restrictions on land supply that drew the most fire. A Bank of Hawai'i publication noted that "the LUC [Land Use Commission] has substantially underallocated land for urban use since the mid 1970s. The housing problem," it added, "will be with us until the urban land underallocation issue is resolved."[33] Other reports echoed similar sentiments. One report on Hawai'i's sugar industry commissioned by the Department of Business and Economic Development concluded that a "conservative estimate of the cost of protecting Oahu's agricultural lands from urban development is $20,000 per house" in 1988 dollars.[34]

The Land Use Commission got the message. Since 1986, more than 13,000 acres statewide have been redistricted urban to allow development, while 5,129 acres have been redistricted on Oahu.[35]

While directed growth seems to have declined in importance relative to affordable housing as the primary emphasis in land policy, the state is involved in two initiatives that would reemphasize growth management. In 1989, the Office of State Planning drafted a bill to amend the state land-use law in order to specify new criteria for the reclassification of land. The new criteria were intended to insure greater protection to watershed, habitats, shoreline areas, forests, wetlands, erosion and flood-prone areas, open space and specific, highly rated agricultural lands. The bill was not enacted, but in 1991–1992 OSP is conducting a statewide review of land uses and state policy.

A second current state initiative is the comprehensive review of the state land-use district boundaries mandated by the legislature in 1985.[36] The Office of State Planning (OSP), which initiated the review in the fall of 1989 for completion in early 1991, has made "growth management" the theme of the review. OSP has commissioned studies of urban land requirements, infrastructure capacities and constraints, and environmental constraints before making recommendations to the LUC on changes in district boundaries.

Both the city and state have developed strategies for dealing with the affordability issue. For some time, the city council has negotiated with developers to insure that a certain portion of the units constructed—usually ten percent—would be affordable. This policy was not enforced uniformly and it is not clear how or whether compliance has been monitored. At the state level, requiring a certain percentage of affordable units, sometimes called inclusionary zoning, was recommended by the 1977 Housing Functional Plan. Prior to 1986, the LUC sometimes asked developers seeking boundary amendments to build a certain percentage of affordable units. In 1987 Harold Masumoto, director of the OSP, went even further by recommending that a petition for a redesignation in central Oahu be denied unless sixty percent of the units were marketed as affordable (80–120 percent of the median income). In reviewing subsequent petitions, the commission has used the sixty percent figure as a goal rather than as a mandate.[37]

The major new housing affordability initiative has been the State Housing Finance and Development Corporation's master-plan new communities. In these efforts, the state acts as a developer. It acquires the land, hires site planners and architects and chooses the contractors. It markets the units, writing provisions into sales contracts to prohibit new owners from quickly reselling the units at a profit. Kumu Iki in Ewa is one of the first such subdivisions, but others have been initiated on Maui and Hawai'i.

## Conclusions

State and county government efforts to construct low-income and special-need housing and to provide subsidies to some housing consumers help alleviate a portion of Hawai'i's housing needs, but housing development by the private sector is the major factor in determining the supply of housing. This emphasis on housing supply makes land-use planning and regulatory decisions by state and county officials central to the economics—and thus the politics— of housing.

The politics of housing in Hawai'i is played out at many levels and settings, but land policy has been central to the debate. Planning and regulating land uses involves making choices. Some land units are designated for development, others are not. Some shoreline areas are designated for preservation, others are zoned for resort development. Areas that once supported small scale agricultural operations are designated for golf course development. These choices are informed by technical analysis conducted by professional planners, engineers, architects and others, but ultimately elected and appointed officials make the choices, usually after several public hearings, using whatever combination of technical and political criteria they want to apply. Hence, land use plans and zoning maps need to be understood as political compromises.

In a sense, Hawai'i's past successes in making those compromises have added to the current development pressures. Hawai'i has become one of the premier playgrounds of the Pacific Basin with all that implies in terms of plans for additional resort developments, second homes for part-time residents, transient rentals, proposals for new golf courses and constant pressures for changes in land use plans and regulations to accommodate even more growth. Shopping malls, golf courses, resorts, and residential subdivisions are proposed and debated. Objections are raised, mitigation measures offered, and proposals are revised. New growth is squeezed, shaped, modified, but usually accommodated in a land use review process that is lengthy, costly and frequently frustrating for all concerned.

Hawai'i's concentration of land ownership, the increasing attractiveness of island land to international investors, the complexity of the land use management system, and conflicts over the use of particular sites all combine to create perceptions of scarcity. These same factors also make it unlikely that the private sector will produce sufficient affordable housing without government incentives or exactions.

## Notes

1. The housing market is segmented in several different ways. One common breakdown is to distinguish among very low income families (those earning less than 50 percent of the state median income); lower income (those earning between 50 percent and 80 percent of the median income); moderate income families (those earning between 80–120 percent of median income) and market income families (those earning more than 120 percent of median income). "Affordable housing " usually refers to housing priced for moderate income families.

2. Christopher Neil, "Thousands Line Up to Tour First Homes of Second City," *Honolulu Star-Bulletin & Advertiser*, A-3, September 7, 1989.

3. Locations, Inc., *Hawai'i Real Estate Indicators*, 1st quarter 1990, p. 6.

4.Bank of Hawai'i, *Construction in Hawai'i*, Honolulu, 1990, p. 22.

5. Calculated on the basis of cost per square foot of living space. Bank of Hawai'i reports that the average condominium is 40 percent smaller than a decade ago. The typical new single-family home is 12.3 percent smaller and the lot is 25.3 percent smaller than a decade ago. *Construction in Hawai'i*, p. (22–24).

6. Peat Marwick, *Rental Housing Development Study for the Island of Oahu*, Prepared for Department of Housing and Community Development, 1989, Exhibit II-L.

7. State of Hawai'i, Department of Business and Economic Development, (DBED) October, *Housing Unit Estimates for Hawai'i, 1970–89*, Statistical Report 213, Honolulu, 1989, p. 2.

8. James W. Hughes, and George Sternlieb, *The Dynamics of American Housing* (New Brunswick, N.J.: The Center for Urban Policy Research, 1987), p. (10).

9. Marwick, *Rental Housing Development Study,* Exhibit II-O.

10. Vickie Ong, "There's No Place Like Home - If you can find and afford it," *Sunday Honolulu Star Bulletin and Advertiser,* February 10, 1991, A-6.

11. Peat Martwick, 1989, p. II-3.

12. DBED *Housing Unit Estimates, p. 8.*

13. Ibid., p. 8.

14. Ibid., p. 7.

15. Ibid., p. 12. 19,421 were federal and 7,287 were state and county housing units.

16. State of Hawai'i, Office of State Planning, Progress Report: Implementation of Priority Guidelines of the Hawai'i State Plan, March, 1989, p. (?).

17. State of Hawai'i, Office of State Planning, *Implimentation of Priority Guidelines of the Hawai'i State Plan*, Honolulu, March, 1989, p. U-19.

18. Willard T. Chow, "Urbanization: Six Propositions," in Joseph R. Morgan, ed., *Hawai'i:A Geography* (Boulder: Westview 1983.), p. 173.

19. *Dalton v. City and County of Honolulu*, 51 Hawai'i 400, 462 P. 2nd 199 (1969).

20. Hawai'i Revised Statutes (HRS), 205.

21. State of Hawai'i, Department of Budget and Finance, 1979, *Land and Water Resource Management in Hawai'i*, Honolulu.

22. (HRS), DBED, 225.

23. *Data Book,* 1988, Honolulu, p. 187.

24. State of Hawai'i, Department of Planning and Economic Development, *The Central Oahu Planning Study: A Summary Report,* Honolulu, 1972, p. 59.

25. City and County of Honolulu, Department of General Planning, (DGP), *Planning for Oahu: Elements of a Residential Policy,* Honolulu, 1971, p. 24.

26. DGP *Planning for Oahu: An Evaluation of Alternative Residential Policies,* Honolulu. 1974, p. 13.

27. Ibid., p. 193.

28. City and County of Honolulu, *City Charter,* 1973, Section 5–408.

29. City and County of Honolulu, Department of General Planning, *General Plan: Objectives and Policies,* Honolulu, 1982, p. 20.

30. City and Country of Honolulu, Department of General Planning, Residential Development Implications of the Development Plans. Honolulu, 1985, p. 39.

31. Susan Jones, "The Development Process and Residential Development in Central Oahu and Ewa," in *Sustainable Development or Suburbanization* (Honolulu: Department of Urban and Regional Planning), 1989, p. IV-16. Luciano Minerloi (ed.)

32. Michael Cieply, "East of Eden," *Forbes,* January 31, 1983, pp. 34–36.

33. Bank of Hawai'i, 1989 (annual) *Construction in Hawai'i,* p. 25.

34. DBED *Hawai'i's Sugar Industry and Sugarcane Lands: Outlook, Issues, Options.* April 1989, p. 20-11.

35. The Hawai'i Sugar Industry and Sugarcane Lands report includes an estimate that about 370 acres per year are required to accommodate housing demand on Oahu. Department of Business and Economic Development, *Hawai'i's Sugar Industry and Sugarcane Lands: Outlook, Issues, Options.* April 1989, p. 20-6.

36. HRS, 205-18.

37. Susan Jones, "Development Process in Central Oahu and Ewa," p. IV-6.

# 10

## PLANNING FOR RAPID TRANSIT ON OAHU: ANOTHER GREAT PLANNING DISASTER?

### *Karl E. Kim*

### Introduction

Part of the title of this chapter is borrowed from Peter Hall's 1980 book, *Great Planning Disasters,* in which a number of famous past planning endeavors (San Francisco's BART, the Sydney Opera House, London's third airport, etc.) are unearthed and painstakingly picked apart. Certainly the book makes for fascinating reading, particularly for those of us who don't have to suffer the consequences of living under the influence of someone else's great planning disaster. This chapter is concerned with a potential disaster in the making, one which could end up some day in another anthology of great planning disasters.

Although planning for Honolulu's rapid transit system has been going on for well over two decades, the prospects for a system are today still uncertain. Some would argue that Hawai'i has already missed the boat on federal funding, that strategic opportunities to lock in new development and transit have been forgone, and that any new fixed-rail system for Oahu is beginning to look more and more like a billion dollar white elephant. Others argue that, short of turning the H-1 freeway into a double-decker highway, a fixed-rail system provides the only means of sufficiently increasing the capacity of Honolulu's already congested transportation system. To the many who have been studying and planning Honolulu's rapid transit system, failure to build a system this time around could also be the makings of a great planning disaster.

The stakes are very high. The proposed rapid transit system is estimated to cost at least a billion dollars—a very expensive project for Hawai'i, where the total combined spending of state and local governments (all four counties) in 1988 was approximately $3.47 billion.[1] Not only are the financial stakes high, but so too are the environmental and societal costs associated with fixed rail. At present, proposals call only for elevated systems similar to those operating in Miami, Vancouver, and Detroit. Even considering the very best technology, an elevated rail system is likely to have a huge impact in a city known for scenic views, urban design (no billboards), and many natural and historic attractions.

It is certainly easy to find harsh critics of rail transit. As John Meyer and Jose Gomez-Ibanez note:

> Almost without exception, the rail extensions and new systems did not live up to their passenger-demand projections, and their discernible impact on urban congestion was a good deal less than expected. The brand-new rail systems were a particular disappointment. Criticisms of these became almost endemic, and some of the most cogent originated with people who had once been among the ardent advocates of rail transit.[2]

New systems in Atlanta, Buffalo, Baltimore, Detroit, Miami, and Los Angeles have experienced both large construction cost overruns and great shortfalls in projected ridership, leading to operating deficits. In spite of more than twenty-five years of federal programs, "mass transit today carries only about 5% of the people who commute to work, the other 95% mainly use automobiles."[3] Given the widespread recognition that "transit is a declining industry," why would any American city, let alone Honolulu, even consider building a new fixed-rail system?

After reviewing the arguments for and against the construction of a fixed-rail system in Hawai'i, this chapter describes some of the potential constituencies who would benefit or lose from a rail system. Planning for rapid transit has evolved into a struggle pitting several different interest groups against each other with a winner-take-all mentality. Without strong leadership directed towards building consensus, and without a concerted effort on the part of local elected officials and the community to face up to Honolulu's transportation problems, the rapid transit system is destined to become a great planning disaster.

## Honolulu's Transportation Problems

Honolulu's transportation problems have been recognized for many decades. In a 1906 report to the Board of Supervisors of

Honolulu County, Charles Mulford Robinson argued that there was a "certain appropriateness" to the "narrow and winding streets, making many a graceful curve and meeting at other than right angles," because the streets were "suited to the place," and "imparted an air of repose and restful deliberation."[4] Robinson urged Honolulu to "shun the checkerboard plan, as you would the plague, and to retain the narrow, winding streets."[5] Yet with the increase in automobiles, growing from 25 in 1905, to 17,439 in 1925, to 98,138 in 1950, attitudes towards traffic and congestion began to change.[6] The 1944 Master Plan Report described serious traffic problems in terms of "accidents, congestion, and delay" and maintained that the "challenge to prepare now for traffic and population increases in Honolulu is real and urgent!"[7] The report went on to state that "Oahu's traffic accident records are factual evidence that traffic requirements are far in excess of the working capacity of existing roadways," that "congestion is increasing the costs of motor vehicle operation and handicapping the whole function of transportation," and that "minor changes in street and intersection design or in traffic control will not accommodate present or future traffic demands."[8]

By the mid-1960s, the need for more concerted transportation planning on Oahu was apparent. The 1967 Oahu Transportation Study, sponsored by the State of Hawai'i and the City and County of Honolulu, in cooperation with the U.S. Department of Housing and Urban Development and the U.S. Department of Transportation, Bureau of Public Roads, stated that it was undertaken "to establish a long-range continuing, cooperative, and comprehensive transportation planning process."[9] The study was the first of its kind in its attempt to be long-range and comprehensive. It contained a set of recommended transportation improvements, including the completion of three highways, H-1, H-2, and H-3, and the construction of a 26-mile, fixed-rail, rapid transit system running from Pearl City to Hawai'i Kai. The study urged completion of both highway improvements and a fixed-rail system by 1985. The study also encouraged that "a short-range interim program be initiated for the purpose of improving and expanding the present bus system to prepare for integration into the express and feeder systems when the fixed facility is ready."[10] While many of the recommended highway improvements have been implemented, the recommendations regarding transit are no further along today then they were more than two decades ago.

## Accommodating Automania

One reason that the recommended highway improvements have been implemented while transit plans have been shelved is the dominance of the car culture in Hawai'i and in the United States as a whole. Since 1950, the number of registered motor vehicles has grown much faster than the population. As depicted in Table 10.1, the number of cars multiplied by almost 6, while the population grew by a factor of only 2.3 over the same period. Put another way, in 1950 there were about 3.6 persons per registered vehicle on Oahu; by 1987, that figure dropped to 1.45. Annual car sales had more than quadrupled over their 1950 levels by 1987. Available census data on means of transportation to work show that approximately 76 percent of the workforce on Oahu commutes by private automobile.[12] Moreover, 85 percent of these vehicles are occupied by only one person, 12 percent have two persons, and only 3 percent have three or more occupants.[13] Figures on vehicle occupancy rates (VORs) collected in 1986 show that, for the most part, the average number of persons per vehicle during the peak rush hour times on the major highways is 1.5 or less.[14] The preferred mode of commuting in Honolulu, as in every other American city, is by private vehicle, and most people would rather drive themselves than form carpools or engage in some type of ridesharing.

In 1980, only eleven percent of the households in Honolulu did not have an automobile.[15] That percentage has surely shrunk in recent years, making it clear that the "car-owning constituencies" dominate. In Hawai'i, as in the rest of the industrialized world, car ownership has become a symbol of success and free choice; it "epitomizes the American way: free men and women freely choosing that most individual and uninhibited way of getting about, all brought about by the interplay of market forces in a free enterprise system."[16]

### Table 10.1: Population, Registered Motor Vehicles, and New Car Sales on the Island of Oahu (1950–1987)[11]

|      | Resident population | Registered vehicles | Annual new car sales |
|------|--------------------|--------------------|---------------------|
| 1950 | 353,020            | 98,134             | 11,917              |
| 1960 | 500,409            | 78,388             | 15,857              |
| 1970 | 630,528            | 318,553            | 33,542              |
| 1980 | 762,565            | 454,316            | 37,104              |
| 1987 | 830,600            | 571,738            | 49,028              |

The reality, of course, is that travel by private automobile is no more an exercise of free-market will than is travel to the moon aboard a NASA spacecraft. While an individual may own a personal vehicle, the moment it leaves a private garage or driveway and enters the public thoroughfare it becomes dependent upon a government built, financed, and maintained system of roadways, and is subject to numerous regulations, codes, and ordinances. The majority of these rules were designed to protect the public from a potentially hazardous form of travel. Still, approximately 45,000 Americans (120 in Hawai'i) die in automobile accidents each year. While numerous new regulations regarding automobile usage are enacted each year (mandatory seat belt laws, stiffer drunk driving penalties, etc.), policies are designed to accommodate rather than control or curtail automobile use.

Honolulu is just as guilty as most other American cities in its failure to control the automobile. The implementation of virtually all of the major planned highway projects is evidence of government policies promoting the automobile as the preferred means of travel. Plans to use congestion pricing (tolls), such as that used in Singapore, to reduce nonessential travel during peak times is not seriously debated among policy makers. Moreover, while there has been talk of a rapid transit system for more than two decades, both automobiles and parking requirements for new buildings have multiplied during the same period.

Though plans of establishing a second city in Ewa have been discussed for years, and construction of a $3 billion megaresort complex in West Beach has started, there is little evidence to suggest a major shift in employment to that area. Such a move will thus disperse population and increase dependency on the automobile. Most of the activity centers (shopping, educational, religious, and cultural) are concentrated in the primary urban center, and virtually all of the growth in office development has occurred in the downtown-to-Waikiki corridor. Since 1975 there have been only 6 office buildings built in suburban areas, and all of these were relatively small (under 85,000 gross square feet). Of the 102 office buildings on the island, 85 are located within the Honolulu district.

More than almost any other city in the U.S., Honolulu has exhibited a linear pattern of development. Part of the reason has to do with the island's topography and the scarcity of developable land on Oahu. While other cities can expand outward, Honolulu's growth has been limited by the ocean and the mountains. Moreover, the development of the tourism industry has served to intensify development along the coastline in Waikiki, separate from Honolulu Harbor and the area which has historically served as downtown. The result is an elongated city form. Given this narrow corridor, it is also not unreasonable to expect that a fixed-rail transit system could provide service to many commuters in the area.

Daily ridership on the public bus system is quite high—over 103,000 in the downtown area, almost 49,000 in Waikiki, and approximately 23,000 in the university area. This gives Honolulu one of the highest bus riderships in the country. Moreover, the number of adult, full-fare passengers has continued to increase since 1980, reaching an all-time high of 42,489,622 in 1987.[17] Honolulu's high level of bus ridership is also reflected in the fact that the proportion of those who commute to work by bus in Honolulu (9 percent) is much higher than the national average for urban areas (5.1 percent).[18] These figures suggest that there may already be a captive market for a fixed-rail system, particularly if it can be well integrated with Honolulu's successful bus system.

One other important factor is Honolulu's large and growing tourist population. Tourists from both mainland U.S. cities and from Asia are often well accustomed to using mass transit facilities. If the five million or so tourists who come to Honolulu each year took one round trip on the fixed-rail system, priced at $2, then the $10 million raised annually could cover approximately half of the estimated operating costs of an automated system.

## What's Wrong With Mass Transit?

Sleek, ultramodern trains whisking large numbers of commuters to work at high speeds may not be compatible with one's notion of Hawai'i. Then again, there is hardly room for pedicabs, quaint little cable cars, or for gondolas to be paddled leisurely up and down the Ala Wai Canal. Honolulu has become a bustling, international city with traffic jams, parking problems, noise and air pollution, and a host of other problems associated with too many cars in too little space. How bad is Honolulu's traffic congestion? While Honolulu did not make the top ten cities in the nation with the worst traffic problems, one recent study found that Honolulu ranks fourteenth among U.S. urban areas in annual vehicle hours of delay, and is the most congested area among those urban areas with less than one million in population.[19] Table 10.2 contains projections of population and motor vehicles for Oahu. Assuming constant rates of motor vehicle

**Table 10.2: Population and Motor Vehicle Projections for the Island of Oahu (1985–2000)[20]**

|      | Resident population | Motor vehicles | Vehicles/mile |
|------|---------------------|----------------|---------------|
| 1985 | 814,600             | 544,976        | 382           |
| 1990 | 859,300             | 574,881        | 403           |
| 1995 | 896,900             | 600,036        | 421           |
| 2000 | 925,000             | 619,303        | 434           |

ownership, the total number of vehicles on Oahu will reach an estimated level of 619,303, by the year 2000, representing a 14 percent increase over 1985 levels. Assuming no growth in the amount of paved roadway, the number of vehicles per mile would increase from 382 to 434. Herein lies one of the major problems with mass transit: simply building a mass transit system will not, in an of itself, reduce the number of cars and the congestion on the highways.

The problem, therefore, with mass transit is that it alone can not solve Honolulu's congestion problems. Experience has shown that people are willing to tolerate much longer commuting times and higher levels of congestion before switching from driving to mass transit. Moreover, as congestion worsens, "motorists will adopt strategies to avoid highly congested situations. The most obvious such strategy is to travel by less congested alternative routes. . . . Drivers can also avoid congestion by changing the time of day or the day of the week they travel. They can also change destinations or forgo a trip altogether."[21] Given the fact the Honolulu's congestion problems occur "only during the peak commuting hour—at other times, the network is considered to be adequate to handle vehicle loads,"[22] there is reason to believe that motorists still have room to make adjustments in driving behavior rather than switch to transit.

There are other inherent problems with mass transit. The term *mass transit* conjures up images of a service provided for the masses—something that Americans with their strong sense of individualism may not particularly care for. While mass transportation may be acceptable for socialist countries (more than 110 cities in the Soviet Union have some form of fixed-rail urban transit system), it might be a very long time before American values change enough so that the public at large views transit differently.[23] One might argue that Americans view mass transit as a big-city phenomenon, if not a decidedly socialistic invention, hardly the type of infrastructure needed for a small, remote island paradise like Honolulu.

Another major image problem affecting mass transit relates to who uses it. Nationwide, transit services are used mainly by people commuting to downtown jobs, young and old people, and those with lower incomes. The young and the elderly make up nearly 40 percent of all transit riders, and workers with household incomes of less than $20,000 represent a forty-four percent share of total transit riders.[24] The fact that transit users tend to come from disadvantaged social or economic groups might also help to explain why a system has not yet been built and why there may be continued opposition to mass transit investments.

Many people see mass transit in general, and fixed-rail rapid transit in particular, as an outdated technology. To some observers, the installation of a fixed-rail system in Honolulu represents a step back in time—an idea which had come and gone some sixty years ago.

## Innovations in Urban Transit Technology

There have been technological developments which make the current proposals for rapid transit much more attractive than earlier proposed systems. These innovations include new control and switching systems, new propulsion systems (linear induction motors, magnetic levitation), and new guideways designs (monorails, suspended vehicle systems). To understand how technology may make the difference between a system which is cost effective, affordable, and attractive and one which is not, some basic distinctions between technologies are necessary.

*Heavy rail systems* include the Bay Area Rapid Transit System (BART) in San Francisco, the Washington Metro System, and the Metropolitan Atlanta Rapid Transit System (MARTA). These are large, expensive, mainly underground systems utilizing an exclusive guideway for moving large numbers of people (up to forty thousand people per hour in each direction).

At the opposite extreme are *light rail systems*. These include electric streetcars and light rail vehicles (LRV) which often share the roadway with other traffic. Examples of light rail systems include San Francisco's Municipal Rail System, parts of the MBTA system operating in Boston, and the new systems built in San Diego and Portland.

*New systems* are a hybrid of heavy and light rail systems—with smaller vehicles, shorter train lengths, and smaller station platforms like light rail, but operating on grade-separated guideways like heavy rail. New systems utilize automated train operation to eliminate the need for drivers and have been able to achieve very low operating headways (time between trains) so that wait time is reduced and passenger system capacities are increased. The newer technologies also make it possible to reduce construction costs while at the same time allowing for more flexible alignments and routing of the system to capture more riders. Because the trains can run on a narrow, elevated guideway, land acquisition costs are lowered. While some alignments may require the condemnation of property, smaller trains are capable of negotiating sharper turns, thereby enabling the system to operate largely upon existing public right-of-ways.

While it is difficult to estimate capital costs, experience has shown that heavy rail systems can cost from $117 million per mile (Washington) to $284 million per mile (Los Angeles). Light rail systems cost considerably less, ranging from $17 million per mile in Portland, Oregon, to $38 million per mile in Edmonton, Canada. Advanced light rapid transit systems fall somewhere in between—Vancouver's Skytrain cost approximately $46 million per mile. Using a rough estimate of $60 million per mile, a fifteen-mile system would cost approximately $900 million. With automation, there is also the potential to reduce operating costs. Driverless trains would enable more resources to be put into system maintenance, security, and other operations.

These technological developments suggest that it may be possible to design a state-of-the-art transportation system in Honolulu that is both demand responsive and service oriented. While an elevated system running through Honolulu will undoubtedly provoke much debate as to the appropriateness of its visual impact, such a system will most certainly provide commuters with a spectacular view of Honolulu's scenery. It is not unreasonable to expect that any elevated rapid transit system built in Honolulu will become the number one tourist attraction in the state.

### The Politics of Implementation

Planning for rapid transit in Honolulu has been a huge, costly, time-consuming endeavor. It has resulted in a seemingly endless flow of studies, community meetings, and legislative debates. There are several explanations as to why a rapid transit system has not yet been built.

One basic problem is that transportation planning is far from an exact science—the comment "whosoever called economics the dismal science probably hasn't been exposed to transportation planning," is truly fitting. Objective analyses are hard to find and problems besieging patronage forecasts, cost estimates, and projected impacts have been well documented. There is still so much uncertainty surrounding cost estimates and patronage in Honolulu that, to date, planning for rapid transit has been largely waged in terms of numbers.

Another problem has resulted because the goal of building a mass transit system may have been too closely connected with the political fortunes of Mayor Frank Fasi. The system is already viewed as "Mayor Fasi's project" because much of the early planning was done during his first twelve-year term in office. As a result, the project may carry some political stigmas that influence how politicians and others view it.

Planning for rapid transit has taken more than two decades, and many of the positions and attitudes toward mass transit have crystalized in that time. In spite of the fact that there have been some technological and design changes, mass transit in Honolulu is not a new idea and many of the arguments and concerns such as patronage, affordability, and environmental impact have been discussed and debated for so long that it is difficult to change attitudes or stimulate new interest in what is perceived to be an old debate. Most politicians have adopted a reactive stance on the city's mass transit plans—a wait-and-see position, which curtails true debate, interaction, and consensus building. Few, if any, allegiances or partnerships which cut across partisan lines have been forged, adding further to the sense that this has been and will continue to be a city project.

Another problem that exists in Honolulu is the difficulty of making comprehensive changes in a transportation system in which state and county agency jurisdictions overlap. While the State Department of Transportation is responsible for the planning and building of the highway system, the city is responsible for local streets and for managing public mass transit. In many states, the highway network serves to connect large urban centers separated by vast distances. In Honolulu, the highway network functions as an integral part of the urban transportation system. This division of responsibilities between the city and the state has meant that transportation planning has not been fully integrated. The Oahu Metropolitan Planning Organization (OMPO), a federally funded organization responsible for the development of comprehensive, coordinated, and continuing plans, has served as a bridge between the city and the state transportation planners. While OMPO has served to increase the quality and quantity of technical information available, it has managed to remain relatively neutral and somewhat removed from the actual politics of implementation.

Tensions between city and state transportation planners became apparent during the controversy concerning the construction of the H-3 interstate highway. H-3 is a 10.7-mile, four-lane divided highway which traverses the Halawa Valley, tunneling through the Koolau Mountains to Haiku Valley on the windward side of Oahu. In spite of the fact that federal highway funds would cover ninety percent of the $740 million construction costs, city transit planners argued that the highway would jeopardize federal support for new mass transit initiatives and that the new highway would not provide needed service to the areas of planned development and growth. The state, on the other hand, argued that more than fifteen years of traffic studies, planning, and design work have demonstrated the need for H-3. The H-3 project illustrates how large, powerful bureaucracies in alliance with organized interest groups (Citizens for H-3, the Chamber of Commerce, the Concrete Suppliers Organization, and various construction unions) and politicians, supported by professional consultants, work to have their key projects approved, funded, and built. While the apparent winner in this conflict is the state and the highway builders, the underlying causes of this controversy have not been addressed.

The fact that H-3 and the interstate highway system have been built and fixed rail has not is evidence that transportation planning in Hawai'i is dominated by forces that would rather see highways and automotive transportation proliferate than improve the quality of public mass transit and increase mobility for those without cars. This has partly to do with the functional separation of highway and mass transit planning, but more with the policies of automobile accommodation and the strength of the automobile-highways industry—both nationwide and in Hawai'i. From this perspective it is easy to understand why H-3 will be built and why maintenance and expansion of the bus fleet—a continuation of the existing approach to mass transit in Hawai'i--may be an easier route to follow than the construction of a new fixed-rail system and the subsequent redefinition of bus service. Allen Whitt, in describing San Francisco's BART system, suggests that the reasons why mass transit has failed have much to do with powerful interests which have intentionally limited the mass transit's potential. He asserts that "BART has largely been a social failure. . . . It has not materially improved the mobility of the Bay Area population, especially the lower-income population. Nor has it significantly improved the urban environment. . . . The system does not do much to lessen the congestion of major traffic arteries. The principal reasons that it does not do these things is because BART is not designed to challenge the dominance of the private automobile in the Bay Area."[25]

Hypothetically, what would it take to challenge the dominance of the car culture in Hawai'i? The technologies or means for accomplishing this goal are known. First, the number of incoming cars would have to be limited by establishing special tariffs or surcharges that would greatly increase the costs of owning a new car or of bringing one to Hawai'i. Second, government could charge road users at prices calculated to reduce travel demand. Travel at peak times by automobile would become more expensive than travel at nonpeak times. Third, further disincentives for automobile use could be enacted—limiting parking lot construction, increasing parking costs, raising traffic and parking violation fines, and other actions that would make driving much more expensive.

These recommendations may sound like an agenda for political suicide in Hawai'i. Even modest proposals for congestion pricing have been deemed "too controversial to seriously consider." Yet, without facing up to the growing dominance and dependency on the automobile, any new mass transit proposal remains hollow. Building a fixed-rail system in an environment in which the car culture continues to be dominant seems a sure prescription for disaster.

Over the past half decade, new transportation initiatives have included not just the fixed-rail system, but also HOV (high occupancy vehicle) lanes, staggered work hours, paratransit/ridesharing, contraflow lanes (changing the direction of traffic during peak times), installation of computerized traffic signaling, changes in bus services, and a host of other ideas to either manage transportation demand or increase the supply of transport services (e.g., Hawai'i Kai–to–downtown ferry service). In spite of the fact that many of these may be good ideas, there is no overall, integrated plan of action—transportation planning in Hawai'i is done in piecemeal fashion by planners sequestered deep within a particular bureaucracy or agency. Not only are mixed signals sent out to the public at large, but such an orientation has promoted unnecessary and unhealthy tradeoffs. Rather than viewing all of the various transportation proposals as part and parcel of the whole transportation mess, H-3 is traded off against fixed rail, staggered work hours are compared against new capital projects, paratransit is seen as way of avoiding the construction of new highways. Honolulu's transportation problems need to be addressed in a more systematic, coordinated manner in which all the various policy options, regardless of who has initiated them, can be evaluated together.

## New Rules to the Planning Game

One of the more significant changes in the environment surrounding the transit issue has been the basis on which the federal government will award capital grants to subnational governments who build fixed-rail systems. The term "local capital overmatch" captures the new spirit of federal financing—that less of a federal share means more of chance of receiving federal funds.[26] Where in the past the federal government could be counted on for providing seventy-five to eighty percent of the capital costs, today the most optimistic estimates of the federal share are in the forty to fifty percent range (to become competitive with other new-start projects, the percentage may have to drop even lower). To some, the federal government's retreat from mass transit may be bewildering—whatever happened to federal concerns about congestion in cities, energy use, and pollution from automobiles? But it is clear that the heyday of federal funding for mass transit has passed.

The decrease in federal assistance will undoubtedly make the question of who pays for and who benefits from transit all the more prominent in the years ahead. The issue of finance is likely to smoke out the various interest groups on the island more than any other of the concerns associated with transit. If broadly based taxes, such as the property, income, or sales taxes are employed, no doubt those concerned over existing tax burdens and services rendered will have something to say. Major legislative initiatives may need to be adopted if, for example, an add-on to the sales tax is used to pay for transit. If state resources are utilized, the Honolulu versus neighbor island tensions are likely to surface. If Honolulu continues to press fixed rail as a local project, the issues of home rule and local autonomy will come up because, even with a billion-dollar rail system, county governments remain subordinate entities of the state. While Honolulu may argue that the transit system is a local public service, the state would ultimately end up bearing the brunt of fiscal responsibility should the city run into financial problems. Given the large operating deficits currently experienced by the city's bus system, and the track record of other new systems started in other cities, there are grounds for concern on the part of state government.

The use of gasoline taxes to pay for mass transit will raise objections among most automobile users, since the heaviest auto users would end up paying the most for a service that they use the least. Yet there is some precedence for this sort of cross-subsidy—a portion of the federal gasoline tax put into the highway trust fund is earmarked for mass transit projects. Such an approach has also been adopted in California, where revenues for the State Transit Assistance Fund are derived from the state gasoline tax. In addition to taxing gasoline sales, other approaches to financing transit include using a portion of the motor vehicle excise tax (Washington State), beer tax revenues (Birmingham, Alabama), payroll taxes (Portland and Eugene, Oregon) and state lottery funds (Pennsylvania and Arizona).[27]

Another approach is tax-increment financing, which has been utilized heavily in Prince George's County, Maryland. Under this approach, districts are established for the purpose of funding improvements. A base-year assessed property valuation is determined, and any taxes collected on property values that have increased above the base year are dedicated to the needed improvements. In all likelihood, such an approach would have only limited potential in Honolulu, because the planned route of the fixed rail system is through already developed areas and the potential for new development or major redevelopment is limited. Some possible exceptions include the Kaka'ako redevelopment area and the Waterfront redevelopment area.

Special assessment districts impose a fee on properties within a district to recover the costs of an improvement made within that district. The fee can be imposed on a one-time basis or on a recurring basis. This approach has been utilized to cover transit costs in Denver, Los Angeles, and Miami. The most difficult aspect is determining the boundaries of the district. In Los Angeles, two special assessment districts were established in which boundaries were based on walking distances of one-half mile and one-third mile. The special assessment rates are uniform throughout the districts and will initially be set at thirty cents per square foot, and will be applied to offices, commercial properties, retail stores, hotels, labor-intensive industrial areas, and income producing residences.[28]

The use of impact fees and development exactions in Hawai'i has not been without controversy (see chapter 8). Yet both represent a potential source of funds for transit improvements. Of the two, the impact fee may be most palatable because it is generally levied where a development is generating new costs, such as increased traffic or strain on the existing infrastructure. The costs of improvements (sewer, water, roads, transit, etc.) are passed on to developers. In some cities, impact fees have been utilized for highway improvements, but Honolulu could consider employing them, as San Francisco has, for transit improvements, especially in those areas where new development is occurring, such as the Ewa plain. Development exactions (sometimes referred to as "negotiated investment") involve developer payments (cash or improvements) in exchange for zoning changes, permit approvals, or development bonuses. There are potential legal problems with exactions, especially since a recent Supreme Court ruling (*Nollan* v. *California Coastal Commission*) which affirmed the principle of rational nexus (see chapter 8).

In addition to stretching the frontiers of public finance, the search for transit funds could also lead to new public-private relationships. The push for privatization has come from both the critics of the public sector and also, more recently, from the federal government itself. George Lave has argued that "two decades of well intentioned federal subsidies have insulated management from the discipline of the farebox and has encouraged the growth of inefficient services."[29] The solution then is to contract out existing services, break apart the large public monopolies, encourage small, demand-responsive services, and deregulate the system of urban transportation. In Hawai'i, given the scale of foreign investment, particularly from Japan, and the interest from worldwide transit suppliers, the notion of a foreign built, owned, and operated rapid transit system is not unrealistic. This raises a whole set of questions and tradeoffs regarding foreign capital and control over local services which local planners and decision makers have not even begun to address.

The new economics of transit involve decreased reliance on federal support. As Honolulu moves further away from the conventional sources of transit finance and into new and largely uncharted waters, the risks and uncertainties in terms of costs and benefits will surely multiply. A decade ago, Honolulu would never have considered operating the fixed-rail system as a franchise. Under the current transit development program, the city is considering the franchise option, whereby the system would be built and operated by a private supplier, with an agreed-upon level of support from the public sector. Of six nonbinding proposals received from transit suppliers, two indicated interest in operating some sort of transit franchise.[30] Incentives for a franchise include the availability of development rights and opportunities to link transit stations with commercial or residential projects, as well as any subsidies paid out by government for providing services.

## Prospects for Rapid Transit in Honolulu

These are difficult times. There is little evidence that the automobile's dominance will lessen. Building a billion-dollar transit system to replace an inefficient bus system seems hardly an appropriate cure for the city's transportation ills. Without hefty support, it is doubtful that the city, state, and private sector can come together in a strong show of local commitment to fixed rail. There are so many other competing needs in the areas of housing, education, and economic development that consensus over how to improve the transportation system seems a long way off. In order to compete with the automobile, the transit system or combined rail/bus system must be able to offer economic savings over driving, reduced travel times, increased convenience, and door-to-door service. That's a tall order for any system, particularly in an environment such as Honolulu, where there has been a long-standing accommodation of the automobile. While changes in rail technology have made the prospects for building an affordable and attractive system in Honolulu brighter than ever before, the fact remains that without greater political will to face up to the city's transportation problems and consensus that rapid transit will provide the best solution, planning any system is likely to be an exercise in futility.

Part of the reason prospects remain so uncertain is that, so far, rapid transit planning has been treated largely as a technical problem, rather than as the political problem that it is in reality. Francine Rabinowitz has described three roles that planners typically play—those of technician, broker, and mobilizer.[31] The technician role is most appropriate in a cohesive community—the type of environment in which there are agreed-upon goals and known means for achieving them. Unfortunately, this is the role that most transportation planners in Hawai'i have assumed—forcing what Christensen has termed "premature consensus."[32] This has resulted in part because of the functional separation of transportation planning activities in the state, but also partly because of the nature of transportation services themselves. While some argue that politics has no business in transportation planning, the reality is that in our system of representative democracy all decision making is saturated with politics. Planners must routinely operate in a political environment, for:

> The structure of the economy organizes autonomy and independence for some people, powerlessness and dependency for others. Planners do not work on a neutral stage, an ideally liberal setting in which all affected interests have voice; they work within political institutions, on problems whose most basic technical components (say, a population project) may be celebrated by some, contested by others.[33]

The community is thus waiting for patronage figures and cost estimates, as if another ten thousand riders per day or another five million dollars per mile in construction costs will help decide whether or not a system should be built.

It is the time to stop treating rapid transit as purely a technical problem. The environment is such that the need for other planning roles—the broker or the mobilizer—is apparent. This is not to suggest that the technician's role will be diminished. There will be increased need for population and employment forecasts, for automobile ownership projections, as well as for patronage and cost estimates. The numbers will have to be verified; hopefully this will be done in an impartial, objective manner.

In order to move from drawing board to construction, however, much more substantive dialogue needs to occur, particularly since the bulk of the costs will be assumed not by the federal government but by the state and city themselves. Following the federally prescribed procedures at the initial planning stages may be sensible, but without building consensus and brokering the various interest in the state, the end result may be that Honolulu will have the dubious distinction of being the only city to twice reject a federally funded rapid transit system. Moreover, Honolulu might choose to adopt a technology or method of implementation that the federal government itself may not be willing to support (e.g., monorail systems or franchise implementation).

The planning of one of Honolulu's greatest public works enterprises needs to be conducted in an open, exciting process. The planning of a transit system provides an opportunity for "social learning and social mobilization."[34] The hard facts are these: a mass transit system is very expensive; it can profoundly affect people's lives and the environment in Honolulu; and now, more than ever before, this island must face up to its problems—of which, transportation is but one—on its own. The bigger question is not whether or not Honolulu will have a rapid transit system, but rather, can this community benefit from the planning process in terms of reaching both shared goals and objectives and the means to achieve them?

## Notes

1. State of Hawai'i, Department of Business and Economic Development, *Data Book 1988,* p. 366.

2. J. Meyer and J. Gomez-Ibanez, *Autos, Transit and Cities.* Cambridge: Harvard University Press, 1981, pp. 10–11.

3. Congressional Budget Office. New Directions for the Nation's Public Works. Washington DC: Congress of the United States, 1988.

4. Charles Mulford Robinson, *The Beautifying of Honolulu,* pp. 3–4. Honolulu, Board of Supervisors, 1906.

5. Ibid., p. 4.

6. R. Schmidt, *Historical Statistics of Hawai'i* (place, publisher, n.d.), table 17.2, pp. 430–31.

7. City Planning Commission, City and County of Honolulu, Territory of Hawai'i Master Plan Report, 1945, p. 11.

8. Ibid., p. 17.

9. Oahu Transportation Study. Honolulu: Oahu Metropolitan Planning Organization, 1967.

10. Ibid., p. 34.

11. Sources include: Schmidt, *Historical Statistics of Hawai'i,* pp. 431–33; DBED, *Data Book,* p. 16.

12. DBED, *Data Book,* p. 477, table 539.

13. Arthur Young, *Promoting and Implementing Paratransit on Oahu: A Plan of Action* Prepared for the State of Hawai'i Department of Transportation, 1987, p. 5.

14. Ibid., p. 6.

15. DBED, *Data Book,* p. 470.

16. Delbert A Taebel and James V. Cornehls, *The Political Economy of Urban Transportation* (Port Washington, New York: National University Publications, Kennikat Press, 1977),p. 5.

17. DBED, *Data Book,* p. 481.

18. U.S. Department of Transportation, Transportation (DOT) Planning Data for Urbanized Areas, Final Report (Washington, D.C.: U.S. Department of Transportation, 1985).

19. J. Lindley, *Quantification of Urban Freeway Congestion and Analysis of Remedial Measures, Final Report* (Washington: Federal Highway Administration, 1986), p. (?).

20. Population projections come from State of Hawai'i, Department of Planning and Economic Development, *Population and Economic Projections for the State of Hawai'i, 1980–2005,* July, 1984, p. 11. Motor vehicles were projected assuming a constant rate of ownership.

21. Meyer and Gomez-Ibanez, *Autos, Transit and Cities,* p. 187.

22. Young, *Promoting and Implementing Paratransit,* p. 8.

23. Chris Bushell, *Jane's Urban Transport Systems, 1989,* (Alexandria, Va.: Jane's Information Group, 1989), p. 5.

24. Ibid., p. 32.

25. J.A. Whitt, "BART and the Gentlemen Engineers," in Urban Elites and Mass Transportation. Princeton: Princeton University Press, 1982, pp. 40–80.

26. Reference Urban Mass Transportation Administration. Procedures and Technical Methods for Transit Project Planning. (Washington, D.C.: Department of Transportation) 1986.

27. U.S. DOT, Alternative Financing for Urban Transportation, Prepared for Federal Highway Administration and Urban Mass Transportation Administration (Washington, D.C.: U.S. Department of Transportation, 1986), p. 1.

28. Ibid., p. 30.

29. George Lave, *Urban Transit: The Private Challenge to Public Transportation* (Cambridge, Mass.: Ballinger Publishing, 1985), p. 2.

30. Department of Transportation Services, Status Report. (Honolulu: City and County of Honolulu, 1989.) Status Report, Feb. 1989, p. 5–2.

31. Francine Rabinowitz, "The Political Roles of the Planner," in *City Politics and Planning* (New York: Atherton Press, 1969), pp. 79–117.

32. Karen Christensen, "Coping with Uncertainty in Planning," *American Planning Association Journal,* Winter 1985, pp. 63–73.

33. John Forester, *Planning in the Face of Power* (Berkeley: University of California Press, 1989), p. 1.

34. See John Friedmann *Planning in the Public Domain: From Knowledge to Action* (Princeton, New Jersey: Princeton University Press, 1987), pp. 181–308.

# 11

## TOURISM IN HAWAI'I: ECONOMIC ISSUES FOR THE 1990S AND BEYOND

### *James Mak and Marcia Sakai*

### Introduction

Tourism is the lifeblood of Hawai'i's economy. In the broadest sense, tourism encompasses all expenditures for goods and services by travelers, and includes purchases for transportation, lodging, meals, entertainment, souvenirs, travel agency and sightseeing services, and various other personal services. Hence, tourism is a conglomerate industry, encompassing the outputs of many industries.

Tourism is an important source of income for many states. The U.S. Travel Data Center estimated that in 1986, U.S. and foreign travelers spent $267 billion on travel in the U.S.[1] Moreover, tourism has been growing faster than the U.S. economy has as a whole, so that between 1975 and 1986, total travel expenditures in the fifty states as a percentage of total state income (i.e., gross state product, or GSP) rose from 5.7 percent to 6.4 percent.[2]

The growing importance of tourism to their economies has not been lost on state lawmakers. Legislators in all fifty states have established state travel offices to promote tourism, funded largely by the public treasury, and more than half the states either have representatives or operate tourist information centers in foreign countries. In fiscal year 1987–1988, the total budgets of the state travel offices totalled $291 million and, in recent years, have grown much faster than the growth of tourist spending.[3]

### How Hawai'i's Tourist Industry Compares

The tourist industry is far more important in Hawai'i than in most other states. However, in 1986, the last year for which state by state data are available, Hawai'i did not even rank among the top

185

ten tourist states. California led the nation with nearly $37 billion in U.S. and foreign tourist receipts, followed by Florida ($22.5 billion), New York ($18.7 billion), Texas ($17.2 billion), and New Jersey ($13.2 billion). For Hawai'i, tourism receipts were less than $5 billion.[4] Nevertheless, among all states, Hawai'i ranked second, next to Nevada, in terms of tourism's contribution to its economy—24% of the GSP.

International travel is more important to Hawai'i than to any other state. While California and Florida led in total foreign travel dollar receipts, foreign travel accounted for one-third of all tourist receipts in Hawai'i in 1986, followed by Washington D.C. (22 percent), New York (10.1 percent), and Florida (9.5 percent).[5] Thus, Hawai'i's travel industry is far more sensitive than those of other states to changes in international economic and political conditions, particularly those in Asia and the Pacific where most of Hawai'i's foreign tourists originate. In 1989, Japan accounted for 20 percent of the total number of tourists coming to Hawai'i, followed by Canada (5 percent), and Australia-New Zealand (4 percent).[6]

## Growth of Hawai'i's Tourist Industry

At the beginning of the twentieth century, Hawai'i's tourist industry hosted small numbers of visitors attracted by romantic tales of the Pacific islands written by Mark Twain and Robert Louis Stevenson.[7] These visitors arrived by steamship, bound for the beaches of Waikiki, the more adventurous also traveling on inter-island steamships to view the activities of the Kilauea Volcano. The period from the late 1800s to the 1920s witnessed the development of hotels providing first-class accommodations, among them the Moana (1901), the Halekulani (1917), and the Royal Hawaiian (1927) in Waikiki, and the Volcano House (1877) on the island of Hawai'i. In 1922 approximately ninety-seven hundred visitors arrived in the islands. Before the interruption of World War II, the number of visitor arrivals had more than tripled, with tourist expenditures (i.e., receipts) increasing from $4.4 million in 1922 to $16.4 million in 1941.

Today, the tourist industry bears little resemblance to that infant business. Shifts in demand and changes in the costs, technology, and organization of tourism have shaped an industry under constant change.

The industry's growth rate has changed over time, essentially following a product cycle pattern of industrial development.[8] The typical product cycle has three phases. The first phase is the brief period when the new product is sampled by first-time buyers. This is followed by the expansion phase, characterized by rapid growth rates. The third phase is the consolidation or maturation phase when the rate of growth of the industry slows, leading ultimately to decline.

In Hawai'i, the first decade of statehood represented the period of rapid growth for the visitor industry. Tourist arrivals increased at an annual compound rate of 19 percent, while visitor expenditures grew at 16 percent. Several factors fueled the growth of tourist travel to Hawai'i.

First, the technological innovation of jet travel, developed during World War II, dramatically reduced the amount of time required to travel from the continental U.S. While steamship passage from San Francisco took nearly a week, propeller plane passage took only ten hours, and the inauguration of Pan American's Jet Clipper service in 1959 reduced travel time further to five hours. The increasing popularity of air travel is indicated by the relative decline in the proportion of passengers arriving by ship. Before 1936, all passengers arrived by ship; by 1959, this proportion was reduced to one-fifth. Today, there is no longer regular passenger steamship service between Hawai'i and the U.S. mainland; ship passage represents a small market niche of less than one percent, providing specialized transportation services to that clientele which prefers the characteristics and amenities of ocean cruises.

Second, not only is air travel faster than ocean travel, it is also cheaper. The development and introduction of wide-bodied aircraft increased the carrying capacity of the jetliners and allowed the total cost of a trip to be spread over more passengers. The 200 passenger stretch-out jets introduced during the late 1960s, for example, increased carrying capacity by 50 percent while increasing costs only 25 percent. Indeed, declining real airfares contributed significantly to increased arrivals, because of the highly responsive nature of vacation travel to the price of air travel. Most of the decrease in the cost of air travel occurred between 1960 and 1970 as real airfares between San Francisco and Hawai'i declined by nearly 50 percent.[9] In 1970, the first Boeing 747 landed in Hawai'i, and, with its four hundred-plus passenger capacity, ushered in the jumbo jet age and mass tourism in Hawai'i.

Third, real incomes in the major U.S. markets increased substantially during the U.S. economic boom of the late 1960s and early 1970s. Until the first energy crisis halted the economic advance in

1973, real personal income per capita grew by nearly 60 percent in the U.S. between 1960 and 1973.[10] One consequence of this greater purchasing power was increased vacation travel, an expenditure typically responsive to increases in income. Thus, what was once a luxury item, affordable by only the wealthy few, was made increasingly accessible by the income gains resulting from U.S. prosperity. Rising affluence also brought increased leisure time for Americans. The combination of higher incomes, lower cost of travel, and faster passage times made it possible for more people to travel frequently and for shorter durations to distant places such as Hawai'i. During the 1960s, the length of the typical American vacation in Hawai'i fell from more than two and a half weeks to less than eleven days.

Adding to the surge in American travel to Hawai'i in the sixties was the growing number of foreign visitors, particularly Japanese. After lifting restrictions on overseas pleasure travel in 1964, the Japanese government began raising the limit on the amount of currency that residents could take abroad.[11] The easing of travel and monetary restrictions, combined with extraordinary domestic economic growth and the declining value of the U.S. dollar in the seventies and eighties, fueled Japanese overseas travel, enabling the Japanese to become one of the major tourist generating nations in the world today. From the very beginning, Hawai'i was the favorite U.S. destination among Japanese travelers.

Since 1970, visitor arrivals have grown at ever slower rates. From 1970 to 1980, the number of tourist arrivals grew at an annual compound rate of 8.5 percent; from 1980 to 1989, visitor arrivals grew at a 6.1 percent annual rate. The state's official forecast, which envisions the continued decline in the growth rate of visitor arrivals well into the twenty-first century, is a clear indication that Hawai'i's tourist industry has entered the maturation phase of its development.[12]

## Shifting Patterns of Hawai'i's Tourist Industry

Although the growth of tourism has slowed in the last thirty years, the numbers on visitor counts fail to show the dramatic changes in the character of the industry in that same time period, and one can hardly portray the industry as static.

In the westbound market, over half of all tourists are repeat visitors, nearly twice the percentage in 1960. Westbound tourists comprise 70 percent of total visitors to Hawai'i; they are largely

Americans and Canadians. Among Japanese visitors, over 30 percent have been to Hawai'i before. Repeat visitors demand different vacation experiences than first-time visitors do; they also spend less money, thus yielding fewer economic benefits to the local community. Thus, if Hawai'i's travel industry has to depend increasingly on repeat visitors to maintain its growth, the marginal economic benefits of growth will diminish over time. Marginal benefits are incremental benefits associated with bringing one more tourist to Hawai'i.

As the share of repeat visitors has increased, the share of tourists traveling on prearranged group tours has also decreased. Group travel constitutes less than 15 percent of all westbound visitors to Hawai'i today, compared to nearly 50 percent in the mid-1970s. Returning visitors are not the only explanation for the decline in group travel to Hawai'i; deregulation of the U.S. airline industry since 1978 had a major impact in reducing the incentive to travel in prearranged groups. Before 1978, U.S. trunk carriers could not compete on the basis of price because of the general price-setting authority of the Civil Aeronautics Board (CAB). Airlines, however, were permitted to engage in differential (i.e., discount) pricing on group travel. Vigorous airline price competition after deregulation reduced the relative advantage previously enjoyed by large traveling groups on prepaid package tours. Technological innovations in communications, such as the widespread use of toll-free telephone numbers, also made individual travel arrangements simpler.

One of the most important changes in Hawai'i's tourist industry since statehood is its growing geographic diversification. In 1959, 46 percent of the westbound visitors were Californians; they now constitute less than 30 percent. Not only has the geographic market changed domestically, it has also changed internationally. In 1959, roughly 80 percent of Hawai'i's visitors were Americans; today that share has fallen to about 65 percent (Table 11.1).

Japan now constitutes the second largest source of tourists (20 percent) after the U.S. In addition, as of 1986, Japanese investors own more than a quarter of all hotel units in Hawai'i.[13] Following the steps made by Japan in the 1960s, both Korea and Taiwan recently reduced restrictions on their own nationals traveling abroad. The 1980s also witnessed the emergence of Europe as the fastest growing travel market. It is conceivable that in the next twenty years Hawai'i could become a truly international travel destination.

Perhaps the most striking change in Hawai'i's travel industry has been the increasing industry fragmentation stemming from the development of the neighbor island destinations. To date, westbound

**Table 11.1: Visitors to Hawai'i by Country/Region (1989)[14]**

| Country/region | Number of visitors |
|---|---|
| United States | 4,294,250 |
| Canada | 352,860 |
| Asia | 1,484,010 |
| Japan | 1,319,340 |
| Taiwan/China | 57,740 |
| Korea | 38,330 |
| Hong Kong | 19,330 |
| Singapore | 15,710 |
| Philippines | 8,290 |
| Indonesia | 8,000 |
| Other Asia | 17,270 |
| Oceania | 288,460 |
| Australia | 186,540 |
| New Zealand | 91,280 |
| Other South Pacific | 10,640 |
| Europe | 205,030 |
| United Kingdom | 94,860 |
| West Germany | 41,900 |
| Other Europe | 68,270 |
| Other Foreign | 17,210 |
| Total | 6,641,820 |

tourists account for most of the travel to the principal neighbor islands of Maui, Kauai, and Hawai'i (the Big Island). Until the mid-1970s, visits to the neighbor islands were typically side trips, from a primary destination base in Waikiki. Many travelers went to the neighbor islands because the trips were part of their inclusive package tours. In the early 1970s, nearly 95 percent of the westbound tourists to the state visited Oahu; over 60 percent visited at least one neighbor island.[15] The proportion of the westbound tourists visiting only the neighbor islands was small—less than 4 percent. With increasing volumes of repeat visitors to the state, more aggressive marketing of neighbor island destinations, a ceiling placed on the number of hotel rooms in Waikiki, and the initiation of direct flights from the U.S. West Coast to the neighbor islands in 1983, tourism on the neighbor islands has grown much faster than on Oahu. Indeed, growth has been highest on Maui, followed by Kauai and the Big Island. By 1989, the proportion of westbound tourists who visited Oahu had fallen to 68 percent, while the share who visited only the neighbor islands increased to around 30 percent. Growing numbers of westbound tourists who used to visit both Oahu and the neighbor islands now bypass Oahu entirely and visit only the neighbor islands during their Hawai'i vacations. With fewer island stops per trip, their average length of stay on each island has risen sharply, although the overall length of stay in the state has fallen slightly to ten days from eleven days during the early 1970s. Among all visitors to Hawai'i, over 60 percent now visit only one island. These changes indicate that Hawai'i's tourist industry is witnessing the fragmentation of what was once a single travel destination into several competing destinations, with each island trying to develop its own distinctive market image.

## Policy Issues Related to Future Tourism Growth

The dynamic nature of Hawai'i's visitor industry and its importance to the economy raises a number of important economic issues: (1) the benefits and costs of more tourism growth; (2) county land use and fiscal autonomy; (3) travel destination promotion; and (4) foreign investment. These issues are explored in greater detail below.

### Benefits and Costs of Tourism Growth

One of the most important issues confronting state policymakers is whether the state should continue to encourage the unconstrained growth of tourism in Hawai'i. Wilkinson has suggested that tourism is nearly inevitable for island microstates as long as international tourism continues to expand.[16] The challenge is to find and implement policies that maximize the benefits and minimize the social costs of tourism.

The principal benefits of tourism are economic—i.e., income, employment, and tax revenues—derived from tourist spending. Until the recent surge in high-spending Japanese tourists to Hawai'i, tourist spending in Hawai'i, adjusted for inflation, grew at a slightly slower pace than tourist arrivals; thus, real expenditures per tourist have declined (see Figure 11.1).

Tourists also impose direct resource costs on the local community. Hawai'i's state and county governments spend money to provide airports, highways, parks, and public services beyond the demands of their own residents. In addition, the tourist industry may have adverse economic impacts on other industries since it employs resources that have alternative economic uses (e.g., land that could be used for agriculture).[17] Ghali has estimated that if there had been no tourism in Hawai'i between 1953 and 1970, the total income loss to Hawai'i would have been surprisingly small.[18]

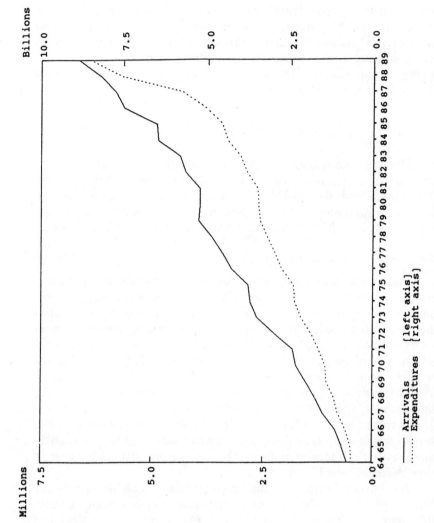

Figure 11.1 Visitor Arrivals and Real Expenditures [CPI-U deflator, 1982–1984 = 100]

Critics of tourism growth argue that the greatest costs imposed by tourists on the local community are the noneconomic environmental and social costs. These costs arise largely because tourism services, unlike other exports must be consumed in the travel destination. Wilkinson noted that because of the local system's increasing inability to absorb the consequences of tourism development, the risk of negative impacts rise as the visitor population grows relative to the local population.[19] In 1989, nearly 6.6 million tourists visited Hawai'i. Because tourists are temporary residents, only 170,000 of them were in Hawai'i on a typical day. Nonetheless, against a small resident population, one of every ten people on Oahu was a tourist; the ratio was one out of every eight on the Big Island, one of every four on Kauai and nearly one of every three on Maui.[20] The combination of small geographic areas and high ratios of tourist populations makes competition, and thus friction, between guests and hosts difficult to avoid.

In a 1982 poll of 600 Honolulu residents, 64 percent of the respondents felt that tourism growth contributed to the decline in the Aloha spirit; the same percentage thought it brought more prostitution; 48 percent felt that tourists aggravated traffic problems in Honolulu; and 38 percent felt that tourism had resulted in overcrowded beaches, hiking trails, parks, and other outdoor places used by the local population.[21] Also, in recent years, there is growing local concern and resentment against nonresident ownership of hotels, golf courses, residential real estate, and other real assets.

Although there are no available empirical estimates of the economic and social costs of tourism growth in Hawai'i, it is not unreasonable to assume that the marginal costs of tourism rise with increasing number of tourists. First, the opportunity cost of resources employed in tourism is likely to increase as more resources are diverted to tourism. Second, the marginal social cost of tourism may also rise with increasing numbers of tourists. Thus, if past trends continue, the marginal benefits of tourism growth will continue to decline while the marginal costs will rise. Beyond some level of tourist population, marginal costs will exceed marginal benefits, and a marketing strategy aimed at attracting more tourists ultimately becomes an imprudent social policy.

Some people would argue that Hawai'i is already beyond the saturation point.[22] This is not the public consensus. In an August 1988 poll of 704 randomly selected Hawai'i voters, sponsored by the *Honolulu Advertiser* and Channel 2 TV, 62 percent of the respondents favored more tourism growth, another 15 percent said that growth was acceptable if done with quality, and only 19 percent were against further growth.[23] The strong public support for more tourism growth suggests that Hawai'i has not yet reached the saturation point; thus, there are additional net benefits to be gained by having more tourists.

However, this is hardly a prescription for a do-nothing policy. In the long run, Hawai'i can have both more tourists and greater total net benefits from tourism by seeking and implementing appropriate public policies to increase the marginal benefits and reduce the marginal costs of tourism. What are some policies which might raise the tourism benefit-cost ratio?

The tourist industry can be encouraged to become more involved and to make greater contributions to educational, social, and charitable activities in the community—activities in which the industry has often been criticized for not doing its fair share.

Public development costs, such as highways, sewers, water systems, and even schools associated with new resort developments can be shifted to developers by using development fees and exactions. To some extent this is already being done in Hawai'i, but not necessarily on a consistent or predictable basis. Typically, only large developers are required to pay fees and exactions. The U.S. Advisory Commission on Intergovernmental Relations (ACIR) recently noted that the sheer difficulty of encompassing all of the public costs of private development in a development fee program makes the establishment of fees and exactions a strategic undertaking.[24] In fact, the counties have chosen to encourage development by imposing development fees encompassing only a limited number and scope of services; thus, developers have not been asked to pay the total costs associated with development. The state and county governments can also discourage geographically dispersed resort development to minimize infrastructure construction costs and social friction between residents and tourists.

Another obvious policy choice is to abandon the current de facto policy of attracting more tourists each year, in favor of a strategy designed to attract tourists who are big daily spenders by using selective marketing, taxation, and land-use planning. Thus, the issue remains the long-standing one of quantity of tourism growth versus quality.

*County Land Use and Fiscal Autonomy*

A second issue related to tourism growth is the autonomy of local county governments in land use-planning and local public finance. The continued rapid growth of tourism on the neighbor islands will induce substantial in-migration of labor to the relatively sparsely populated outer islands, requiring costly government expenditures to provide the public services demanded by both tourists and residents. The recent study by the ACIR found that, given the current distribution of the functional responsibilities between the state and the county governments in Hawai'i, tourism growth imposes a greater financial burden on the county governments than on the state government. Yet, an earlier state government study found that, relative to what each level of government spends to provide public services to tourists, tourist spending generated far more tax revenues to the state government than it did to the county governments.[25] Counties are also experiencing intensified fiscal pressures from state (and federally) imposed environmental protection mandates without compensating fiscal resources. Additionally, county governments are compelled by Hawai'i collective bargaining laws to pay the same wages as the state government, although the latter has greater financial resources.

At the same time, and unlike other states, local (i.e., county) governments in Hawai'i are severely limited by the state government in their taxing authority. County governments in Hawai'i are not permitted to levy their own sales or income taxes. The property tax is the only major tax over which the counties have full authority. Thus, this highly unpopular property tax contributes a significantly higher percentage of local government revenues in Hawai'i than in most other states.

The state government also tightly controls local land use through its Land Use Commission (LUC). County governments opposed to (or in favor of) specific resort developments must petition the LUC to reject (or approve) the developers' proposed applications for land-use reclassification. State law also permits the state government to override county zoning laws, as in the Kakaako redevelopment and the construction of the proposed state convention center in Waikiki. The power to control land use and override county zoning laws not only allows the state government to determine the social impacts developments have on the local community, it also affects property assessment values and hence county property tax revenues. Thus, the high degree of state control in taxing authority and land use makes it very difficult for the counties to control local development and finance public services. The obvious solution is for the state to grant the counties greater autonomy in taxing authority and land-use planning.

Of the two, achieving greater county autonomy in land-use planning will be far more difficult, give that the abolition of the LUC is improbable. The issue, then, is an intergovernmental one. At present, the relationship between the commission and the counties is strained. The challenge for the 1990s is to find a mechanism by which to improve communication and to foster joint decision making.

### Promotion of Travel Destinations

One issue which has not received any public attention is the appropriate future role of the Hawai'i Visitors Bureau (HVB) in the promotion of Hawai'i travel. HVB is a private not-for-profit corporation contracted by the state to promote travel to Hawai'i; over 90 percent of its budget is derived from the state general fund.[26]

As Hawai'i's tourist industry continues its transformation into a multiplicity of destinations, a single marketing organization will face increasing difficulty in promoting them. The neighbor islands have already formed individual organizations to promote travel to their own islands, financed by industry and county government contributions. This new competitive environment raises a number of questions relevant to the future role of the HVB. What are the appropriate future functions for the HVB, and especially its neighbor island chapters? Should the state government also finance the neighbor island destination marketing organizations as it does the HVB, or should their financing be left to the neighbor island travel industries? Should the county governments help fund county travel promotion and by what means? Thus, the issues for the 1990s are who should be promoting Hawai'i travel and who should pay for it.

### Foreign Investment

If the experiences of the past thirty years are repeated, the growing internationalization of the travel industry will be accompanied by greater inclination on the part of foreigners to invest in Hawai'i assets. Estimates of the volume of foreign investments in Hawai'i vary widely.[27] The state estimates that cumulative foreign investments in Hawai'i totalled $8.7 billion through the end of 1989. The Japanese have the largest investment position in Hawai'i, accounting for over 80% of accumulated investment by all foreign countries. Of all investment types, investment in hotel and tourism-related properties have dominated in terms of value.

As a regional economy, Hawai'i has historically depended on external investment flows to finance the capitalization of both its commodity-based production of sugar and pineapple and its service-based production of tourism. This dependence is a direct result of the constraints on the availability of locally generated investment funds, imposed by Hawai'i's relatively limited resource base and economic output.

The recent surge of Japanese investments into Hawai'i can be attributed to several economic conditions. First, the declining value of the dollar encouraged foreign direct investment, because U.S. businesses and real estate became less expensive to acquire as dollar-denominated selling prices fell in terms of foreign currency. Second, Japanese-owned dollars accumulated from continuing foreign trade surpluses created a large pool of investment funds with which to acquire foreign investments. To the extent that the capital inflows have served to broaden the resource base of Hawai'i's tourist industry, foreign investments have been economically beneficial.

However, there is growing concern over the negative impacts of speculative buying, and a growing sense of loss of local control over prime tourism properties. Japanese golf course acquisitions, followed by sales of high-priced, exclusive club memberships in Japan, have raised concerns that local players will soon be priced out of this popular recreational and sporting activity. At present there are 28 golf courses in Honolulu, with 40 others in various stages of planning. Proposed new golf courses are seen as a threat to future housing prices in the state. Local exasperation with foreign ownership is compounded by formidable cultural and communication barriers between foreign owners and local residents.

Thus, the issue of the effects of foreign investments in Hawai'i's tourist industry does not concern their economic contribution, but rather their perceived negative social impacts on the local community. The previous discussion of the tradeoff between the benefits and costs of tourism emphasizes the benefits of encouraging the tourist industry to make greater contributions to educational, social, and charitable activities in Hawai'i. The challenge in the 1990s is to find ways to improve communications between investors and residents so that foreign owners can learn to be good citizens and local residents can learn to be good hosts.

## Conclusion

In Hawai'i's statehood year, less than a quarter of a million tourists came to Hawai'i. Today, the industry is more than twenty times larger, and has reached the mature stage of its development. Hawai'i's tourists are more geographically diverse than they were three decades ago. They are more knowledgeable about Hawai'i travel, more independent and price sensitive, and more selective about the island they visit. No longer is Hawai'i a single destination; the industry has become fragmented as the neighbor islands have emerged as serious challengers to Oahu's Waikiki. The changes witnessed by Hawai'i's travel industry raise important policy questions for the 1990s and beyond. The state faces many critical policy decisions, of which this chapter has highlighted a few.

## Notes

1. U.S. Travel Data Center (USTDC), *Impact of Travel on State Economies, 1986* (Washington D.C., 1988).

2. USTDC, *Impact of Travel, 1975–1986* issues; U.S. Department of Commerce, Survey of Current Business (Washington, D.C., May 1988), pp. 34–45.

3. USTDC, *Survey of State Travel Offices, 1988–89* (Washington D.C., February 1989). See also earlier issues.

4. USTDC, *Impact of Travel 1986;* and U.S. Department of Commerce, U.S. Travel and Tourism Administration, *Impact of Foreign Visitors' Spending on State Economies, 1985–86* (Washington D.C.: September 1988). In 1989 6.6 million tourists spent nearly $11 billion and accounted for 30% of total household income in Hawai'i.

5. Ibid.

6. Hawai'i Visitors Bureau (HVB), *1989 Annual Research Report* (Honolulu, 1990), p. (8). Data on Hawai'i tourist arrivals and expenditures (cited below) were obtained from various issues of the HVB *Annual Research Report,* HVB, *1988 Visitor Expenditure Survey* (Honolulu, 1989), and the State of *Hawai'i Data Book, 1990* (Honolulu, 1991).

7. A detailed account of the early history of Hawai'i tourism can be found in L. J. Crampon, *Hawai'i's Visitor Industry, Its Growth and Development* (Honolulu: University of Hawai'i, School of Travel Industry Management, 1975).

8. Simon Kuznets, *Secular Movement in Production and Prices* (New York: National Bureau of Economic Research, 1930).

9. Robert Ebel, James Mak, and James Moncur, "The Future of Hawai'i's Major Exports," in M. Gahli, ed., *Tourism and Regional Growth* (Leiden: Martinus Nijhoff Social Sciences Division, 1977), p. 40.

10. Ibid.

11. James Mak and Kenneth White, "Tourism in Asia and the Pacific," in C. H. Lee and S. Naya, eds., *Trade and Investment in Services in the Asia-Pacific Region* (Boulder: Westview Press, 1988), pp. 121–49.

12. *Population and Economic Projections for the State of Hawai'i to 2010, Series M-K* (Honolulu: November 1988). Expected rates of growth of visitors are 3.5 percent per year, 1990–95; 3.0 percent per year, 1995–2000; and 2.5 percent per year, 2000–2010.

13. DBED, "Foreign Direct Investment in Hawai'i: Opportunity or Threat?" *Quarterly Statistical & Economic Report, 2nd and 3d Quarters, 1987* (Honolulu: 1987).

14. Hawai'i Visitors Bureau, *1989 Annual Research Report*, p. 5.

15. Most Japanese tourists still take only day trips to the neighbor islands.

16. Paul F. Wilkinson, "Strategies for Tourism in Island Microstates," in *Annals of Tourism Research*, 16 (1989), pp. 153–77.

17. Peter Diamond, "On the Economics of Tourism," *East Africa Economic Review*, 1 (December 1969), pp. 53–62; Moheb Gahli, "The Contribution of Tourism to Hawai'i's Growth," in S. P. Ladany, ed., *Management Science Applications to Leisure Time Operations* (New York: North Holland Publishing Co., 1975), pp. 124–33.

18. Gahli, "Contribution of Tourism."

19. Wilkinson, "Strategies for Tourism."

20. County population data were obtained from the DBED, *Data Book 1990* (Honolulu: 1991). p. 16.

21. Juanita Liu and Turgut Var, "Resident Attitudes toward Tourism Impacts," *Annals of Tourism Research* 13 (1986), pp. 193–214. In the same poll, respondents felt that tourism gave residents a greater variety of entertainment, valuable educational experiences, more historical and cultural exhibits, positive feelings about the state, more parks and recreational areas, and better maintained roads and public facilities.

22. See, for example, Luciano Minerbi, "Tourism in Hawai'i," *Economic Issues of Tourism, a Consultation* (San Anselmo: Center for Responsible Tourism, 1989.

23. Poll results reported in James Mak, Gail Tamaribuchi, and Lyle Hendricks, *Hawai'i's Economy* (Honolulu: State of Hawai'i, Department of Education, August 1989), p. 47.

24. Robert W. Rafuse, Jr., et. al., "Intergovernmental Fiscal Relations in Hawai'i," in State of Hawai'i, *Tax Review Commission, Working Papers and Consultant Studies*, vol. 2 (Honolulu: December 1989), p. 282.

25. State of Hawai'i, Department of Planning and Economic Development, *State Tourism Study, Public Revenue-Cost Analysis* (Honolulu: 1978).

26. HVB, *Annual Report, 1988–1989* (Honolulu: 1989).

27. Marcia Sakai, "Nonresident Investment in Hawai'i," in *Tax Review Commission Working Papers and Consultant Studies,* vol. 2, (Honolulu: December 1989), pp. 321–338.

# 12

## CRIME AND JUSTICE IN HAWAI'I

### A. Didrick Castberg

The average television viewer on the U.S. mainland might think that the state of Hawai'i is crime ridden, given the series of popular programs based on the problem, from "Hawai'i Five-O" through "Magnum P.I." to "Jake and the Fatman." As is invariably the case, television depictions of crime and the response to it in Hawai'i diverge significantly from reality. There is crime in Hawai'i to be sure, but, as we shall see, crime and the system intended to deal with it in Hawai'i are quite similar in most respects to the mainland U.S., with a few notable exceptions. The exceptions are the result of the unique geographical, cultural, and political characteristics of the state.

### Institutions

Article I of the Hawai'i Constitution is a bill of rights, which closely matches the Bill of Rights of the federal Constitution, although it contains sections dealing with equality of the sexes (section 3) and privacy (section 6), specific protections not found in the U.S. Constitution. Virtually all of the sections dealing with criminal procedure read the same as their federal counterparts, with a few minor exceptions. For example, section 7, dealing with search and seizure, includes a clause concerning "communications sought to be intercepted," specifically including all forms of communication subject to search and seizure provisions.[1] Section 11 provides for the appointment of independent counsel to advise the grand jury, a grand jury indictment being required in all felony proceedings; section 12 specifically allows for release on recognizance; and section 14 requires a jury of twelve in felony cases and for the appointment of counsel in any case where the offense is punishable by imprisonment. Overall, the Hawai'i Constitution differs from the U.S. Constitution as regards criminal procedure in its greater specificity and increased protections for the accused.

## Law Enforcement

The primary law enforcement agencies in the State of Hawai'i are the police departments of the four counties.[2] Since there are no separately incorporated cities or towns in Hawai'i, law enforcement in each county is countywide. Because the counties (and even parts of some counties) are separated by significant expanses of water, there is in effect no intercounty law enforcement possible, nor is there a state law enforcement agency with general law enforcement responsibilities. There are, then, four police departments in the state: Hawai'i County Police Department; Honolulu Police Department; Kauai Police Department; and Maui Police Department. Even though police departments are a county function, all non-supervisory police officers in the state are represented by the State of Hawai'i Organization of Police Officers (SHOPO), which bargains with the individual counties to arrive at common salaries and benefits for its members (supervisory-level law enforcement personnel are represented by the Hawai'i Government Employees Association).

In addition to these departments there are agencies with limited law enforcement responsibilities. The state sheriff is responsible for courtroom security, the transportation of defendants to and from court, and the execution of orders relating to the courts as the chief justice may direct.[3] The sheriff's office has recently undergone reorganization as a result of criticism of its assumption of law enforcement duties beyond the scope of its statutory function, and for currying political favor by handing out honorary sheriff's badges to legislators and other influential individuals.

There are other agencies with limited law enforcement powers, including prison guards and officers of the State Department of Fish and Game, harbor police, and marine police. Still, the vast majority of law enforcement is conducted by the four county police departments, with the city and county of Honolulu having the greatest share due to its population.[4] Honolulu accounted, for example, for 76 percent of the major offenses reported to the police in 1989.[5]

The county police departments are administratively indepen-dent of each other and of the state, with state law establishing only general guidelines for county law enforcement, such as the powers and duties, and the selection and dismissal of the chief.[6] There are no statewide standards for recruitment or training of police officers, nor is there any statewide certification, although the recruitment and training of officers is very similar from county to county. Hawai'i County, for example, requires prospective police officers to pass a qualifying examination, a physical examination, a physical qualify-ing test, an oral interview, and a background check. Less than ten percent of those who initially apply are selected for recruit training. Recruit training lasts six months and includes the standard topics taught in most modern police academies.

*Crime Data*

Police officers in Hawai'i are faced with virtually all of the prob-lems facing their mainland counterparts, plus some others. Table 12.1, gives a breakdown of major offenses reported to police in the state in 1989. Less serious offenses, excluding traffic violations, to-taled 121,060.[8]

The vast majority of offenses are in the City and County of Ho-nolulu, on the island of Oahu. As can be seen in the Table, 12.2, clearance rates (percentage of offenses cleared by an arrest) vary by county as well.

**Table 12.1: Major Offenses, State of Hawai'i, 1989[7]**

| *Offense* | *Total reported* |
| --- | --- |
| All part I ("major") offenses* | 65,328 |
| Murder, non-negligent manslaughter | 53 |
| Negligent manslaughter | 69 |
| Forcible Rape | 479 |
| Robbery | 914 |
| Aggravated assault | 1,462 |
| Burglary | 14,379 |
| Larceny | 47,257 |
| Motor vehicle theft | 4,330 |
| Arson | 387 |

*Note that drug offenses are not listed under part I offenses; they are a separate category in FBI statistics, even though they are considered major crimes.

## Table 12.2: Major Offenses by County, 1989[9]

|          | Part I offenses | Clearance rate | Population |
|----------|-----------------|----------------|-----------|
| Honolulu | 52,436          | 13.9           | 841,600   |
| Hawai'i  | 6,860           | 23.8           | 122,300   |
| Kauai    | 2,781           | 20.7           | 51,000    |
| Maui     | 7,251           | 13.2           | 97,200    |

### Organized Crime

Organized crime does not seem to be much of a factor in Hawai'i, although there have been allegations from time to time that a "godfather" of organized crime exists in the state. Japanese organized crime figures, or *yakuza,* have attempted to establish ties between Japan and gangs in Hawai'i, but strict enforcement of immigration and customs regulations, as well as effective intelligence on the part of both countries, has severely hampered such attempts. Similarly, efforts have been made to establish links between West Coast and Hawai'i gangs, primarily for distribution of drugs, with little success. The fact that Hawai'i is an island state makes it much easier to resist such attempts.

### Marijuana

Marijuana, on the other hand, is a major cash crop in Hawai'i and a major challenge for state law enforcement. It was estimated by the U.S. Drug Enforcement Administration (DEA) that the harvest value of marijuana grown in the state in 1987 was $1.33 billion, while the state attorney general has said that marijuana is a $10 billion per year business.[10] Whatever its size, marijuana presents many problems for law enforcement. It is grown on all major islands, and detection and eradication is a challenge. The island of Hawai'i, the major source (97 percent) of marijuana in the state, presents particular problems due to its size—4,060 square miles, or about the size of Connecticut. The island is mountainous, rich in tropical growth, and sparsely populated, making the detection and seizure of marijuana difficult and expensive. Large sums of money are spent on green harvests and other eradication campaigns that rely primarily on helicopters and the military. The eradication efforts in 1989 included not only police and national guard resources, but the DEA, and the Air Force, and the State Department of Land and Natural Resources.[11]

The effectiveness of the effort devoted to fighting marijuana finally is questionable. Hawai'i County police reported that 1,564,434 plants were destroyed in 1989, down from 1.7 million in 1987 and 1.8 million in 1988, and conclude that it is a sign of "the turning of the tide in the marijuana fight."[12] Despite these efforts the substance is still readily available and enjoyed by broad segments of Hawai'i's population. There are, in addition, increasing calls for its legalization, or, at least, decriminalization. Many law enforcement officials are, of course, opposed to both proposals. Public opinion is mixed on the subject.

## Prosecution

Prosecution, like law enforcement, is a county function. The Hawai'i County prosecutor is elected in a partisan election, as is Kauai's, while the Honolulu election is nonpartisan. Maui's prosecutor is appointed by the mayor with the approval of the county council. Deputy prosecutors are hired by the prosecutor and are not subject to civil service rules.

Ironically, the nonpartisan Honolulu prosecutor's office seems to be the most political. This is very likely a function of its jurisdiction over Honolulu, both the governmental and financial center of the state. The prosecutor who lost his bid for reelection in 1988 was the subject of a great deal of controversy as a result of his charges that some criminals were close to elected officials, his criticism of the state judiciary, and his rocky relations with the Honolulu Police Department. The prosecutors in the other three counties have much less visibility and are less controversial, and they often run unopposed in those counties where they are elected. Service as county prosecutor does not seem to be a stepping stone to political office, although prosecutors are frequently appointed to the judiciary.

Plea bargaining is the norm in every county, much as it is elsewhere in the U.S. While occasionally controversial, it nevertheless is widespread and, given Hawai'i's sentencing laws, rarely affects maximum sentences.[13] County prosecutors in Hawai'i are making a concerted effort to prosecute career criminals and frequently have a special section or prosecutor devoted to the task. Plea bargaining in these cases is not the norm, although it will certainly take place if necessary. Because the Hawai'i Constitution requires indictment by grand jury for all felony offenses, the prosecutor spends a good deal of time preparing cases for and presenting evidence to that body.[14]

Due to the inherently one-sided nature of the grand jury, provision is made in the constitution for an independent counsel, an attorney who is essentially on call to the jury when a legal question arises. This provision to some extent reduces the rubber-stamp nature of the grand jury, but true bills of indictment nevertheless are returned in the vast majority of cases presented by the prosecutor.

The attorney general (AG) is appointed by the governor, and has general prosecutorial powers. These powers are rarely exercised, however, as the primary role of the AG is in civil cases. The AG has been involved in some major criminal cases in the state, but most prosecution is county in nature. The AG may provide assistance to the counties, and is required by statute to act as a clearinghouse for information on resources to assist law enforcement and, in general, provide coordination for law enforcement statewide.[15]

## Defense

Those accused of committing criminal acts may be represented by retained counsel, assigned counsel, or a public defender. The majority of defendants are indigent, and hence are represented by a public defender. However, an indigent defendant may be represented by counsel appointed by the court in the case of conflicts of interest in the public defender's office. The public defender's office is a state agency under the Department of Budget and Finance, and the state public defender is appointed by the Defender Council, a panel of five members appointed by the governor.[16] Public defenders receive equivalent pay to prosecutors, although they have fewer resources, such as investigators and clerical support. In 1986, the last year for which figures were available, there were 98 full-time public defenders and 291 prosecutors in the state, with expenditures of the former totalling $3,233,000 and the latter $9,142,000.[17] In general, public defenders feel that they are at a disadvantage compared to prosecutors, but whether this is in fact true and whether, if it is true, it has any systematic impact is difficult to say. It is clear, however, that public defenders do win cases and do plea bargain effectively, if *effectively* is defined as succeeding in having charges reduced or dropped in a majority of cases. Public defenders have also won some landmark state supreme court decisions, such as the 1974 case of *State* v. *Kaluna,* which provided greater protection against searches and seizures to Hawai'i criminal suspects than was afforded them under the U.S. Constitution.[18]

## Courts

The Hawai'i judicial system is graphically represented in Figure 12.1. Although district courts and circuit courts are shown at the same level on this chart, the former is a lower court and therefore inferior to the circuit court. The lines indicate the route of appeals, all of which go directly to the supreme court, which may then retain the case or send it to the intermediate court of appeals. The tax and land courts are also administratively equivalent to the circuit courts.

District courts are nonjury trial courts with exclusive jurisdiction in misdemeanor and petty misdemeanor cases. Preliminary

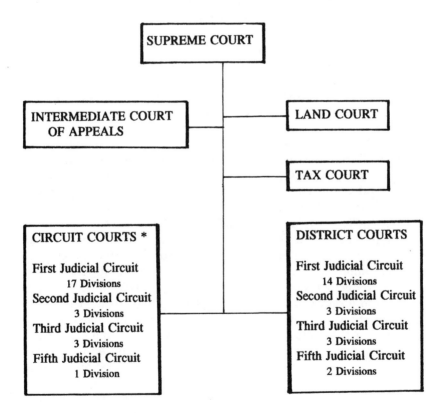

\* Includes Family Courts

Figure 12.1:   Hawaii Judicial System.

hearings in felony cases also are heard in district courts. A defendant who is charged with a misdemeanor and wishes a jury trial is transferred to the circuit court. Circuit courts are courts of general jurisdiction with exclusive jurisdiction in felony cases. Juvenile cases are heard in family court, a division of the circuit court. The intermediate court of appeals and the supreme court are courts reached on appeal. Generally speaking, cases involving the formulation and development of law are assigned to the supreme court, while cases involving "trial court error or application of settled law" are assigned to the intermediate court of appeals.[19]

There are thirty-two district judges statewide, serving terms of six years. At the circuit court level there are a total of twenty-four judges, who serve ten-year terms. There are three judges on the intermediate court of appeals and five justices on the supreme court, all serving terms of ten years.

District court judges are appointed by the chief justice from a list of six names for each vacancy submitted by the Judicial Selection Commission, while all other judges and justices are appointed by the governor from such lists submitted by the commission. The Judicial Selection Commission is composed of nine members, three of whom are appointed by the governor, two by the chief justice, one each by the senate president and speaker of the house, and two by the Hawai'i Bar Association. All serve for six years. In addition to soliciting nominations for judicial vacancies, the commission decides whether judges who want another term will be reappointed.

The system described was designed to reduce the influence of partisan politics while increasing the role of merit in the selection of judges and justices, and is a variation of the Missouri Plan of judicial selection found in many states. It is doubtful that politics can ever be completely removed from judicial selection, but the system at least reduces the more overt forms of partisan bias. Although judges and justices in Hawai'i do not have party labels, it is safe to say that the vast majority are Democrats and that most of them have been active in one way or another in the party. And while there are judges from most of the ethnic groups represented in Hawai'i, there is only one female judge at the circuit court level and none at the appellate court level. In 1990, the terms of six circuit court judges expired, allowing the governor (who was reelected in 1990) to replace them. Governor Waihee will in his second term have the opportunity to replace four supreme court justices, all members of the intermediate court of appeals, and eleven additional circuit court judges.[20] Thus, the current governor will have a major impact on Hawai'i's judiciary.

Judges do not have a great deal of latitude in sentencing since most offenses are punishable by indeterminate terms. This means that the judge must sentence the offender to the maximum term allowed by law, leaving the parole board to determine how long the offender will serve. Judges do have the discretion to impose sentences not involving incarceration for most offences.

The public's perception is that judges are lenient.[21] Whether this perception is based on a thorough appraisal of sentencing patterns or simply on a few well-publicized cases, it is widespread and has resulted in community groups engaging in court monitoring; in a few isolated cases there has been picketing of courts to protest leniency in sentencing. Public opinion seems to have had some influence on sentencing patterns, as well as on legislative toughening of penalties.[22]

## Corrections

Correctional facilities in Hawai'i consist of community correctional centers (jails) in each county, mimimum-security prison camps on the slopes of Mauna Loa on the island of Hawai'i (Kulani) and at Waiawa on Oahu, and a medium and a maximum security prison on Oahu. There are male and female juvenile detention facilities on Oahu as well. In late 1989, a little over one-third of the nearly three hundred positions for guards (or adult corrections officers—ACOs) were unfilled, creating problems for the corrections system.[23] These problems exacerbated the chronic overcrowding found in Hawai'i's prisons.[24] This overcrowding has been the subject of a lawsuit by the Hawai'i chapter of the American Civil Liberties Union (ACLU), a suit that was temporarily settled through a written agreement between the Department of Corrections and the ACLU. The difficulty encountered in filling the vacant positions seems to be a function of the working conditions, pay, and, more recently, the low unemployment rate in the state. The prison system suffers from inadequate educational and training programs as well, and there have been repeated allegations of brutality by ACOs. To address these issues more effectively, in 1988 a prison administrator from Colorado was brought in to oversee the corrections system; he resigned early in 1991, having made a number of improvements.

The polyglot ethnic mixture of Hawai'i's population is found also in its corrections system, but not in the same percentages as in the population, as Table 12.3 illustrates:

**Table 12.3: Representation of Ethnic Groups in Hawai'i's Prisons[25]**

| Ethnicity | % in population | % of prisoners |
|---|---|---|
| Black | 2.5 | 5.7 |
| Caucasian | 33.4 | 25.3 |
| Chinese | 6.2 | 1.0 |
| Filipino | 15.2 | 8.1 |
| Hawaiian/part-Haw. | 12.5 | 34.3 |
| Japanese | 22.3 | 4.6 |
| Other, unknown | 7.9 | 21 |

Those overrepresented in the prison population—most notably Hawaiians and part-Hawaiians, who account for one-third of all prisoners—are members of ethnic groups that tend to be lower socioeconomic status. It is not clear what accounts for this disparity, although a similar pattern exists on the mainland for other ethnic groups.

The Department of Corrections is a new entity, created by the legislature in July 1988. Prior to that time, corrections was a division of the Department of Social Services and Housing (DSSH), now the Department of Human Services. Given the problems facing the corrections system it was felt that separation from DSSH and full departmental status might be a positive step. In 1990, the Department of Corrections became part of the Department of Public Safety, an umbrella agency that also includes the sheriff's office. The removal of the sheriffs from the judiciary is an attempt to clean up an office that has been the focus of scandals and allegations of political influence.

The Hawai'i Paroling Authority falls under the Department of Corrections, and is responsible for determining the minimum sentence to be served by incarcerated felons. It consists of three members appointed by the governor for four-year terms from a list of three names for each vacancy, submitted by a panel composed of various professionals and one individual from the general public.[26] Just as judges have been criticized for their leniency in sentencing, so too has the paroling authority for paroling felons who subsequently commit serious crimes. While a few well-publicized cases may be responsible for this perception, there is little question that the parole system is at best imperfect. This problem is not limited to Hawai'i and exists in almost every state in the nation. The overcrowding of the prisons puts considerable pressure on the Paroling Authority. The difficulty of predicting future behavior with any degree of accuracy, together with the heavy case loads of parole officers, makes it almost inevitable that some prisoners will be paroled who will commit additional crimes.

The Hawai'i correctional system is in a period of transition, and the 1990s may prove to be crucial in determining the future of corrections in the State of Hawai'i. Public concern is substantial, but the costs of providing more facilities and personnel are great, and taxes in Hawai'i are already some of the highest in the nation. Some major changes will have to be made, but what they are and how much they will cost is unclear.

Hawai'i has made a relatively rapid transition from a plantation economy and culture to a modern business and tourism-based economy and heterogeneous culture, and such rapid transitions often bring social problems—problems that are now becoming a major factor in the social and political life of the state. There seems little doubt that substantially more resources will have to be devoted to the criminal justice system in Hawai'i, hopefully together with some original thinking, in order to make the state safer for its residents and not jeopardize the all-important tourist industry.

## Notes

1. Section 7 has as its intent a restriction on wiretapping or electronic eavesdropping. The Fourth Amendment to the U.S. Constitution could not have applied to such procedures when it was written and has been applied only through subsequent Supreme Court interpretation. This, of course, depends upon which justices happen to be on the court when a particular case is decided.

2. There are four counties in Hawai'i: Hawai'i, Honolulu (a city and county), Kauai, and Maui. Each county is geographically defined by the island that bears its name, with the exception of Maui County, which includes the islands of Molokai and Lanai, and each county is governed by its own mayor and county council.

3. Hawai'i Revised Statutes, 601–33.

4. The 1990 population of Honolulu was 908,019; the population of Hawai'i County was 135,080, Kauai County, 67,963, and Maui County, 137,190. Figures from Department of Business and Economic Development, DBED, *The Population of Hawaii, 1990*. Honolulu, 1991, p. 13.

5. *Major* means part 1 offenses, a category used by the FBI for its crime statistics; Hawai'i Criminal Justice Data Center figures, *The State of Hawaii Data Book, 1990.* Honolulu, 1990, p. 104. (Hereafter: DATA BOOK).

6. (HRS), 52–35 through 52–37; HRS, 52–32.

7. Hawai'i Criminal Justice Data Center, DATA BOOK, p. 105.

8. Ibid. These offenses are referred to as "part II" crimes, using the FBI designation, and include most misdemeanor offenses, or those crimes punishable by not more than one year in jail.

9. Crime statistics supplied by Hawai'i Criminal Justice Data Center, DATA BOOK, p.107; July 1989 population figures from Hawai'i State Data Center, Department of Business and Economic Development, DATA BOOK, p. 17.

10. *Honolulu Star Bulletin,* July 20, 1988 p. A–14, from estimates provided by the Drug Enforcement Administration (DEA) and the National Organization for the Reform of Marijuana Laws. Attorney General's estimate reported in *Hawai'i Tribune-Herald,* December 27, 1989, p. 1, 8.

11. Ibid. The DEA maintains a helicopter and personnel in the County of Hawai'i and works in conjunction with the county police department in marijuana eradication. The Department of Land and Natural Resources has been involved in a controversial program of spraying marijuana found growing on state land with herbicides and with diesel oil. The Air Force sent two RF–4C reconnaissance aircraft to the island of Hawai'i in November 1989 to photograph suspected marijuana-growing areas with infrared film, presumably to be used by the DEA.

12. *Hawai'i Tribune-Herald,* December 27, 1989, p. 1. Marijuana figures supplied by Hawai'i Criminal Justice Data Center.

13. The Hawai'i Penal Code requires judges who intend to incarcerate a felon to sentence that person to the maximum provided by law. See the discussion on page 210.

14. This right may be waived, although this is not frequently done.

15. HRS, 28–10.5

16. HRS, 802–8, 9.

17. Criminal Justice Data Center figures, DATA BOOK, p. 112.

18. 55 Hawai'i 361. The case involved the strip search of a woman suspected of committing an armed robbery. The woman took a small package from her underwear and gave it to the matron performing the search. The matron opened the package and found some capsules which subsequently proved to be Seconal, a controlled substance. The search would have been

reasonable under the U.S. Constitution, but was held to be unreasonable under the Hawai'i Constitution.

19. State of Hawai'i, Hawai'i Supreme Court, *The Judiciary: Annual Report,* 1986, p. 22. Figures for the number of judges do not include perdiem, or part-time, judges.

20. *Honolulu Advertiser,* Sept. 24, 1989, pp. A–1, A–4. The current governor replaced one supreme court justice who retired in December 1989.

21. James C. F. Wang, *Hawai'i State and Local Politics* (Hilo: Wang Associates, 1982), pp. 508–9. Public perception may be based at least in part on the sentencing of marijuana growers by state and federal judges. The former rarely sentence a first offender to incarceration whereas federal judges normally sentence first offenders who grow marijuana on federal property to at least five years in federal prison.

22. The 1988 legislature increased the penalties on several offenses and further restricted the discretion of judges by making probation not applicable for certain cases. Efforts to reduce leniency in sentencing seem to have been especially successful on Maui, following the granting of probation to a rapist several years ago.

23. *Honolulu Advertiser,* Sept. 23, 1989, p. A–1.

24. The most recent prisoner population figures (for the fiscal year 1987–1988) show a maximum capacity for all adult facilities of 2505 and an average monthly headcount of 2117 (State of Hawai'i, *Department of Corrections Annual Report FY 1988,* Honolulu, 1989, p. 27). The average, however, includes both overcrowded facilities and those not filled to capacity. Transfers to ease overcrowding are not always feasible due to the classifications of the inmates.

25. Prisoner figures from the Department of Corrections; 1990 population figures from U.S. Census, both as reported in the *Sunday Star-Bulletin & Advertiser,* July 7, 1991, p. A6.

26. The panel consists of the chief Justice of the Hawai'i Supreme Court, the director of the Department of Social Services, the head of the Hawai'i Correctional Association, the president of the Hawai'i Bar Association, the head of the Hawai'i Council of Churches, a member of the public appointed by the governor, and the president of the Hawai'i chapter of the National Association of Social Workers. (HRS, 353–61).

# 13

## EDUCATION IN HAWAI'I: BALANCING EQUITY AND PROGRESS

*Thomas W. Bean and Jan Zulich*

At all levels, education in the fiftieth state is engaged in a slowly evolving reform movement. At the heart of this reform is the issue of centralization. In this chapter, we briefly trace the historical roots of Hawai'i's unique centralized public school system. We then compare some of the positive and negative aspects of our public schools to those of other state systems. Higher education in Hawai'i also comes under scrutiny. Throughout the chapter, we compare Hawai'i's system to the social and political foundations that underpin educational change in America. Our central guiding question is: Can Hawai'i's centralized system balance equity and progress?

### Background

Those of us who are preparing teachers in the State of Hawai'i are bound by the policies and procedures of the State of Hawai'i Department of Education (DOE). We adhere to its policies for accrediting our programs, hiring public school faculty, and orchestrating staff development sessions for the teachers in diverse urban and rural communities across the seven-island chain.

Hawai'i is the only state with a single, centralized school system. Serving more than 167,000 students in over 225 schools, Hawai'i's public schools are influenced by the prestatehood practices and beliefs of King Kamehameha III. In 1840, he enacted the first public school laws in Hawai'i, initiating a shift from missionary influence to secularization of the public school system. Kamehameha mandated English, rather than Hawaiian, as the language of instruction. These early efforts to provide equal educational opportunity for all students fueled the rationale for Hawai'i's centralization. By 1898 when Hawai'i was annexed to the United States, Hawai'i's system was regarded by the United States Congressional Subcommittee on Education as equal to mainland systems of education.[1]

Today, per pupil funding allocations average $3000 per year, comparable to many urban and suburban mainland districts. Teacher-to-student ratios are similar to mainland classrooms, with one teacher for twenty-six students. Hawai'i spent $475 per pupil in 1986 and ranked fiftieth in the nation, while Minnesota, a state that is number one in successfully graduating high school students, ranked 5th, with $745 per pupil.[2]

Hawai'i's classrooms are truly multicultural. The student population is comprised of 29 percent Caucasian, 23 percent Japanese, 17 percent Hawaiian, and 11 percent Filipino. In addition, there are 5 percent Chinese, 5 percent Puerto Rican, 2 percent Black, 1 percent Korean, 1 percent Samoan, and 10.5 percent students of mixed ethnicity. In contrast to Hawai'i's students, 60 percent of Hawai'i's nine thousand teachers are Japanese-American.[3]

When Japanese immigrants came to Hawai'i over a hundred years ago as plantation laborers, they adhered to the cultural emphasis of *katei kyoiku,* the value of family education.[4] Because of this strong emphasis on education and a desire for economic success, Hawai'i's Japanese-Americans attained middle-class standing, many within the teaching profession, in a single generation.

Presently, statewide efforts to recruit minority teachers from underrepresented groups are in progress. For example, the recent governor's task force on Filipino representation in teaching found that only five percent of the state's teachers are of Filipino ancestry, yet eleven percent of Hawai'i's students are Filipino.[5] In addition, thirty-nine percent of the nonnative English-speaking students in public schools speak either Ilokano or Tagalog, both of which are Filipino languages. Teachers arriving in Hawai'i who have successfully achieved certification in the Philippines must pass the National Teachers Examination, a standardized test required for certification in Hawai'i and other states. Because this test intimidates many nonnative speakers of English, intensive test-taking workshops are offered to assist these experienced teachers in the certification process. It is too early to gauge the impact of these task force efforts on increasing the representation of Filipino teachers in Hawai'i's classrooms.

Unlike other states, Hawai'i does not support its schools through property taxes. Schools are supported by general revenues of the state, special state funds, and federal grants. The state legislature has the power to levy taxes, placing control of educational finance within the centralized biennial budget process. The legislature appropriates revenues and the governor approves fiscal expenditures for the public schools. This means, then, that numerous education initiatives compete in the complex political arena of the legislative process. A bill must run the gauntlet of the house and senate education committees, multiple hearings, and conference committee compromises before it can be signed into law, or vetoed if the governor so chooses.[6] Thus, major reform efforts became Sisyphian labors. Their initiation is controlled by the lengthy and volatile legislative process, and if approved, further shepherded by the Department of Education. Over the past few years, state budget surpluses have been mounting in an expanding economy, and the economic and political climate is ideal for educational reform. Still, the processes available to initiate and implement needed reforms remain cumbersome at best.

The statewide system is governed by a single Board of Education (BOE) consisting of a thirteen-member panel elected by citizens for four-year terms. The board appoints a state superintendent who also serves on the governor's cabinet. District superintendents appointed by the state superintendent administer the seven school districts, some including schools on more than one island. A district school advisory council (SAC) serves each district. The governor appoints council members, further centralizing what might be a powerful local voice in school-based reform. These SAC's advise the Board of Education and district superintendent about community concerns. In the community surrounding each school, parent-community networking centers attempt to integrate school and community goals. Unlike locally controlled school boards across many mainland communities, these advisory groups have little control over school-based issues.

Hawai'i schools, like those in the mainland, are accredited by the Western Association of Schools and Colleges. Island schools pursue eight curricular objectives set forth by the DOE. These objectives focus on enhancing basic skills, self-concept, decision making, independence in learning, physical and emotional health, career development, beliefs and values, and sensitivity and creativity. Students are required to attend school between the ages of six and eighteen for 176 days each year. High school graduation requires twenty credits in the areas of English, social studies, math, science, physical education, health, guidance, and electives. In addition, students must pass the fifteen required skills in the Hawai'i State Test of Essential Competencies. On the Sixth Annual State Education

Performance Chart, Hawai'i was about average in the number of students who graduated from high school: the national average graduation rate is 71.6 percent and Hawai'i successfully graduated 70.8 percent, a ranking of thirty-third in the nation.[7] In comparison, Minnesota ranked first with a 90.6 percent graduation rate while California graduated 55.5 percent of its high school students. Clearly, there is room for improvement in Hawai'i's schools. In a small community with a local school board, change may occur quickly. However, in a large centralized system spanning schools on seven islands, change occurs slowly. Centralization and the development of bureaucratic structures is a more common feature of contemporary education than we might care to acknowledge.

## Control of Public Education

There has been a steady expansion of bureaucratic structures that disperse decision making and control across a number of groups, including school boards and politicians.[8] As schools and districts have become consolidated, teachers and parents find themselves increasingly distant from policy decisions that affect them. While the Hawai'i Board of Education is, unlike many state boards, elected rather than appointed by the governor, even elected boards are limited in their decision-making power. The increasing intervention of state and federal mandates for categorical aid programs, additional regulation in the form of court decisions related to desegregation, and teacher union contract negotiations, all conspire to limit the influence of boards of education. However, there is wide variation across the country in state support of schools and the relative influence of boards, the legislature, and various grass roots interest groups. For example, in a decentralized system like New Hampshire's, the state's share of education support is only 8.5 percent. Hence, its influence over local issues is likely to be negligible. In contrast, Hawai'i state government provides 90 percent of the school funding and thus has substantial control over educational policy making. The Hawai'i State Superintendent of Education, appointed by the Board of Education, maintains a close working relationship with the legislature, governor, and the board.

### The Hawai'i Plan

A study of Hawai'i schools conducted by Berman-Weiler and Associates confirmed much of what Hawai'i's parents, teachers, and children have known for a long time: Our centralized system is too "top-down," offering limited opportunities for teacher, parent, and community "grass roots" involvement in curricular issues.[9] Similarly, in a Carnegie Foundation study of teacher involvement in decision making, Hawai'i teachers felt they were not very involved in shaping the curriculum. For example, in terms of selecting new teachers, 9 percent claimed they were involved while 91 percent asserted they were not. In the area of school budget decisions, 57 percent felt involved while 43 percent did not.[10] These figures were comparable to the perceptions of other teachers across the country. If Hawai'i's recent effort to institute community-and school-based management is successful and produces follow-up studies, we should expect to see changes in these perceptions of teacher powerlessness in the next few years.

In addition to charting well-known problems in Hawai'i's schools, the Berman-Weiler report offered some recommendations. Among those related to control of education, eight were advanced, some of which are fairly radical in light of the current system. The authors recommended: (1) instituting locally elected school boards; (2) having individual schools determine their curricular programs and select teachers; (3) establishing a measure of accountability by having the DOE provide school "report cards" to parents; (4) providing DOE technical assistance to schools, especially those that failed to perform well on the school report card measure; (5) reconstituting the DOE to take a central role in research and development; (6) making the BOE members partially elected and partially appointed; (7) having the BOE appoint the superintendent; and (8) allowing parents to select school sites.

The one recommendation that enjoyed a great ground swell of support from various constituencies was adopted, and will be phased in over the next few years is the establishment of community-and school-based management. The community-school–based management recommendation has now been signed into law by the governor into law. We will consider its impact on our centralized system next.

## School-and Community-Based Management

This particular reform gives some decision-making functions to the individual schools. Ironically, it is structured in such a way that decentralization in curricular decision making is accomplished through the centralized approval of the DOE and BOE. In essence, the board determines the system-wide budget and overall goals that schools must achieve. But any school that develops an individual plan for meeting these goals and allocating resources may apply to the BOE for a waiver from certain administrative rules and collective bargaining provisions that might impede the new program.[11] It is argued that each community of parents, faculty, and students will feel a strong sense of ownership in the creative solutions they devise for their school's problems. In addition, individual schools are likely to develop particular strengths in science and technology, the arts, and other curricular areas. Parents will want the freedom to enroll their children in a particular school because of its unique strengths. School choice, a Berman-Weiler recommendation not adopted by the legislature, is directly related to the development of community-and school-based management.

*School Choice and Curricular Reform*

Currently, the major route to school choice for parents and students in Hawai'i is through district exemptions, essentially waivers for parents enrolling their children in schools outside their normal district boundaries. During the 1988–1989 school year, 13,563 exemptions were granted. Fully 12,519, or 93 percent, were granted for noncurricular reasons such as child care, convenience to grandparents, or job location. Only 1,044, or 7 percent were related to a special curricular offering at the selected school.[12] These are not very surprising statistics. In addition, urban traffic and rural distances mitigate against parents opting for a school that is a major inconvenience to attend, even if it features special offerings not attainable elsewhere. Finally, in Hawai'i, neighborhood ties are often quite strong and bolstered by extracurricular activities linked to the neighborhood school.

Historically in Hawai'i, school choice has centered on the many private schools available. Private schools in Hawai'i provide an option for parents able to afford their generally high cost. About seventeen percent of Hawai'i's children attend some 150 private schools.[13] The demand for existing spaces far exceeds availability, indicating increasing pressure for school choice. For example, in 1989 Punahou had 150 kindergarten spaces available and 555 applicants. At the junior high level, 475 applicants competed for 110 seventh grade slots.

In our judgment, solid school-based management programs will form a good foundation for other reforms that will influence individual classrooms and students. If schools truly institute excellent magnet programs in such areas as the arts, science, and technology, some of the hundreds of applicants to the state's private schools may opt for a potentially excellent public school.

## Control of Public Education in the Future

In a recent analysis of education reform in the United States, Chris Pipho described our nationally diverse, "crazy quilt" system as one that must certainly seem bizarre to foreign visitors.[14] For example, New York has thirty-two local school boards, while Chicago is shifting to local school councils consisting of six parents, two teachers, a principal, and two community members in each of 595 school sites. These school councils are expected to develop plans for school improvement. Thus, while centralization has been the norm for Hawai'i, even systems that we would regard as decentralized are subdividing further in the interest of local involvement. Just how far will Hawai'i be willing to go to balance equity and diversity? In our somewhat skeptical view, we see a number of social, economic, and political factors that support a cautious appraisal of change in Hawai'i's centralized system.

The perception of education as an experience that prepares future citizens for advancement up the economic and social ladder has deep roots in the success of many immigrant groups in Hawai'i. The success of our centralized system in producing leading citizens from both urban areas and small plantation towns demonstrates the value of an interest in equal opportunity.[15] Moreover, neighborhood schools, especially in the rural areas, are the center of attention for sports and related social events. Families are not anxious to have their children travel either long distances or through the maze of urban traffic to leave the neighborhood setting under the present system. Whether they would do so if the opportunity for a superior educational experience were available in a magnet school some distance away remains uncertain. In addition, parental involvement in school-based management may be dominated by an elite group of parents who are not working multiple jobs to cope with our high cost of living.

Economic factors also support the continuance of a centralized system. Our schools are dispersed across seven islands in the chain. Were we to embrace local school boards similar to those on the mainland, and a system of property tax collection to fund local schools, inequities in resources would become more pronounced. Moreover, the island economy is vulnerable to downturns in discretionary spending related to tourism and to shifts in military spending and foreign investment. If, or when, a recession occurs, our current budget surplus will diminish. Efforts to insure an equitable distribution of schools funds rests with the Board of Education rather than with small community school boards that may be ill prepared to cope with shifts in our economic wellbeing.

Political forces, especially the growing interest on the part of the governor in playing a high profile role in education reform, further serve to continue a centralized system. The entrenched legislative process is unlikely to change in the near future. The Department of Education's role as the broker for federal categorical aid programs, and an increasing public tendency toward litigation in conflict resolution, suggests a growing rather than diminishing bureaucracy.

Hawai'i's 1989 legislative session, in which some education reforms were signed into law, indicates the degree to which the state is likely to forgo centralized control. Basically, the legislature and governor embraced school-based management, carefully monitored by the centralized Board of Education. They also approved the development of early childhood education programs and a special school facilities fund to generate eight hundred million dollars over ten years to upgrade badly deteriorated schools and add new buildings. Unarguably, these are important reforms that are likely to have a real impact on Hawai'i students and teachers. Will subsequent legislative sessions move toward true decentralization with elected local school boards? In our view, for the social, economic, and political reasons we mentioned earlier, this is highly unlikely. Hawai'i is making small, cautious changes to nudge public schools into greater decentralization while retaining an emphasis on educational opportunity for all its citizens.

This same focal point of how best to balance equity and progress can be applied to an analysis of the beleaguered university system. There are some strong parallels between public school efforts to change a centralized governing body and the University of Hawai'i campuses as they struggle to compete for a decreasing number of faculty and on increasingly diverse student body.

## Background on the University of Hawai'i

The University of Hawai'i system includes a main campus in the Manoa Valley area of Honolulu which serves over 20,000 students.

The sprawling Manoa campus is regarded as a research institution in the Carnegie Foundation's classification scheme for more than thirty-three hundred institutions of higher education.[16] Universities within this category typically generate over 33.5 million dollars in research grants and produce over fifty doctoral level graduates each year. The University of Hawai'i system places special emphasis on oceanography, volcanology, astronomy, and cross-cultural studies. Two smaller campuses serve students primarily at the undergraduate level. The University of Hawai'i at Hilo has a population of 3,750 students. Recently, this campus began offering a postbaccalaureate professional certificate for teachers. Its sister institution, the University of Hawai'i at West Oahu, currently serves 500 upper-division students. However, this suburban area is expected to grow dramatically to become Honolulu's second city. In addition, the statewide university system also includes seven community colleges. These community colleges serve students on Oahu as well as on the outer islands of Maui, Hawai'i, and Kauai. Their curriculum encompasses both vocational programs and general education courses that may be transferred to the University of Hawai'i system.

The University of Hawai'i student population, like that across the country, is increasingly nontraditional.[17] Nontraditional students are defined as twenty-five years old or older, married or divorced, in single-parenting roles, and employed at least part-time. In Hawai'i's university system, women comprise over fifty-five percent of the student population. Fully forty-five percent are part-time students seeking their degrees in evening and weekend courses. They are an average of 26.2 years old and view child care as a critical support service. The Manoa campus is only able to serve 104 children; Hilo serves just twenty in a Head Start program. The issue of child care is expected to continue heating up in future legislative sessions. An extensive state-funded after-school program now serves families.

## Control of Higher Education

The University of Hawai'i system is governed by a single board of regents based in Honolulu and appointed by the governor, a university president on the Manoa campus appointed by the board, and a chancellor serving both the University of Hawai'i at Hilo and the University of Hawai'i at West Oahu. The chancellor reports to the president of the Manoa campus. In addition, another chancellor oversees the community colleges, and provosts govern the individual campus sites.

Thus, as in Hawai'i's public schools, the university system is highly centralized and its flow of resources is intimately linked to the political climate of the legislature. In recent years the university system, particularly the University of Hawai'i at Hilo, has experienced budget shortfalls and difficulty in recruiting and retaining faculty, resulting in a pervasive desire to tackle these problems and move ahead.

Although the University of Hawai'i at Manoa is, in the Carnegie Foundation's system, a premier Research I university, it lacks the autonomy characteristic of similar institutions on the mainland. About a third of the professoriate nationwide teach and conduct research in major institutions such as the University of California at Berkeley, where the pursuit of knowledge is paramount.[18] Faculty enjoy a substantial amount of autonomy, carrying out their work in decentralized colleges or schools with little interference from top-down administrative mandates. In contrast, another third of the professoriate can be found in comprehensive universities where unionization is a common feature designed to counter what faculty perceive as a capricious, top-down managerial style. Adequate travel money, computers and other resources are available sporadically, and feelings of inertia and powerlessness prevail. At present, the University of Hawai'i system and its faculty union, the University of Hawai'i Professional Assembly, are grappling with just these issues. If it is to become a truly great university system, faculty recruitment, retention, and development must receive more support.

Some would argue that greater autonomy for individual campuses is the solution to the tug of war for resources that characterizes legislative sessions. For example, Senator Malama Solomon, Chair of the Senate Higher Education Committee, proposed that the University of Hawai'i at Hilo have its own president who would report to a separate board of regents for the campus.[19] Recently, Ernest L. Boyer, President of the Carnegie Foundation for the Advancement of Teaching, studied the university governance issue in Hawai'i. In contrast to Senator Solomon's proposal, Boyer recommended maintaining a single board of regents, viewing separate boards as unnecessary duplication of functions.[20] Moreover, he argued that separate boards would result in isolated and conflicting agendas. Boyer further recommended standardizing course offerings across the three campuses and instituting public "Regents Forums" where nonagenda items could be brought to the board's attention.

The issue of who controls higher education in Hawai'i, the governor, the legislature, a single board or multiple boards, the president or the faculty, will continue to be a hot political issue for the time being. However, as in our analysis of public school control in the future, we can advance some tentative predictions for higher education in Hawai'i.

## Control of Higher Education in the Future

Decision making in the university system parallels our characterization of the public schools. Analyst Robert Birnbaum finds that the elements of power and control in universities are increasingly dispersed across the faculty, who concern themselves with curricular and personnel issues, and the president, the chancellors, and board of regents who focus on budgetary issues. As the University of Hawai'i system and other systems across the country grow in size, professional administrators replace rotating faculty administrators, further separating faculty from many of the decisions that affect them. Faculty then respond to this centralization of control by centralizing their own participation in the form of collective bargaining which, in Birnbaum's view, "ritualizes disruptive conflict."[21]

An unfortunate byproduct of centralization is a growing sense of powerlessness on the part of campus administrators, faculty, and students. In Birnbaum's view, the most startling realization for faculty and administrators is the recognition that not only individuals at lower levels have limited ability to exert influence upward, but that those higher in the university organization also exert little upward influence. In such a system, university presidents may feel more like middle managers than campus leaders. A single centralized board of regents may have little time to become familiar with multiple campuses.

Given these undesirable features of centralization and the growing awareness that the University of Hawai'i system is lagging behind other multiple-campus systems across the country, why does Hawai'i insist on maintaining this arrangement?

Birnbaum argues that centralized models of decision making in higher education subscribe to a trade off in which the center provides needed services to the various campuses in exchange for approval and compliance. Faculty in the University of Hawai'i system have tacitly accepted this arrangement for many years. In our analysis, this overly centralized system is no longer serving Hawai'i's university students at the level they deserve. The university system needs its own "Hawai'i Plan" to break the cycle of inertia. While the faculty union grapples with issues related to salaries and benefits, many of the infrastructure issues remain. Problems of deferred maintenance, inadequate secretarial support, limited and sometimes nonexistent faculty travel budgets, limited faculty development programs, and other infrastructure problems pervade our campuses. Although a Research I university, the University of Hawai'i shares many of the features of lesser institutions. To what extent is this likely to change?

As we suggested in our discussion of modest tinkering within the public schools, change is a laborious process in a centralized system. It seems unlikely that the forces influencing decision making in the centralized university system will suddenly embrace separate boards for individual campuses, or any other radical reforms. Attempts at equitable distribution of resources are more difficult to achieve in the university environment where market forces related to a shortage of business, computer science, and engineering faculty produce inequities in salaries. A merit system might help balance these inequities, but developing faculty-supported criteria for merit can take years. Like the school system, the university must vie for resources in the biennial legislative arena. The university system has less clout because attendance is a matter of choice. Public schools exert greater voter influence because of their compulsory nature as well as their greater visibility to a larger segment of the community. They strive for a conservative posture that engenders trust and confidence. Conversely, universities seek to be on the cutting edge of knowledge, challenging the status quo, questioning and prodding conventional wisdom. The very behaviors that are rewarded in the university milieu are sometimes viewed as unacceptable within the surrounding community.

Finally, leadership within Hawai'i's university system is now, as in many centralized systems on the mainland, largely symbolic. In reality, decisions that influence progress in the system are made very slowly within a multilayered, legal-rational system that buffers individuals from criticism and litigation. Although this system is, on the surface, quite cumbersome, progress is not impossible to achieve. Efforts to improve recruitment and retention within the university system are underway. University of Hawai'i President Simone ranked this issue as his number one priority for the near future. Faculty salaries at the University of Hawai'i at Manoa rank in the fortieth percentile for comparable universities on the mainland.[22] This harsh reality, coupled with major infrastructure problems and Hawai'i's high cost of living, have caused an exodus of faculty over the past few years—faculty the system wanted to retain. However, the public's desire for educational reform should have some positive impact on the University of Hawai'i system. Otherwise, in the case of the education program at the university, we will be in the ironic position of preparing teachers in a university environment that is inferior to that of the public schools.

In summary, both the centralized public school and university systems are likely to retain their present governance structure in the future. Budgetary issues will remain tied to the biennial legislative process with an emphasis on maintaining equity. Faculty, administrators, parents, and students will be able to nudge the system toward change through school-based management in the public schools and collective bargaining in the university. Will we be able to achieve a level of progress comparable to that of similar systems on the mainland? That remains to be seen.

## Notes

1. Jan Zulich, "Hawai'i's School System Is One of a Kind," *Phi Delta Kappan* 70 (7), (March 1989), p. 546.

2. Thomas Kaser, "How Berman Report Changed Public Schools in Minnesota," *The Honolulu Advertiser,* March 19, 1989, p. A–6.

3. Zulich, "Hawai'i's School System," p. 546.

4. Ibid.

5. *Pamantasan: Report of the University of Hawai'i Task Force on Filipinos* (Honolulu: University of Hawai'i at Manoa, Spring 1988), p. 3.

6. Jerry Burris, "The Making of a Law—Hawai'i Style," *The Honolulu Advertiser,* February 13, 1989, p. A–6.

7. Thomas Kaser, "Isle Passed (or Failed) School Study," *The Honolulu Advertiser,* May 4, 1989, p. B–1.

8. Joel Spring, *American Education: An Introduction to Social and Political Aspects,* (New York: Longman, 1989), p. 172.

9. Paul Berman, Jo Ann Izu, Robert McClelland, and Patricia Stone, *The Hawai'i Plan: Educational Excellence for the Pacific Era* (Honolulu: Berman Weiler Associates, 1988), p. 4.

10. Ernest L. Boyer, *Teacher Involvement in Decisionmaking: A State-by-State Profile* (The Carnegie Foundation for the Advancement of Teaching, Princeton, N.J.: 1988), p. 9.

11. *Hawai'i's Schools and You: School/Community-Based Management* (Honolulu: Hawai'i State Department of Education, 1989), p. 3.

12. Thomas Kaser, "School "Choice" Plans Not Choice, Expert Says," *The Honolulu Advertiser,* May 21, 1989, p. A–3.

13. Thomas Kaser, "Percentage in Private Schools Depends on Who Gets Counted," *The Honolulu Advertiser,* April 14, 1989, p. A–6.

14. Chris Pipho, "Sorting Out Local Control," *Phi Delta Kappan* (February, 1989), pp. 430–431.

15. Zulich, "Hawai'i's School System," p. 546.

16. "Carnegie Foundation's Classifications of More Than 3,300 Institutions of Higher Education," *The Chronicle of Higher Education,* July 8, 1987, p. 22.

17. Jim Borg, "Career Women Are UH's New Boom," *The Honolulu Advertiser,* February 7, 1989, p. D–3.

18. Burton R. Clark, "The Academic Life: Small Worlds, Different Worlds," *Educational Researcher* (June 1989), p. 4.

19. Dave Smith, "Solomon's Fight With UH Heats Up," *Hawai'i Tribune Herald,* March 19, 1989, p. 8.

20. Thomas Kaser, "Some UH Changes Are Urged," *The Honolulu Advertiser,* April 5, 1989, p. A–11.

21. Robert Birnbaum, *How Colleges Work: The Cybernetics of Academic Organization and Leadership* (San Francisco: Jossey-Bass, 1988), p. 16.

22. Albert J. Simone, *UH President's Report,* April 4, 1989, p. 1.

# 14

## HAWAIIAN LABOR:
## THE SOCIAL RELATIONS OF PRODUCTION

*Edward D. Beechert*

### Background

Hawai'i's unique political economy has created a labor history equally distinct from that of mainland agriculture and the other plantation economies of the Pacific. The Europeans arrived in Hawai'i at a critical juncture in a struggle for supremacy among the chiefs. Western technology and tactics were quickly adopted by the Hawaiian chiefs, transforming both the nature of the struggle and altering the traditional Polynesian culture and economy. The outcome was a system based vaguely on the Hawaiian traditional political system, converted to an oligarchical aristocracy. Land had been held by the lesser chiefs, at the direction of the high chief. Power struggles had little impact on the commoner until the scale of warfare demanded larger forces and the bloodshed escalated the costs. The fragile rhythms of the Hawaiian subsistence system were badly disrupted. The adoption of a system of production for wealth rather than community maintenance was the initial step in reducing the *maka'ainana* (commoners) to a proletarian status.

A significant step in that process was the development of the sandalwood trade. On the death of Kamehameha in 1819, there were no further restraints on the chiefs, who promptly used their traditional chiefly powers to gather and sell sandalwood for their personal profit.[1] The political economy was further altered in 1825, on the death of Kamehameha II (Liholiho). The chiefs agreed on the succession of his son under a regency and further proclaimed that land would not be redistributed, but would remain the heritable property of the lesser chiefs. This was the first step in the long march toward the privatization of property. In succeeding years, further steps toward fee simple ownership were taken. Some effort was made to protect the commoners' right to land, but these were largely ineffective.

The oligarchical system resulting from this early experience facilitated the rapid transfer of effective control to the newly arrived mercantile class. The Hawaiian commoner was effectively out of the political system.[2]

## The Imported Economy

The rapid decimation of the Hawaiian population from epidemic diseases created a problem for those looking to development of Hawaiian resources. To the western eye, Hawai'i was vastly underdeveloped. Traditional Hawaiian agriculture and marine resources concentrated land development in suitable areas, leaving large areas untouched. Both English and American arrivals brought with them ideas derived from the traditional plantation systems of the Caribbean and the United States. Fortunately for the Hawaiians, rivalry between the major powers, England, United States, and France, served to prevent the annexation by one of these imperial actors in the early stages of Hawai'i's experience with the outside world.

The development of maritime activities was based upon Hawai'i's location in the Pacific. Partly because of Spanish hostility and lack of resources on the Pacific coast, captains making the transit into the Pacific via Cape Horn had few choices other than to make for Hawai'i to refurbish and replenish their ships. From 1821, the discovery of the northern whaling grounds brought New England ships and merchants in large numbers. These merchants formed the nucleus of the factoring system which in later years emerged to dominate the sugar industry. The financial, marketing, and supply services led directly to control of the individual plantation companies. Added to that influence was the arrival after 1820 of the New England missionaries to convert the Hawaiians to Christianity.

Both groups sought, for different reasons, to develop Hawaiian resources. The missionaries were appalled at what seemed to them an evil indolence on the part of the Hawaiian commoner. In traditional Hawaiian society, work was performed for the maintenance of the clan and the community. There was no concept of wealth or its accumulation. Work as an expression of virtue or salvation was a new, foreign idea: one largely rejected by the Hawaiian people. The mercantile community realized that the vast tracts of land, once they were available, would require large amounts of labor. Their thinking ran along traditional plantation lines: coffee, cotton, sugar, and even silk and rubber were envisioned as potential crops. For several reasons, there were obstacles in the way of such development. Slavery was out of the question. The New England missionaries were avid abolitionists at home and fervent in their opposition to such ideas in Hawai'i. The use of Asian sources for a supply of labor was hedged with problems of international rivalry and the hostility of the Hawaiian chiefs.

The question of Hawaiian sovereignty was always a delicate one. The rapid decline of the Hawaiian population placed that sovereignty in jeopardy, leading the successors to Kamehameha to search for new population sources which could also furnish the expected needs for labor. The "Labor Question," as it came to be known, remained in one form or another until the end of immigration, which effectively occurred in 1934.


## The Plantation Economy

The Hawaiian commoner proved to be more resistant than his chiefs to Western ways. Despite vigorous efforts to introduce the concept of wage labor and a cash economy, the Hawaiians were selective in their response. Around the port cities, Hawaiians quickly acquired the reputation of demanding high wages. The rural people remained largely out of the emerging economy when possible. The imposition of a head tax (payable in cash) in 1842 reduced that possibility considerably. But even the tax still did not produce the volume of labor necessary for large-scale agriculture.

The first commercial sugar plantation at Koloa, Kauai, in 1835, obtained its labor from local chiefs who commandeered their subjects. This was ineffective and was replaced with a wage paid in scrip. The abuses connected with this system produced a strike by the Hawaiians in 1841. Given the small scale and uncertainties of the fledgling plantations, the scarcity of labor did not present any great difficulties despite the constant discussion of the importance of securing "cheap, docile" labor.

A combination of the reluctance of Hawaiians to submit to the low wage expectations of would-be developers, the rapid decline in their numbers, and the ambitious plans to develop the land contributed to the creation of a liberal, Western-style constitution in 1850 to facilitate economic development. This was accompanied by an indenture law, modeled on the laws of New York and Massachusetts for apprentices and the master-servant relationship. Although similar to other indenture laws, this law was tempered by the prohibition in the constitution of Hawai'i of involuntary servitude and debt peonage, and extended to imported workers the full legal rights of citizens. In theory, at least, the indentured worker enjoyed legal protection from the abuses characteristic of other plantation economies.[3]

The uneven development of the sugar industry between 1850 and the outbreak of the American Civil War in 1861 saw very few Chinese workers imported to Hawai'i. Hawaiians continued to make up the basic work force until the expansion of planting exceeded the number of Hawaiians available. The economy of Hawai'i at this point was oriented toward the whaling industry and the supplying of ships with provisions.

When the Reciprocity Treaty of 1876 brought Hawaiian sugar into the U.S. tariff subsidy, plantation acreage multiplied and the numbers of imported workers rose rapidly, bringing into play new forces of opposition. The large numbers of Chinese imported during the 1870s gave rise to an anti-Asian movement in Honolulu and the nonplantation community. Rising anti-Chinese sentiments in Hawai'i and the U.S. mainland forced the search for non-Asian labor supplies. Portuguese workers and smaller numbers of other Europeans were added to the workforce. The Hawaiian legislature, nominally controlled by Hawaiians, was a center of anti-Asian labor agitation. This facade of Hawaiian sovereignty, reinforced by the dependence on the U.S. market for sugar, limited the power of the planter class. Attempts of the legislature to restrict Chinese labor recruiting and to cut off the subsidy of the U.S. tariff led to a drastic change in Hawai'i's government. In 1887, a new constitution was forced on the king by the planters and their threat of armed revolt. The new document severely restricted the electorate and limited the power of the king. Despite these steps, the legislature amended the Masters and Servants Act several times between 1850 and the overthrow of the monarchy in 1893, working to loosen the penal aspects and to make the indenture less onerous.

This tendency was sharply reversed upon the overthrow of the queen and the establishment of the republic. Ruling by executive committee decree, the republic quickly reduced the indenture to a condition of servitude, restricting imported workers to plantation work on threat of deportation. The republic accelerated the flow of Chinese and Japanese workers, hoping to establish a sufficiently large work force before annexation would cut off the Chinese source.[4] Given the rate of expansion of the sugar acreage and the high rate at which indentured workers left the industry, Hawai'i planters faced a continual shortage of workers, resulting in a higher wage scale than was thought desirable. The difficulty of maintaining a reserve pool of workers was never satisfactorily resolved before annexation dramatically altered the pattern.

## Annexation and Federal Law

Annexation to the United States had been a goal of the business community for many years. A treaty had been negotiated in 1854 with Kamehameha IV, who died before the final details were completed. Although England and France toyed with annexation of Hawai'i on several occasions, U.S. interests in Hawai'i were decisive in preventing the completion of the process. The inescapable fact that the West Coast was the only feasible market for Hawaiian sugar conditioned the relationship of Hawai'i to the mainland. The certain loss of Chinese labor sources, and the likely loss of Japanese workers, either from changes in Japanese government attitudes or the rising resentment of the Pacific coast states to Japanese emigration had to be weighed against access to the market. When the McKinley Tariff of 1890 removed the sugar subsidy, in effect abrogating the Reciprocity Treaty, Hawai'i suffered a severe depression. The importance of becoming a territory of the U.S. was hammered home. The uncertainty of labor supplies meant only a threat of higher wages; the loss of the subsidy, roughly two cents per pound of raw sugar, was an economic reality.[5]

The Organic Act of 1900, which created the Territory of Hawai'i, opened up the opportunity for worker resistance. Shifting from individual and small-group responses to abuses, the workers began immediately to organize themselves and present demands backed by the threat of strikes. Although somewhat more than half of the sugar workers were free day workers upon annexation, the presence of the indentured work force had limited worker resistance. This forced a dramatic change in the structure of the political economy of the plantation system. The Hawaiian Sugar Planters' Association (HSPA), was created in 1895 to deal more effectively with the problems created by the overthrow of the Hawaiian monarchy and the potential relationship with the U.S. Congress. It now was concerned with organizing itself to deal with the threat of organized labor.

The struggle for control of the job site was fought vigorously from 1900 forward. Increasingly large-scale strikes by Japanese workers culminated in the strike of 1909. With Japanese immigration severely restricted by the Root-Takahara Agreement of 1907, the planters faced even greater difficulties in maintaining a pool of labor sufficiently large to hold down wage demands.

The Japanese Higher Wages Association of 1909, a combination of urban intellectuals and plantation workers, although largely unsuccessful in their strike of Oahu plantations, nonetheless achieved a degree of unity of Japanese workers on all sugar plantations, and inflicted considerable damage on Oahu production. They also forced significant changes in the wage structure and plantation social welfare after the strike.

The impact of the strike was most evident in the search for new supplies of labor. Efforts to use Puerto Rican workers in 1900 had been costly and stimulated effective opposition in Puerto Rico. The pacification of the Philippines by 1909 opened the door to that possibility. The Philippines were the last resort of the beleaguered sugar industry. Despite the many theories of racial control of the work force, of using segregation and ethnic rivalries to divide workers, little action was taken in the face of the chronic shortage of workers. The strikes of 1909 and 1920 clearly demonstrated the inability to produce efficiently by using scab labor. The skill of the experienced plantation worker was not easily replaced.

Each new level of organization by the workers and the planters moved the labor relations of Hawai'i closer to the mainland experience. The radicalism of the early twentieth-century labor movement which so frightened the American power structure had its counterpart in Hawai'i. Repressive labor legislation designed to control labor, such as criminal syndicalism laws, antipicketing and antiriot statutes, and a severe criminal trespass law, overlaid with a program of welfare capitalism, shaped and blunted labor's response. But the combination was unable to contain the workers' struggle for dignity and better working conditions. The heyday of welfare capitalism, the decade of the 1920s, saw a massive investment in community-building programs designed to focus the loyalty of the plantation worker to the company. The basic failure of such programs was vividly illustrated in the strike of 1924. Filipino workers, over a period of eight months, struck twenty-three of the forty-five plantations. Ill planned, conducted with little or no leadership, the strike, like that of 1920, was technically lost. The impact on the industry, however, was sharp. Losses to the industry exceeded all expectations. Losses were particularly severe on plantations that were not struck, as incoming labor supplies were diverted to the struck plantations, forcing sharp cutbacks in production.[6]

## Welfare Capitalism

Shocked by the impact of the seemingly futile strike, the industry engaged an industrial survey firm to explore the failure of the welfare program and restructuring of the work force which had taken place after the 1920 strike. The firm quickly identified one of the principal causes of worker dissatisfaction: incompetent and untrained supervisors using tactics which were dubious with unfree workers and disastrous with a mobile, free labor force. It was recommended that meaningless twelve-hour shifts in the mills should be replaced with three eight hour shifts. But plantation camp amenities were still inadequate, and better mechanization was needed to relieve some of the drudgery of field work.

Except for the mechanization proposals, the report was rejected by the industry as radical and unworkable. Efforts were continually made to reduce labor costs through mechanization. Beginning in 1906, this effort focused on loading, transport, and cultivation.[7]

A factor common to sugar production in the Pacific area was the steady restriction and elimination of immigrant labor supplies, which began in mid-nineteenth century and picked up strength until the final elimination of indentured labor systems in English possessions in 1914. Racist sentiments and the rising cost of Melanesian labor had transformed the Australian sugar industry from a plantation economy to small-holder farming, with government-operated mills. Elsewhere, producers were forced to deal with the upward pressure on wages created by this constriction. In Hawai'i a combination of mechanization and a paternalistic welfare system was used to maintain a stable, low-wage plantation system.

The colonial status of the Philippines was a key element in this effort. Rising opposition to Filipino labor in the western United States brought congressional efforts in 1928 to eliminate this source of labor. Eventually this goal was reached in the Philippine Independence Bill of 1934 which immediately cut off the Filipino's status as an American national. This left Hawai'i's plantations only citizen labor for its production forces—a condition always before held to be impossible for any plantation economy.[8]

## Urban Labor

The urban labor force of Hawai'i, minute by comparison, was nonetheless molded by the plantation experience. The economic expansion touched off by annexation brought mainland trade unions with it. The development of naval facilities at Pearl Harbor entrenched a small work force of skilled craftsmen who brought their mainland organizations with them. Shortly after annexation, Honolulu had a Central Labor Council, made up of American Federation of Labor craft unions.

The fragility of the economic expansion, the small size of the urban workforce, and the steady stream of workers leaving the plantation inhibited successful labor organizing. The AFL unions all barred Asians from membership. A situation soon developed in which skilled Asian craftsmen dominated the construction industries and reduced the Caucasian-only unions to a low level.

Just as their mainland counterparts declined in the decade of the 1920s, so did the urban union workforce in Hawai'i. The Honolulu Central Labor Council surrendered its charter in 1928 when the per capita payments of the member organizations fell below the subsistence line. Trapped in the racism of the mainstream labor movement and cut off from the radical elements of labor, the Honolulu unions were more than marginal. As the U.S. Commissioner of Labor bluntly put it in 1929, "there are no union contracts in force in Hawai'i." The relatively small size of the urban economy and the concentration of economic control were formidable obstacles when coupled with the draconian antilabor legislation of the decade of the 1920s.[9]

## The New Deal

The U.S. Navy and the Army had long argued for a commission status for the islands as a way of meeting what they perceived to be the threat of an Asian majority. In 1930–1932, it appeared that Hawai'i would lose its status as a territory and be placed under a military commission government. Narrowly escaping the fate of Guam and American Samoa, Hawai'i faced yet another challenge in 1934 that would dramatically alter its political economy and transform the sugar industry.

Annexation in 1900 had provided the protection of the subsidy so essential to the survival of the industry. The Roosevelt administration in 1934 secured the passage of the Jones-Costigan Act. Hawai'i was defined as an "off-shore" sugar producer and subjected to a sharp cut in its production quota. The act was basically designed to assist mainland sugar producers and to restore the Cuban sugar industry, with its heavy American investment. Although Hawai'i challenged this "foreign" status in court, the court ruled that Hawai'i was subject to the legislative will of Congress. With skillful lobbying, the HSPA succeeded in reducing the cut. The event signalled the arrival of a new power—federal regulation of local economic affairs.

The depression of the 1930s brought the federal government into the workings of the sugar industry through the relief measures for agriculture. The Agricultural Adjustment Act (AAA), Social Security, and the National Labor Relations Board (NLRB), all in 1935, and the Fair Labor Standards Act of 1938 (FSLA), transformed the industrial relations of the sugar industry. This legislation ensured the intervention of the federal government and the imposition of wage, hour, and production controls on all aspects of the sugar industry.

The sugar industry, on the advice of lawyers that these controls would be declared unconstitutional, as the National Industrial Recovery Act (NIRA) had been, ignored the NLRB and the AAA. As an agricultural industry, they assumed that they would be exempt from these provisions. The quotas of the AAA and the subsidies attached to them, however, contained a trap not anticipated.

In order to receive the subsidies, the industry had to show that it was in compliance with all appropriate federal statutes. The determination of what portions of the industry were covered was with the agencies. The AAA and Social Security soon determined that the transportation and manufacturing portions of the sugar industry were indeed covered. With the passage of the FSLA, minimum wages and hours were mandated for those segments. This immediately presented problems for the industry. With year-round operations, the custom was to move workers around to various tasks during the season. This was particularly true during one or two months when grinding was halted during the year. When the planters claimed the housing and health perquisites furnished the workers as a wage payment to meet minimum wage standards, they were promptly assessed Social Security taxes on that portion for mill workers. The

Hawaiian industry was notorious for the lack of meaningful job descriptions, each plantation having evolved its own system. Federal agricultural regulators demanded uniform job classifications. The workers were quick to see the advantages of equal pay for equal work offered by these new procedures.

As a concession to the perceived radical threat, labor legislation granted to the American worker, for the first time since 1789, the right to organize. Even before this legislation, Hawaiian workers were moving to organize, spurred by the example of Pacific coast maritime workers with whom they had a long familiarity. Longshoremen in Hilo and Honolulu had participated in the San Francisco strike of 1934 and returned to Hawai'i determined to organize the waterfront. Their ambition quickly spread to the plantations.

Plantation organizing began in 1937 when the left-oriented United Cannery, Agricultural, Processing and Allied Workers of America (UCAPAWA) issued a charter to organizers on Kauai. A sophisticated use of federal subsidy legislation, labor law, and brilliant organizing skills marked this campaign. Jack Hall organized the workers of Kauai into a political caucus which, in 1938 and 1940, removed two territorial senators who represented and owned a majority of the sugar production on Kauai.

The organizing spirit reflected in the Pacific coast maritime struggles in 1934–1936 was quickly picked up in Hawai'i, spreading from the waterfront to urban unions. Almost defunct in 1930, the unions began a revival in 1938 with the sharp expansion of military activities in Hawai'i. The Pacific Contractors' Consortium undertook the reconstruction of Pearl Harbor into a major military base in 1938, bringing in thousands of workers. These craft workers deposited their union cards in the small Hawaiian locals in order to maintain their pension and death benefits. Local nonunion workers heard about the AFL craft unions from these workers. The militant, radical maritime unions, and the craft unions who brought mainland wages and working conditions, sharply raised the class consciousness of the Hawaiian workers.

## The Transformation of Hawai'i

In 1937, the ILWU longshore unit in Honolulu filed unfair labor practice charges against Castle and Cooke, resulting in the first NLRB hearing in Hawai'i. The end result, although only a partial victory for the union, led to the establishment of an NLRB office in

Honolulu. The field examiner found a carefully constructed facade of companies and legal entities which masked a very few people. He commented:

> The relationship is so close, the acts of one melt into the acts of another with no line of demarcation, that it is impractical when discussing the occurrences to separate in each case the different companies.[10]

The power noted by the NLRB examiner was about to be altered by the sweeping changes brought on by the depression and the Roosevelt administration programs. Long-standing agitation finally resulted in the cutting off of the Philippines in 1934 as a source of cheap and abundant labor for U.S. agriculture. The loss of imported labor forced an acceleration of mechanical harvesting to meet the quotas assigned to Hawai'i.

By 1937, the labor shortage forced the industry to leave some cane unharvested. An admittedly inefficient and expensive mechanical harvesting system was put into use in 1938 and steadily improved. Under the spur of union wages and working conditions, this mechanization process accelerated after 1946. The use of wartime machinery, particularly hydraulic-operated equipment, was rapidly adapted to sugar cultivation and harvesting.

### Post-War Evolution

World War II's transformation of the Hawaiian economy brought mainland wage standards and practices to the industry. Immediately after the lifting of martial law in 1944, the ILWU longshoremen petitioned their headquarters for an organizing drive that would include the plantations. Perhaps spurred by the impatience of the Hawai'i members who had commenced to recruit without waiting for approval from San Francisco, the ILWU set up a Hawai'i division with the explicit goal of organizing the sugar and pineapple industries on an industrial union basis. Selecting Jack Hall, who had organized successfully for UCAPAWA, to be Division Director, and Frank Thompson of Sacramento as the organizer, the campaign was launched in June of 1944.[11]

Bringing the principles of industrial unionism to Hawai'i's major industries quickly transformed the labor relations of the hitherto paternalistic oligarchy. Between the first industry-wide strike in 1946 and the climactic 128-day 1958 strike, the industry was transformed into a highly mechanized, disciplined industry presided over by nearly equal powers. After 1958, the bargaining continued to be sharp and often difficult, but the existence of the union was no longer challenged.

The change in the industry was fundamental. More was involved than simply a matter of mechanization of the work processes and a consequent reduction in the size of the work force. The very structure of the companies was altered. Caught up in the expansion mood of the corporate world of the 1960s, most of the Big Five sugar agencies branched out widely, to a greater extent than previously, with investments in nonagricultural areas. Prior to this, the agencies had operated in lines related to local merchandising and the production of sugar. Always quick to invest the large profits derived from the sugar subsidy, this pattern was one of corporate expansion—conglomerate style. American Factors and Castle and Cooke were the most aggressive in seeking new investment areas. Tourism bulked large in their plans. Ultimately, Castle and Cooke, American Factors, and C. Brewer were transformed into corporations no longer closely held by Hawaiian interests. The most startling example of this shift was the purchase of AmFac by a Chicago real estate investment firm. Theo H. Davies divested itself of all of its sugar interests. New management, with new areas of interest, reduced the sugar component of these old-line firms. Of the Big Five, only Alexander and Baldwin remains an Hawaiian corporation, solidly based in sugar and owning some ninety-seven percent of Matson Navigation.

This shift from largely local control to control by corporations outside Hawai'i significantly affected the work situation. For the workers, two problems arose. One was the rapid reduction in the agricultural work force, sharply reducing the union membership. The second problem was to find alternative areas of employment, both for its members and for future workers. As early as 1952, the ILWU foresaw the effects of mechanization on employment. In 1957, the union launched a major organizing drive. "To ward off the threats of mechanization and automation . . . it behooves us to institute an intensive organizing drive." The sharp reduction in sugar and pineapple operations which has occurred in the 1980s, and the distinct possibility that many of the remaining plantations will cease production, confronts the union again with a crisis.

The development of the service sector, notably tourism, as the principal employer for the foreseeable future has brought back some of the old problems. Modern unionism in the form of the ILWU and the Hotel Employees and Restaurant Employees (HERE) put an end to the crude racism which once characterized the tourist industry. However, a more subtle form of discrimination marks the tourist industry as the new "plantation." Locals tend to resent the subservient attitudes they must assume for tourists. They are further alienated by workers who come from the mainland for a short stay in Hawai'i, financing their visits by work in hotels and restaurants. These workers tend to regard the unions as unimportant. Local residents, facing the limited employment opportunities of Hawai'i, regard the transients' attitude as endangering their achievement of reasonable working conditions.

Rising resentment among some of the ethnic groups threatens the outwardly calm labor and social situation. Filipinos resent the domination of the civil service and professional areas by Japanese-Americans, and other minorities are demanding a better share of such opportunities. Public policy politics tend to be dominated by incessant talk of economic development. Yet, in fact, the prospects for technological development and financial services, the political favorites, are not good, given Hawai'i's built-in high costs, small population, and geographic isolation. Native Hawaiians have started a Hawaiian nationalist movement. Shut out of housing, denied access to land by the incredible prices and concentration of ownership, this low-income group has managed to raise the public consciousness on these issues.

Construction and the continuous expansion of the tourist industry are no longer viable means of sustaining the Hawaiian worker. Unions in Hawai'i will likely have to shift their concerns from immediate working conditions to embrace questions of housing, welfare rights, and meaningful education. A service economy presents the labor movement with the need to develop both new organizing techniques and a shift in legislative lobbying. The effort promises to be as difficult as was the original organizing movement in the post-War years.

## Notes

1. Lt. Charles Wilkes, *Narrative of the United States Exploring Expedition During the Years 1838, 1839, 1840, 1841, 1842*, (5 vols, London, Wiley and Putname, 1845); vol. 4, p. 218; Ralston, Caroline, *Grass Huts and Warehouses: Pacific Beach Communities of the Nineteenth Century* (Honolulu, The University Press of Hawaii, 1978) pp. 128–129.

2. Ralph Kuykendall, *The Hawaiian Kingdom, 1778–1854*, vol. 1, pp. 119–20.

3. See Hugh Tinker, *A New System of Slavery* (Oxford University Press, 1974). See Beechert, *Working in Hawai'i: A Labor History* (University of Hawai'i Press, 1985), pp. 306–310; for details of labor history events, see chapters 5, 8, 10 and 11.

4. U.S. law prohibited indentured contract labor and Chinese were barred from entering the United States. The Japanese government was also changing its attitude toward labor recruitment, threatening that source.

5. William Taylor, *The Hawaiian Sugar Industry*, unpublished Ph.D. diss., University of California, 1935, p. 68.

6. John E. Reinecke, "The Filipino Piecemeal Strike of 1924–1925," is a massive documentary history of this strike. See Beechert, *Working in Hawai'i*, p. 220, for data on industry losses.

7. See Beechert, "Technology and the Plantation Labour Supply: The Case of Queensland, Hawai'i, Cuba, and Louisiana," in A. Graves and B. Albert, eds., *The World Sugar Economy in War and Depression, 1914–1950* (London: Routledge, 1988), p. 131–142.

8. See especially, Jay Mandle, *The Roots of Black Poverty* (Durham, N.C.: Duke University Press, 1978), p. 10; George Beckford, *Persistent Poverty: Underdevelopment in Plantation Economies in the Third World* (Oxford: Oxford University Press, 1972), p. 67.

9. U.S. Department of Justice, *Law Enforcement in the Territory* (G.P.O., 1932), pp. 184–85, details the political structure and some of the economic concentration of power.

10. National Labor Relations Board, 12th Region, International Longshoremen's Association and Castle and Cooke, Ltd, Case XX-C-55, Honolulu, August 14, 1937, George O. Pratt, Examiner. When the case was filed, the ILWU had not been separated from the ILA. See also the report of James Shoemaker, U.S. Department of Labor, *Labor in the Territory of Hawai'i, 1939* (G.P.O., 1940), pp. 39–40.

11. Beechert, *Working in Hawai'i*, p. 292ff.; Sanford Zalberg, *A Spark is Struck: Jack Hall and the ILWU in Hawai'i* (Honolulu:; University of Hawai'i Press, 1979), p. 105ff.

# 15

## *KŪPAʻA ʻĀINA\**: NATIVE HAWAIIAN NATIONALISM IN HAWAIʻI

### *Haunani-Kay Trask*

I do not feel . . . we should forfeit the traditional rights and privileges of the natives of our islands for a mere thimbleful of votes in Congress; that we, the lovers of Hawaiʻi from long association with it should sacrifice our birthright for the greed of alien desires to remain on our shores.

Kamokila Campbell before Congress on statehood for Hawaiʻi, 1946

Our country has been and is being plasticized, cheapened, and exploited. They're selling it in plastic leis, coconut ashtrays, and cans of "genuine, original Aloha." They've raped us, sold us, killed us, and still they expect us to "behave". . . . Hawaiʻi is a colony of the imperialist United States.

Kehau Lee on evictions of Hawaiians from Native lands, 1970

The time has come to create a mechanism for self-government for the Hawaiian people. The question of Hawaiian sovereignty and self-determination needs to be dealt with now.

Mililani Trask before Congress on Hawaiian sovereignty, 1989

### Introduction

Spanning nearly fifty years, these statements by Native Hawaiians contradict the official celebrations which occurred in Hawaiʻi in 1989, marking the thirtieth anniversary of statehood as the bringer of prosperity and self-government to Hawaiʻi's Native people.[1] Today,

---

\*Kūpaʻa ʻĀina: = hold fast to the land.

glass and steel shopping malls with layered parking lots stretch over what were once the most ingeniously irrigated taro lands, lands that fed millions of Hawaiians over thousands of years. Large bays, delicately ringed long ago with well-stocked fishponds, are now heavily silted and cluttered with jet skis, windsurfers, and sailboats. Multistory hotels disgorge over six million tourists a year onto stunningly beautiful (and easily polluted) beaches, closing off access to locals. On the major islands of Hawai'i, Maui, O'ahu,and Kaua'i, meanwhile, military airfields, training camps, weapons storage facilities, and exclusive housing and beach areas remind the Native Hawaiian who owns Hawai'i: the foreign, colonial country called the United States of America.

But colonization has brought more than physical transformation to the lush and ancient islands of Hawai'i. Visible in garish "Polynesian" revues, commercial ads using Hawaiian dance and language to sell vacations and condominiums, and the trampling of sacred *heiau* (temples) and burial grounds as tourist recreation sites, a grotesque commercialization of everything Hawaiian has damaged Hawaiians psychologically, reducing their ability to control their lands and waters, their daily lives, and the expression and integrity of their culture. The cheapening of Hawaiian culture (e.g., the traditional value of *aloha* as reciprocal love and generosity now used to sell everything from cars and plumbing to securities and air conditioning) is so complete that non-Hawaiians, at the urging of the tourist industry and the politicians, are transformed into "Hawaiians at heart," a phrase that speaks worlds about how grotesque the theft of things Hawaiian has become. Economically, the statistic of thirty tourists for every Native means that land and water, public policy, law and the general political attitude are shaped by the ebb and flow of tourist industry demands. For Hawaiians, the inundation of foreigners decrees marginalization in their own land.[2]

The State of Hawai'i, meanwhile, pours millions into the tourist industry, even to the extent of funding a booster club—the Hawai'i Visitors Bureau—whose TV and radio propaganda tell locals, "the more you give" to tourism, the "more you get."[3]

And what Hawaiians "get" is population densities like Hong Kong in some areas, a housing shortage owing to staggering numbers of migrants from the continental United States and Asia, a soaring crime rate as impoverished locals prey on flauntingly rich tourists, and environmental crises, including water depletion, that threaten the entire archipelago. Rather than stem the flood, the state is projecting a tidal wave of 12 million tourists by the year

2010, and encouraging space facilities and battleship homeporting as added economic "security."[4]

For Hawaiians, this latest degradation is but another stage in the agony that began with the first footfall of European explorers in 1778, shattering two millennia of Hawaiian civilization characterized by an indigenous way of caring for the land (called *mālama 'āina*). Introduced diseases, from syphilis and tuberculosis to small pox, measles and leprosy, killed Hawaiians by the hundreds of thousands, reducing the Native population (estimated between 800,000-1,000,000 at contact) by ninety-five percent in just over a hundred years.[5] Gunboat diplomacy by Western powers and missionary duplicity against the Hawaiian chiefs forced the transformation of Hawaiian land tenure from communal use to private property by the middle of the nineteenth century. Called the Great Māhele, this dispossession of the Hawaiians' birthright—their ancestral *one hānau*, birthsands—allowed foreigners to own land. As the Hawaiian people continued to die off in multiple epidemics throughout the nineteenth century, the *haole* (white) foreigner bought up more land until, by 1888, three-quarters of all the arable land was controlled by *haole*.[6] In this way, as one scholar has remarked, "Western imperialism had been accomplished without the usual bothersome wars and costly colonial administration."[7]

In the meantime, Protestant missionizing constantly attacked Native customs from the *hula* to Hawaiian sexual practices while individual missionaries acquired vast acreages of Hawaiian land. Finally, in 1893 the American military overthrew the constitutional Hawaiian government headed by Queen Lili'uokalani, with the familiar justification of "protecting American lives and property." Resistance by Hawaiians was crushed and an all-haole puppet government called the Republic of Hawai'i was put in place in 1894, with forced annexation to (and citizenship in) the United States following in 1898. The ruling planter's party, composed primarily of missionary descendants, governed Hawai'i as an oligarchy throughout the territorial era. Despite Native opposition, Hawai'i became a state in 1959.[8]

As a result of these actions, Hawaiians became a conquered people, their lands and culture subordinated to another nation. Made to feel and survive as inferiors when their sovereignty as a nation was forcibly ended by American military power, Hawaiians were rendered politically and economically powerless by the turn of the century. Today, Hawaiians continue to suffer the effects of American colonization even after the alleged democratization of statehood.

Preyed upon by corporate tourism, caught in a political system where they have no separate legal status from which to control their land base (over a million acres of so-called "trust" lands set aside by Congress for Native beneficiaries but leased by their alleged "trustee," the State of Hawai'i, to non-Natives), Hawaiians have been reduced to twenty percent of the resident population in their own land.[9]

Despite the presence of a small middle class, Hawaiians as a people register the same profile as other indigenous groups controlled by the United States: high unemployment, catastrophic health problems, low educational attainment, large numbers institutionalized in the military and prisons, occupational ghettoization in poorly paid jobs, and increasing out-migration that amounts to diaspora.[10] The latest affliction of colonialism—corporate tourism—has meant a particularly insidious form of cultural prostitution. The *hula*, for example, has been made ornamental, a form of exotica for the gaping tourist. Far from encouraging a cultural revival, as tourist industry apologists contend, tourism has appropriated and prostituted the accomplishments of a resurgent interest in things Hawaiian (e.g., the current use of replicas of Hawaiian artifacts such as fishing and food implements, capes, helmets, and other symbols of ancient power to decorate hotels). Hawaiian women, meanwhile, are marketed on posters from Paris to Tokyo promising an unfettered, "primitive" sexuality. Burdened with commodification of their culture and exploitation of their people, Hawaiians exist in an occupied country whose hostage people are forced to witness (and, for many, to participate in) their own collective humiliation as tourist artifacts for the First World.

## An Awakening

Misery, however, has a surprising ability to call forth resistance. Out of land struggles in rural areas threatened with development was born a Native rights movement, similar to movements of other colonized Native peoples, like the Tahitians and the Maori, in the Pacific. Beginning in 1970, the Hawaiian Movement evolved from a series of protests against land abuses, through various demonstrations and occupations to dramatize the exploitative conditions of Hawaiians, to assertions of Native forms of sovereignty based on indigenous birthrights to the land and sea.

As they organized to fight land development, Hawaiians also experienced a cultural flowering focused on Hawaiian language immersion preschools, traditional *hula* and religious practices, and the farming of taro, the Hawaiian staple which, in Hawaiian genealogy, is the *kuaʻana* or elder sibling of the Hawaiian people. Indeed, never since the fateful coming of the *haole* had Hawaiian culture enjoyed such a renewal. Along with the push for a land base came the growth of cultural pride.

This cultural and political awakening was preceded by a fundamental transformation in Hawaiʻi's economy. From dependence on military expenditures and cash crops of sugar and pineapple in the first half of the twentieth century, Hawaiʻi's economy shifted to an increasing dependence on tourism and land speculation with rising investment by multinational corporations in the second half of the century.

Concentrated land ownership, a problem since the onslaught of plantation agriculture in the 1800s, had actually increased during the twentieth century. Small landowners controlled less than ten percent of the land. The military, the state, large private estates, and foreign and American developers owned the remainder. As a result, large landlords drove up the price of land, capitalizing on the post-statehood rush toward commercial, especially hotel, development.

Already economically exploited and culturally suppressed, rural Hawaiian communities, which had been relatively untouched during the plantation period, were besieged by rapid development of their agricultural areas beginning in the late 1960s. These communities—among them Hāna, East Molokaʻi, Keaukaha, Nānākuli, Waiʻanae, Waimānalo, Kahaluʻu—had managed to retain many traditional practices such as taro farming, fishing, and the spoken Hawaiian language. Given the effects of educational and religious colonization by the missionaries in the nineteenth century and the great decline in the Native population, these Hawaiian communities, although remnants of a once dynamic civilization, were nevertheless crucial to the perpetuation of Hawaiian culture. Their threatened extinction by urbanization and other forms of development was correctly perceived by many Hawaiians as a final attempt to rid their ancestral homeland of all Hawaiians. In many ways, it was predictable that the Hawaiian Movement would begin and flourish in rural areas where the call for a land base would be the loudest.

## Native Versus Local Rights

At the beginning of the seventies, communities often took a stand in terms of the rights of "local" people. The term *"local"* included both Hawaiian and non-Hawaiian long-time residents of Hawai'i. The assertion of their rights to live on the land was opposed to the rights of property owners like the state, developers, and private estates.

But as the decade wore on, the assertion of indigenous Hawaiian rights as historically unique from the rights of immigrants to Hawai'i began to characterize more community struggles. Independent of their "local" supporters, Hawaiians began to protest development by occupying lands, or by resisting eviction from land scheduled for development. They also protested through mass demonstrations, legal actions, and through cultural assertions such as the construction of fishing villages. These forms of protest placed the Hawaiians' demand to live and transmit their culture on a specified land base at the front of the Movement. The rights of "locals" were not thereby opposed. But Hawaiians' historic and cultural claims to the land as the *first* and *original* claimants were increasingly seen, at least by Hawaiians, as primary.[11]

A typical eviction struggle (and one that began the Movement) occurred in 1970 in Kalama Valley on the island of O'ahu where the single largest private landowner in the State of Hawai'i—Bishop Estate—evicted farmers for an upper-income residential development by Kaiser-Aetna. The resistance called forth an outpouring of support from around the state. And although the organizing core, Kōkua Hawai'i, lost the battle, the issue of land use and land rights would characterize public debate for the next twenty years.

## Claiming a Land Base

The merging of land-rich but capital-poor landowners with out-of-state corporations became a familiar pattern. This combination enabled large resorts, replete with golf courses, condominiums, and restaurants to spring up near beaches and on conservation land around the islands. Mostly descended from American missionaries and other entrepreneurs, the landowners, like Campbell Estate, Castle and Cook, Dillingham, American Factors, Alexander and Baldwin, and others, linked up with American and Japanese multinational corporations to develop the Kona Coast on the Big Island of Hawaiʻi, the east end of Molokaʻi, the Waiʻanae Coast on Oʻahu, the south and north shores of Kauaʻi, and the west side of Maui. Such resort and residential development spurred anti-development battles wherever it occurred.[12]

In the meantime, Native political organizations moved to reclaim a land base. Legal corporations (e.g., the Hawaiian Coalition of Native Claims), political groups (the A.L.O.H.A. Association), and loose-knit community coalitions argued for reparations from the United States for its role in the overthrow of the Hawaiian government in 1893, for forced annexation in 1898, and for the consequent loss of Hawaiian nationhood and sovereignty. Beyond this, legal claims were made (e.g., by groups like *Hoʻāla Kānāwai*—"awaken the law") to the Native "trust" lands totalling nearly a million acres, but mismanaged by the state and federal governments. And finally, claims to a land base were brought as a right of residence by virtue of indigenous status, called aboriginal rights.[13]

Along with these claims had come concerns over military expropriation and abuse of lands. The American military controls nearly thirty percent of the most populated island, Oʻahu. Military lands, including "trust" lands, were taken by Executive Order during periods when the United States was at war.[14]

By 1976, this concern had exploded over Kahoʻolawe Island, smallest of the eight major islands, military bombing target since 1941, and site of traditional Hawaiian worship. Occupation by Native activists rallied Hawaiians statewide around several issues: destructive military land use in an archipelago where land is scarce; the assertion of the Native land use ethic—*mālama ʻāina*—in opposition to military use; and the failure of the state to protect the land for the public. In 1990, after the death of two activists and the designation of the island as a national historic site, the bombing was finally halted, but the controversy surrounding military misuse of land has expanded to include illegal military use of Native trust lands (for which the military pays, in some cases, less than a dollar a year), and the general presence of the military on all islands.[15]

By 1980, abuse of Hawaiian Homes trust lands (nearly 200,000 acres) by the state and federal governments had been challenged by demonstrations, occupations, and law suits because of the extent of illegal use for airports (e.g., Hilo, Kamuela, and Molokaʻi airports), military reservations (e.g., Lualualei Valley), public schools (e.g. Nānākuli and Molokaʻi high schools), public parks (e.g., Anahola and Waimānalo beach parks) and county refuse sites (e.g., Molokaʻi dump), even private homes (e.g., Kawaihae residential lots). By 1991 there were over 20,000 people on the Hawaiian Homes waiting list, while illegal usages and other non-Native uses existed on more than 130,000 acres of trust lands. Particularly galling to beneficiaries was their status as wards of the state, without litigation rights to challenge illegal uses in both state and federal courts.[16]

The other trust—on ceded lands—had *never* been used by the state for Hawaiians, despite their beneficiary status. Thus, as Hawaiians came to link abuse of the trust lands with land dispossession at the time of the overthrow and annexation, they coalesced around a unified push for a land base. Land and money restitution from the American government for its historic role in the loss of Hawaiian domain and dominion could be coupled with Native control of the trust lands to form a land base as the anchor of Native sovereignty. In the decade of the eighties, various arguments for Hawaiian sovereignty were put forward by defendants in eviction arrests (e.g., at Sand Island and Mākua Valley), by Hawaiian activists at the United Nations and other international forums, and by lawyers and political groups seeking redress for all manner of Native rights violations. International networking included exchanges of nationalists to Nuclear-Free and Independent Pacific conferences and Third World gatherings throughout the Pacific, the Americas, and Asia. What started as a call for restitution in the seventies had broadened into a clear demand for Native sovereignty in the eighties.[17]

The strength of this push was not lost on politicians at both the state and federal levels. Long discounted as a minor voice because of their poor voting participation in the American-imposed electoral system, Hawaiians had come more and more to represent a potential pivotal swing group in elections. If organized, they could turn narrow defeats into narrow victories. Towards this end, Hawaiian claims were professed by candidates to the 1978 State Constitutional Convention, in various campaigns for the legislature and eventually the state house, and even in congressional races. The results were seen in an increase in elected Hawaiian officials beginning in the late seventies, in the appointment of two presidential commissions in 1981 to review both the Hawaiian Homes trust and the conditions of Hawaiians, and in the creation of an Office of Hawaiian Affairs (OHA) in the Constitutional Convention.[18]

## The OHA Story

The Office of Hawaiian Affairs, though ostensibly for representation of Hawaiian rights by Hawaiians (the only group allowed to vote for its all-Native trustees), was actually devised as an extension of the state. OHA was powerless as a mechanism of self-government, having no control over the trust lands (i.e. no legal status to stop their takings or misuse), and no statutory strength to prevent abuses of Hawaiian culture (for example, disinterment of Hawaiian remains and destruction of Hawaiian sites).

OHA trustees were not paid, resulting in a high turnover as board members moved on to gainful employment. Indeed, three members from the first board quit after one term to run for the legislature, using their visibility as trustees to aid in voter identification. Two chairpersons of the board misused OHA monies while in office, although only one was dismissed for the offense. Over its many years of existence, OHA has been plagued by scandals, some sex-related, others concerning mismanagement of funds, falsification of credentials, and misrepresentation of programs to the state legislature.[19]

Beyond its trustee problems, OHA was accused by many Hawaiians of being a "do-nothing" organization because most of its funding went into personnel, office space, and administration, rather than programs for Native beneficiaries. Moreover, without a secure source of funding, the office was constantly embroiled with the state in legal battles, often inconclusive, over a share of the trust land revenues. In the end, OHA was reduced to just another interest group begging at the door of the legislature.

But the worst aspect of OHA was that it served as a false front to the Movement: although overflowing with pro-Hawaiian rhetoric, OHA supported destructive development, such as state geothermal energy projects on Hawaiʻi island that endangered pristine Native forests and threatened pollution of nearby communities and potential destabilization of the volcanic area where geothermal wells would be sunk. A megaresort called West Beach (one-fifth the size of Waikīkī), was supported by several OHA trustees, despite overwhelming evidence that its hotels, marinas, restaurants, and golf courses would damage fisheries, obliterate historic sites, and forever pave over fertile lands. Finally, projects like these had the active support of the local Democratic Party, the reigning political force since statehood.[20]

While OHA closed ranks with the Democratic Party, there was a proliferation of sovereignty groups seeking some form of Native political control of a land base. One of these groups, *Ka Lāhui Hawaiʻi*, was born out of a core watchdog association that had lobbied for the Federal-State Task Force on the Hawaiian Homes Commission Act. After the Task Force report documenting both abuses of trust lands and recommendations, the community group called a constitutional convention of its own in 1987, with 250 delegates from around the archipelago meeting to create a constitution and to elect interim officials.[21]

## The Emergence of Native
## Hawaiian Sovereignty Groups

As a Native initiative for self-government, *Ka Lāhui* was a repudiation of OHA as the sole representative of the Hawaiian people. Within three years of its first convention, *Ka Lāhui's* membership had grown thirty times to 7,500, suggesting more than that Hawaiians did not support OHA. *Ka Lāhui's* large membership was a sign of how many Hawaiians supported sovereignty on the model of American Indian nations. *Ka Lāhui* served as a focus for discontent over continued state abuse of the trust lands and revenues, and it raised an issue that OHA had ignored: inclusion of Hawaiians in federal Indian policy that recognized over 300 Native nations in the United States while not extending this recognition to Hawaiians.

By the end of 1988, the issue of sovereignty was identified with the issue of nationhood. While OHA worked on a reparations package to be presented to Congress, a sovereignty conference was hosted at the state capitol. Six major groups presented positions on the structure of the Native land base, a mechanism for Hawaiian governance, and political strategies for the achievement of nationhood. The groups included *Na 'Oiwi o Hawai'i* (supporting more community education before any mechanism for government was established), the Protect Kaho'olawe 'Ohana (supporting decentralized, island-based, autonomous entities), *E Ola Mau* (a health professionals group supporting *Ka Lāhui*), the Council of Hawaiian Organizations (supporting a constitutionally established mechanism on a separate land base), the Institute for the Advancement of Hawaiian Affairs (supporting secession), and *Ka Lāhui Hawai'i* (supporting federal recognition of Hawaiians as a Native nation with all the rights of nationhood extended to Indian nations). Although OHA board members had been invited to participate, they declined.

All groups developed their arguments from the prior existence of the Hawaiian nation, the culpability of the United States in the loss of Hawaiian domain and dominion in 1893, the unilateral change in

Native citizenship that came with forcible annexation in 1898, and the internationally recognized right of all peoples to self-determination. The specifics of the Native Hawaiian–U.S. relationship had been linked with the universals of the human rights position to form a powerful defense of Hawaiian sovereignty.[22]

In the simplest terms, sovereignty was defined, in the words of *Ka Lāhui Hawai'i*, as

> the ability of a people who share a common culture, religion, language, value system and land base, to exercise control over their lands and lives, independent of other nations.

Given that the Hawaiian form of government had been overthrown in 1893, the first order of business for Hawaiians emerged as the creation of a mechanism for self-government.[23]

### Self-Governance and Sovereignty Versus Reparations

What that mechanism will look like is still hotly debated by sovereignty groups today. But the level of commitment is so high that when Senator Inouye's Indian Affairs Committee came to Honolulu to hear testimony on reparations in the summer of 1988, Native groups argued for self-government, not merely reparations. In 1989 a series of repeat forums yielded the same response from the communities.

The most compelling defense of Hawaiian sovereignty was put to the Senator as an extension of current federal policy regarding Native people controlled by the United States. In the 1970s, President Nixon had officially changed U.S. Native policy from wardship to self-determination. The policies of termination (through which Indian tribes would cease to have federal recognition and therefore tribal land rights as well as other treaty rights) were to be replaced by a commitment to aid and encourage tribal self-government. This aid was to come not only in monies for economic development projects on reservations, but also as specific recognition of tribes by the federal government. Today, the U.S. government recognizes over 300 Indian nations. Under existing U.S. policy, relations between the federal government and these Indian tribes are described as "Nation-to-Nation."

In the Hawaiian case, there has not been any federal recognition of a Native claim to self-government. It is as if, in terms of federal policy, Hawaiians are still in the stage of "termination" rather than self-government. In practice, federal policy had straddled two poles, acknowledging Hawaiians as Natives for some purposes (such as educational and health programs) but refusing to grant them the privileges of Native recognition in terms of self-government.

Inouye was stunned by this argument. He could not fail to see the injustice of federal recognition for one Native people but not another. Pressured by Hawaiians' calling for self-government, and cornered by the press at the hearing, Inouye finally acknowledged that "If native American Indians have sovereignty, it's difficult to argue Hawaiians do not." As a self-proclaimed champion of Indian rights, Inouye had been forced to recognize the equal claims of another Native people (who were also from his home state) to self-determination.[24]

The 1988 public statement by Inouye that Hawaiians had a claim to as much self-government as Indians was a recognition in itself of how far the Movement had progressed. For years, the debate had been whether or not Hawaiians deserved reparations. Governor Waiheʻe had stated openly that he would be satisfied with an apology for the overthrow from the American government. OHA, meanwhile, had supported a large reparations package to be dispersed through its offices.

But the reparations game had been surpassed by a historic evolution in Hawaiian consciousness. Faced with this reality, and sensing that they had been underprepared and out-organized at the summer hearing (where they had argued for reparations), OHA came out for sovereignty. Acknowledging themselves a state agency, they nevertheless asserted that OHA should be the governing structure of the Hawaiian nation.

This position was problematic for several reasons: OHA was not representative of all Hawaiian communities and never had been, because voting procedures overweighted the most populous island of Oʻahu, resulting in a skewed representation for trustees from the Neighbor Islands; any lands or monies transferred by the federal government to OHA would go to the state, *not* to the Hawaiian people, since OHA was a state agency; this would mean *less*, not more, control by Hawaiians over their future. Finally, giving OHA nation status would be akin to calling the Bureau of Indian Affairs (BIA) an Indian nation.

Nevertheless, OHA issued a detailed "Blueprint" for reparations in 1989 arguing their prior status as the representative organization of the Hawaiian people. Ignoring the argument for inclusion into federal Indian policy, OHA's Blueprint made no claims against the State of Hawaiʻi, despite documented abuse of its trust relationship to Hawaiians. Instead, all claims were made against the federal government for the overthrow and annexation, with the recommendation that OHA be allowed to have control of the trust lands.[25]

In February of 1990, after 30 months of closed-door negotiations, OHA and the governor's office concluded an agreement to settle ceded land claims against the state. In the settlement, Hawaiians lose their right to 1.4 million acres of ceded lands and OHA receives $80 million in 1991 and $8.5 million every year thereafter. Thus, money rather than land is at the heart of the settlement.

Clearly, the Office of Hawaiian Affairs, the governor, and Senator Inouye have begun to move in concert to: (1) support continued state and federal control of Native trusts; (2) refuse to transfer control of the lands to Native Hawaiians but give OHA some monies from the trusts; and (3) allow a measure of autonomy on some portion of Hawaiian Homes lands but only for agricultural and residential purposes, not for commercial or industrial purposes, with allowable water use for agricultural purposes only.[26]

The *Ka Lāhui* response to this potential deal has been carefully enunciated since 1987. The land base of the Hawaiian Nation should include all of the 200,000 acres of Hawaiian Homes lands, half of the 1.4 million acres of the ceded lands, and additional lands provided in restitution for the overthrow. Moreover, and perhaps most critically, Hawaiians must be recognized as a Native nation within the purview of federal policy on other Native peoples in the United States.[27]

While OHA and the Democratic Party bosses move to foreclose real self-determination for Hawaiians, it is likely that their combined efforts will increase OHA's legitimacy in the eyes of the Federal government. Of course, OHA will need more than the State of Hawaiʻi to move Congress to accept a restitution package. Given repeated attempts during the Reagan years to abrogate all Indian treaties and to create "national sacrifice areas" on reservation lands, settlement of Hawaiian claims through congressional action will remain doubtful for some time to come.

## Waiting for Self-Determination

While all this political maneuvering continues, of course, the marginalization and exploitation of Hawaiians, their culture, and lands also continues. Historically, the decline of Hawaiians and their culture is traced directly to land dispossession. Therefore, any attempt to address Hawaiian claims which does not return Hawaiians to control of their own land is doomed to fail.

If OHA is successful, the Hawaiian people will be burdened with yet another agency, non-Hawaiian in design and function, *set in place to prevent rather than fulfill Native autonomy*. Like Indian tribal councils created by the federal government to short-circuit Indian self-determination in the early twentieth century, OHA will be a top-down institution whose architects envision an extension of the State of Hawai'i (easily influenced by the ruling Democratic Party) rather than a Native initiative for self-government.

Given the growing number of sovereignty groups, however, OHA's position will not go unchallenged. *Ka Lāhui Hawai'i* and other representatives of the sovereignty roundtable, *Ka Pākaukau*, will dog OHA at every step—both in Washington, D.C., and in Hawai'i. The central argument for Native control will be heard if not heeded.

Elsewhere in the Pacific, Native peoples struggle with the same dilemma. The Maori, like the Hawaiians, are a minority in their own land, have been dispossessed through conquest and occupation by a foreign white people, and have suffered psychologically from cultural suppression. They, too, have been demanding a form of sovereignty, seeking identity and cultural integrity by returning to the fight for tribal lands. And they have supported Hawaiian resistance, as fellow Polynesians and as fellow colonized people.

In Tahiti, meanwhile, a strong independence movement has captured the mayorship of the second largest city while uniting antinuclear, labor, and Native nationalist forces to resist French colonialism. With others in the Pacific, the Tahitians have spearheaded the Nuclear-Free and Independent Pacific Movement.

Aborigines, Kanaks, East Timorese, and Belauans focus world attention on well-known cases of genocide and military imperialism. And for each of these indigenous peoples, there is the familiar, predictable struggle for self-determination.

But if Hawaiians are not alone in the Pacific, they are certainly unsupported in their own islands. While the United Nations moves to declare 1992 the Year of Indigenous People and to devise conventions and standards for the rights of Native peoples worldwide, the general public attitude in Hawai'i remains one of resistance to the recognition of Hawaiians as Native and, therefore, both eligible and deserving of self-government. More than any single actor or agency, the general American ideology that "everyone is deserving of the same treatment because everyone is an immigrant" works against the recognition and settlement of Hawaiian claims. The two ruling elites in Hawaiʻi, the Japanese and the *haole*, express their racism against Hawaiians by claiming Hawaiʻi as their own, conveniently ignoring the overthrow, forced annexation, and continued land theft. Neither is there any acknowledgement that the privileges of these groups rest on the continued dispossession of Hawaiians. As in the metropole, so in the colony: the settler classes deny their history.

In such a hostile atmosphere, it is certain that whatever successes Hawaiians do achieve in the struggle for self-determination will be won slowly and at great expense. But, as in the times of their ancestors, there will always be Hawaiian voices speaking for the land and the people born from her. Unlike all other peoples in the islands, only Hawaiians are truly children of the land.

## Notes

1. First quote is from testimony by Kamokila Campbell, wealthy heir to the Campbell Estate, before the Larcade Committee, U.S. Congress, House Committee on Territories, *Statehood for Hawaiʻi Hearings*, H. 263, 79th Congress, 2d sess., January 7–18, 1946, p. 482. Second quote is from an interview with Kehau Lee in the *Hawaiʻi Free People's Press*, vol. 1, 1971. Third quote is from testimony by Kia ʻĀina (Governor) of Ka Lāhui Hawaiʻi, Mililani Trask, before Senator Inouye's Committee on Indian Affairs, Honolulu, summer 1989.

2. For a discussion of state policy based on the rapid expansion of the tourist industry and its crucial influence on in-migration and population growth, see Eleanor Nordyke, *The Peopling of Hawaiʻi*, 2d edition (Honolulu: University of Hawaiʻi Press, 1989), p. 134–72. In 1990, Hawaiians numbered around 225,000. The tourist count was projected to 6.5 million by the end of the year.

3. In the 1989–1991 biennium budget of the Hawaiʻi State Legislature, the Hawaiʻi Visitors Bureau received over $15 million.

4. Nordyke writes, in *The Peopling of Hawaiʻi*: "In 1980 the gross density of Waikīkī, including over 17,000 residents, 43,000 nonresident visitors, and 32,000 workers employed in the area was about 93,000 persons per square mile—one of the most densely populated regions in the world" (p. 150). For examples of the socioeconomic and environmental problems resulting from tourism see *Hawaiʻi Business*, April, 1985; Jon Matsuoka and Terry Kelly, "The Environmental, Economic, and Social Impacts of Resort

Development and Tourism on Native Hawaiians," *Journal of Sociology and Social Welfare* 15 (4) (1988); David Stannard, "Tourism Called a Phony 'Happiness' Industry," *Honolulu Star-Bulletin*, June 9, 1986; Meda Chesney-Lind, "Salient Factors in Hawai'i's Crime Rate," University of Hawai'i School of Social Work, 1983; and the 1989 Declaration of the Hawai'i Ecumenical Coalition on Tourism which calls for a ban on all resorts in rural Hawaiian communities, among other things. Unpublished but available from the American Friends Service Committee, Honolulu, Hawai'i. Finally, for state projections of tourist industry growth see Nordyke, *Peopling of Hawai'i*, p. 256.

5. For Hawaiian population estimates, see David Stannard, *Before the Horror: The Population of Hawai'i on the Eve of Western Contact* (Honolulu: University of Hawai'i Press, 1989). For a discussion of the impact of *haole* diseases on Hawaiians, see his "Disease and Infertility: A New Look at the Demographic Collapse of Native Populations in the Wake of Western Contact," in *Journal of American Studies*, 24, 1990, p. 325–350.

6. For the Hawaiian relationship to the land and an analysis of the impact of the Great Māhele on this relationship, see Lilikalā Porton, *Land and the Promise of Capitalism*, Ph.D. dissertation, University of Hawai'i— Mānoa, 1986.

7. Neil Levy, "Native Hawaiian Land Rights," *California Law Review*, 63 (July 1975), p. 857.

8. For the original report on the overthrow and native sentiment against annexation, see Hon. James Blount, the *Blount Report*, U.S. 53d Congress, House of Representatives, ed. sess., 1894–1995. For the modern controversy over the culpability of the United States in the overthrow, see *Native Hawaiians Study Commission Report*, vols. 1 and 2, U.S. Department of the Interior, 1983. For an analysis of the Territorial period, see Noel Kent, *Hawai'i: Islands under the Influence* (New York: Monthly Review Press, 1983).

9. For a discussion of the trust lands see vol. 2 of the Study Commission Report and the report of the *Federal-State Task Force on the Hawaiian Homes Commission Act*, U.S. Department of the Interior, 1983.

10. For current statistics on Hawaiians, see *Native Hawaiians Study Commission Report*, vol. 1; also see *E Ola Mau: Native Hawaiians Health Needs Study* (Honolulu: Alu Like, 1985).

11. For a more detailed account of the Hawaiian Movement in the context of colonialism, see my "Hawaiians, American Colonization, and the Quest for Independence," *Social Process in Hawai'i* 31 (1984), pp. 101–36.

12. Kent, *Hawai'i Islands under Influence*. See also, Haunani-Kay Trask, "The Birth of the Modern Hawaiian Movement: Kalama Valley,

Oʻahu," *Hawaiian Journal of History*, 21 (1987), pp. 126–153. For the relationship between missionary descended landowners and development of resort and commercial properties, see George Cooper and Gavan Daws, *Land and Power in Hawaiʻi* (Honolulu: Benchmark Books, 1985).

13. For an argument for sovereignty based on the overthrow and annexation as well as aboriginal rights, see Melody MacKenzie, "Towards Reparations/Restitution," and "Sovereignty: Honoring the Native Claim," prepared for the second volume of the *Native Hawaiians Study Commission Report*, available from the Native Hawaiian Legal Corporation.

14. For a summary of military landholdings in the context of Hawaiʻiʼ politics in the Twentieth century, see Ian Lind, "Ring of Steel: Notes on the Militarization of Hawaiʻi," *Social Process in Hawaiʻi* 31 1984, pp. 25–48. For a list of Hawaiian Homes trust lands taken illegally through Executive Orders, see the report of the *Federal-State Task Force on the Hawaiian Homes Commission Act*, Department of the Interior, 1983, pp. 265–289.

15. For an early study of the Protect Kahoʻolawe ʻOhana in the context of Hawaiian cultural revival, see Myra Jean Tuggle, "The Protect Kahoʻolawe ʻOhana: Cultural Revitalization in a Contemporary Hawaiian Movement," M.A. thesis, University of Hawaiʻi, 1982. For a later study, see "Kahoʻolawe Island, Hawaiʻi Cultural Significance Overview," by Tom Keane for the U.S. Navy, 1986, available from Hamilton Library, University of Hawaiʻi and the reply from the Protect Kahoʻolawe ʻOhana, available from their attorney, Cynthia Thielen, Honolulu, Hawaiʻi.

16. For the most complete review of the problems with the Hawaiian Homes trust as well as some solutions, see the report of the *Federal-State Task Force on the Hawaiian Homes Commission Act*. The report carefully documents illegal uses, wrongful takings, and below-market rentals. Recommendations are also made, including a right to sue for aggrieved beneficiaries in both State and Federal courts. Waiting list numbers are available from the Department of Hawaiian Home Lands, State of Hawaiʻi.

17. For a summary of the practice, enunciation, and theoretical underpinnings of sovereignty in the Hawaiian Movement, see my article, "Hawaiians and Human Rights," *Honolulu Star-Bulletin*, November 26, 1984. For a discussion of Hawaiian claims to nationhood in the content of American Indian nationhood, see *Ka Lāhui Hawaiʻi*, a booklet available from the Center for Hawaiian Studies.

18. The presidential commissions grew out of a decade of political activism around the issues of reparations and the abuse of the Hawaiian Homes trust. The Native Hawaiians Study Commission issued its report, including a minority report in Volume 2 in 1983. By coincidence, the Federal-State Task on the Hawaiian Homes Commission Act issued its report in the same year. Both reports are excellent for background material on the two issues.

19. This list of problems was compiled from ten years of minutes from OHA monthly meetings (available from the Office of Hawaiian Affairs, Honolulu, Hawai'i). Perhaps the only good thing that can be said here is that the sunshine laws appear to have worked.

20. OHA's support for geothermal energy projects and for West Beach was, and remains, controversial both within Hawaiian communities and within the OHA Board of Trustees. Neither project was supported by the board unanimously.

21. *Faces of the Nation*, a video produced for *Ka Lāhui* by NaMaka o Ka'āina Video explaining the origins and structure of *Ka Lāhui Hawai'i* contains valuable information about the governing body of *Ka Lāhui*. The Constitution of the Nation is contained in a booklet, *Ka Lāhui Hawai'i*, available from the Center for Hawaiian Studies, University of Hawai'i, Honolulu, Hawai'i.

22. Trask, "Hawaiians and Human Rights."

23. This quote is from the booklet, *Ka Lāhui Hawai'i*, p. 10, available from the Center for Hawaiian Studies.

24. *Honolulu Star-Bulletin*, August 22, 1988.

25. *Blueprint for Native Hawaiian Entitlements*, September 1989, available from the Office of Hawaiian Affairs, Honolulu, Hawai'i.

26. This information came from a *Ka Lāhui* bulletin leaking information regarding an impending settlement between the state and OHA with the support of Inouye's office. The bulletin, dated January 26, 1990, is available from the Center for Hawaiian Studies, University of Hawai'i, Honolulu, Hawai'i.

27. Ibid., p. 2.

# CONTRIBUTORS

*Peter S. Adler* is the Director of the Center for Alternative Dispute Resolution, a program to find nonlitigated solutions to public and organizational conflicts located in the Judiciary of the state of Hawai'i. He has a Ph.D. from Antioch University in sociology. Prior to assuming his current position he was executive director of the Neighborhood Justice Center in Honolulu. He is a frequent contributor to professional journals on the topic of conflict resolution processes and mediation.

*Thomas W. Bean* is professor and chair of the education department at the University of Hawai'i at Hilo. He was formerly a professor and graduate coordinator of the reading department, California State University, Fullerton. Dr. Bean received his Ph.D. in reading from Arizona State University. Bean teaches courses in secondary reading and graduate course work in educational research. He is the co-author of four contemporary texts entitled: *Content Area Reading: An Integrated Approach* (1989); *Content Area Reading: Improving Classroom Instruction* (2d ed., 1986); *Improving Communication Through Writing and Reading* (1984); and *Rapid Reading for Professional Success* (1983).

*Edward D. Beechert* is a professor of history at the University of Hawai'i at Manoa. He holds the B.A., M.A., and Ph.D. from the University of California at Berkeley. Specializing in U.S. labor and economic history, Beechert has published extensively. His most recent works include, *The Port of Honolulu: A History* and *Patterns of Resistance: Plantation Labor in the Pacific.*

*Dan Boylan* received a Ph.D. (University of Hawai'i) in American studies. He's taught at the Tuskegee Institute, the University of Iowa, the University of Hawai'i at Manoa, and West Oahu College, where he is currently a professor of history. Boylan's interest in Hawai'i politics grew out of his involvement in the John A. Burns Oral History Project. Between 1975 and 1980, Boylan interviewed many of the major actors in the post-World War II development of Hawai'i's Democratic Party.

Since 1978, Boylan has written a dozen feature-length articles on Hawai'i's politics for *Honolulu* magazine. He currently contributes a monthly political column to that publication.

*David Lee Callies* is a professor of law at the William S. Richardson School of Law, University of Hawai'i at Manoa. He is a graduate of the University of Michigan Law School where he was managing editor of the *Journal of Law Reform* and he received an LL.M. from the University of Nottingham (England). He is the author of *Regulating Paradise: Land Use Controls in Hawaii* (1984) and coauthor (with Robert Freilich) of *Cases and Materials on Land Use* (1986); (with Fred Bosselman) *The Quiet Revolution in Land Use Control* (1971); and (with Bosselman and John Banta) *The Taking Issue*. He presently teaches property, land use, and state and local government law, and serves as a consultant to state and county government agencies on land use and local government matters.

*A. Didrick Castberg,* professor of political science, teaches courses in legal systems, law and politics, freedom and civil liberties, American politics, and technology at the University of Hawai'i at Hilo. He holds a Ph.D. in political science from Northwestern University. Castberg publishes in the areas of constitutional law, criminal justice (U.S. and Japan), and public policy (energy). On the Hilo Faculty since 1974, he spent the 1986–1987 academic year in Japan on a Fulbright and sabbatical.

*Jeffrey L. Crane* holds a Ph.D. in sociology from Notre Dame University and is currently a professor of sociology and Associate Dean, College of Arts and Science at the University of Hawai'i at Hilo. His primary interests are in critical and interpretive social theories, social and cultural change, and social psychology. Crane has published and presented papers in the areas of critical theory, semiotics, mythology, health care, sociology of science, and mass culture. He is currently working on a *Sociological Fact Book* on the State of Hawai'i for Harper and Row, and an anthology of theoretical essays titled *The Laughing Picaro*. Crane is a past president of the Hawai'i Sociological Association and a frequent consultant for agencies such as United Way, Hilo Hospital, and the Commission on the Handicapped.

*David Hammes* received his B.A. in economics (magna cum laude) from Humboldt State University in Arcata, California, and his Master's and Ph.D. degrees from Simon Fraser University in Burnaby, British Columbia, Canada. He teaches macroeconomics, money, and banking, monetary theory, and the history of economic thought at the University of Hawai'i at Hilo. Dr. Hammes's research interests in public finance, methodology, economic theory and national income statistics are reflected in his publications of the book *Shaping Our Nation* (1988) and articles in *The Review of Income and Wealth* (1987), *Economic Inquiry* (1983 and 1987), *Philosophy of the Social Sciences* (1984), *Kyklos* (1989), and the *Revue Francaise d'Economie* (1988).

*Dean Higuchi* received his B.A. and M.A. in political science with an emphasis in public policy and futures studies from the University of Hawai'i at Manoa. He is a technical information specialist at the U.S. Environmental Protection Agency, Pacific Islands Contract Office in Honolulu. Although he studies a wide range of pacific environmental issues he has a particular interest in water quality and solid waste management.

*Karl E. Kim* received his undergraduate education at Brown University where in 1979 he received the Samuel C. Lamport Prize in economics and sociology. His Ph.D. is in urban and regional planning from the Massachusetts Institute of Technology. Since 1984, he has been an assistant professor at the University of Hawai'i at Manoa in the department of urban and regional planning, where he teaches courses on computer applications, planning theory, and infrastructure planning. He has been the principal investigator to numerous state and federal projects, has also served as a consultant to the City and County of Honolulu rapid transit planning.

*Kem Lowry* is chair of the Department of Urban and Regional Planning, University of Hawai'i. He received his Ph.D. from the Department of Political Science, University of Hawai'i, in 1976. He has been a visiting scholar at the Institute for International Relations and Development in Asia, Sophia University, Tokyo; visiting faculty at the Department of City and Regional Planning, University of North Carolina; and a fellow at the Marine Policy Program, Woods Hole Oceanographic Institution. He has published articles on land use, coastal management and evaluation in journals including *American Planning Association Journal, Urban Law Annual, Publius, Environmental Impact Assessment Review, Policy Studies Review, Ocean Yearbook*, and *Coastal Zone Management Journal*.

*James Mak* is a professor of economics at the University of Hawai'i at Manoa. He was born in China and raised in Shanghai

(China) and Kobe (Japan). He received his Ph.D. in economics from Purdue University. His current areas of specialization include Hawai'i's economy, the economics of tourism, and more recently, Pacific Island economies. Mak is on the editorial boards of the *Journal of Travel Research* and the University of Hawai'i Press. In addition, he is a member of the Hawai'i State Council on Revenues, and has served on the Hawai'i Visitors Bureau Market Research Committee, Governor's Committee on Hawai'i's Economic Future, and the Chamber of Commerce Education Committee. He has also served as the executive director of the Hawai'i Council on Economic Education.

*Norman Meller* is political science professor emeritus of the University of Hawai'i at Manoa. In 1955 he received a Ph.D. in political science from the University of Chicago. He served as director of the Legislative Reference Bureau of the University of Hawai'i from 1947 until 1955. When he left the bureau he became chairman of the political science department and was later named director of its Pacific Islands Studies Program, a graduate program emphasizing teaching, research, and publishing on the Pacific. His published works include three monographs, twice as many books, and a considerable number of chapters in edited books and articles in learned journals.

*Deane Neubauer* is professor of political science at the University of Hawai'i, Manoa. He holds a Ph.D. from Yale University. He joined the political science department at the University of Hawai'i in 1970, and served as chair from 1975 to 1978. From 1980 to September of 1988 he served as dean of the College of Social Science. Neubauer's work is oriented in policy phenomena to which he attempts a variety of approaches, focusing on democratic theory questions, comparative policy analysis, health politics, urban politics and currently the politics of medical malpractice. His work is characterized by political economy themes to these subject matters, often by problematizing the normalized liberal frames which orient policy study in the United States.

*Ronald A. Oliveira*, formerly a professor of economics at the University of Hawai'i at Hilo is currently an analyst with the Oregon Public Utilities Commission. He received his B.S. (with honors) in agricultural economics from the University of California at Berkeley. His Master's and Ph.D. degrees in agricultural economics were both earned at the University of California at

Davis. His professional areas of specialization include natural resource economics, regional economic modelling, applied econometrics and forecasting, and public finance. Oliveira has published manuscripts in a variety of professional journals including the *Journal of the American Statistical Association, American Journal of Agricultural Economics, Land Economics, Environment and Planning, Western Journal of Agricultural Economics, Canadian Journal of Forest Research, Forest Science*, and the *Journal of Leisure Research*.

*Richard Pratt* has a Ph.D. in political science from the University of Hawai'i. He is an associate professor of political science and the director of the public administration program at the University of Hawai'i at Manoa. Pratt's research interests include public policy in Hawai'i, health politics and policy, and the political dimensions of work. His publications have appeared in a variety of journals including the *Journal of Health Politics, Policy and Law*, the *Journal of Multivariate Behavioral Research*, and the *Journal of Social and Biological Structures*.

*Marcia Y. Sakai* holds a Ph.D. degree in economics (1985) from the University of Hawai'i at Manoa and also holds an M.A. in mathematics (1971). Her interests are in regional economics, labor economics, public finance policy, and economic education. She has written and reviewed papers in tourism and in state and local tax policy. She currently is a staff economist for the Hawai'i State Public Utility Commission.

*Zachary Smith* received his B.A. from California State University and his M.A. and Ph.D. from the University of California at Santa Barbara. He has been teaching political science and public administration at Northern Arizona University in Flagstaff since 1989. He taught at the Hilo branch of the University of Hawai'i from 1982 to 1989 and has also taught at Ohio University and the University of California at Santa Barbara. Smith has published seven books as well as many articles on environmental and natural resource policy topics as well as on American politics and public administration.

*Richard J. Tobin*, a professor of political science at the State University of New York at Buffalo, received his Ph.D. from Northwestern University. The author of *The Social Gamble: Determining Acceptable Levels of Air Quality* and *The Expendable Future: Evaluating Public Policies for the Protection of Endangered Species* as well as articles in numerous professional journals, professor Tobin has interests in a broad range of environmental topics.

*Haunani-Kay Trask* traces her genealogy to the island of Kaua'i on her father's side and to Hana, Maui, on her mother's side. She currently resides in Kane'ohe, Ko'olauloa, O'ahu. Professor Trask is a member of the Hawaiian Nationalist Movement and a political consultant to *Ka Lahui Hawai'i*. She teaches at the University of Hawai'i at Manoa where she is director of the Center for Hawaiian Studies.

*Jan Zulich* is an associate professor in the Education Department, University of Hawai'i at Hilo. She received her Ph.D. in secondary education with an emphasis in curriculum from Indiana University. Zulich teaches courses in classroom management, a graduate seminar in critical issues in education, and introduction to education. Her publications include an article on Hawai'i's school system in the *Phi Delta Kappan* journal and research on dialogue journals in preservice teacher preparation. Zulich's professional interests include work in cooperative learning and a long-range study of preservice teacher's stress through case study analysis of dialogue journal entries.

# INDEX

Abercrombie, Neil, 80
Acid Rain, 121
Adams, Romanzo, 53
Administrative reorganization, 15, 18
Aging, office of, 18
Agriculture:
  crops, 231
  department of, 15, 18
  land, 151, 156, 158, 159
  preservation of, 139
  state district, 136–137, 139–140
Airports, 15
Akaka, Dan, 80
Alternative Dispute Resolution (ADR): 104
  Center for, 106, 109
American Arbitration Association, 106
American Indians, 254–255
Anderson, D. G. "Andy", 71, 81
Annexation: 14, 233–234, 244–246
  the courts, 21
  and land development, 136
  military presence, 245
  missionary role, 246
  overthrow of Hawaiian government, 246
A+ Program, 94
Apportionment and reapportionment, 19, 20
Arbitration, 104, 106
  See also Mediation, court ordered
Ariyoshi, George, 71, 76, 93, 96, 97, 101, 157
Attorney General, 16, 18, 208

Baker v. Carr, 15
Banks, 15
Before the Horror, 54
Board of Realtors, 106

Boards and Commissions, 17, 18
Budgeting:
  base, 87
  Budget and Finance, Department of, 90, 92–94
  centralized staffs, 86
  crises, 71–74, 83–85, 97
  "Current Service Base," 87
  cycle, 87
  earmarking funds, 18
  executive, 17, 18
  "fair share & base," 87
  Planned Program Budgeting System (PPBS or PPB), 85, 89–94, 98
  role of, 86
  state strategies, 88, 95, 99
  surplus, 97–98
Bunye, Vicky, 72
Burns, John A., 80, 89, 97, 101
Buses. See Mass transit

Campbell, Kamokila, 244
Canoe districts, 19
Capital Improvements Budget, 95
Castle and Cooke, Inc.:
  interlocking companies, 240
  NLRB case, 239–240
Caucasians, 71, 75, 81
  See also Haole
Cayetano, Ben, 72, 80, 94
Ceded Lands Trust, 251, 256
Christensen, Karen, 182–183
Clean Water Act, 122
Colonization, 245–247
Commission on Water Resource Management. See Water
Conservation, 14, 15
Constitution:
  Amendment, 20

Bill of Rights, 203
  Hawaiian, 232, 233
  Hope Chest Constitution, 19
  Reapportionment Commission, 20
  search and seizure, 203, 208, 212–213
  state, 14, 16–20, 25, 26
Constitutional Convention:
  (1950), 16
  (1978), 17, 19, 20–22, 97, 109, 158
Consumer protection, 15
Contractual arbitration, 104
Corrections Department, 210–214
Cost of living, 45
Courts, state, 15, 21, 209–210
Crime, 63–64, 205–206

Date-Lau Case, 144–145
  *See also* zoning
DBCP. *See* Pesticide use
Deeded land, 23
Democratic Party of Hawaii. *See*
  Political parties
Demographics. *See* Population
Development agreements, 140, 142–143
  *See also* Land use
Directed growth. *See* Growth manage-
  ment
Districts:
  local government, 14
  state conservation, 136–137, 139
  urban, 136–137, 139
Drug Enforcement Administration,
  206, 213

Economy:
  imported, 231–232
  Plantation, 232–234
EDB. *See* Pesticide use
Edelman, Murray, 98
Education: 14, 15
  Board of, 17, 18, 22
  funding, 217, 218
  future of, 222–223
  governance, 218, 219
  Hawaii plan, 219, 220
  higher:
    governance, 225, 226, 227
    University of Hawaii, 224
  school choice and curricular reform,
    221, 222

school-community-based
  management, 220, 221
Employment:
  government, 43, 44
  growth by sector, 34, 37
  levels by sector, 34, 36
Endangered species, 129
Environmental Protection Agency
  (EPA), 118, 119, 121–126
Environmental quality:
  and development, 119, 125, 128,
    131–132
  economic impacts, 120
  and immigration, 117
  impact assessments, 119, 122
  laws, 118, 119
  Office of, 119
  programs, 130
  protection, 130–131
Ethnicity:
  crime, 63–64
  group, 58–59
  health risk, 60
  income, 62
  *See also* Population
Executive:
  branch, 16–18
  budget, 96–98
  history, 13

Fasi, Frank, 71–72, 75–76, 80, 122,
  161, 176
Federal:
  Federal Mediation and Conciliation
    Service (FMCS), 104
  lands, 23
  legislation, 88
  regulation, 238
Felix, John Henry, 72
Fifth Amendment, U.S. Constitution,
  137–138
Filipinos: 71–72, 79, 81
  labor, 235–236
Fish & Wildlife Service (FWS), 128, 129
Fiss, Owen, 105
Fixed rail. *See* Mass transit
Fong, Hiram, 80
Fono, 113
Foreign investment: 42
  and tourism, 199

Forester, John, 186
Forestry, 15
Friedmann, John, 186
Froman, Jr., Lewis A., 102

Gamey-Ibaney, Jose, 168
Garbage collection. *See* Solid waste
Gill, Tom, 80, 101
Government:
    local, 14, 16, 21, 24–26
    monarchy, 13, 14, 19, 21
    preempting federal functions, 15
    reorganization, 16, 18
    Republic. *See* Republic of Hawaii
    territory, 16, 21, 24
Governmental functions, division of, 15
Governor:
    item veto, 18
    monarchy, 14, 19
    state, 14, 16–18, 22, 23
    territorial, 13, 17
Great Mahele, 30, 136
Gross state product:
    alternative measures of economic
        activity, 40–41
    by components, 32
    relative to other national economies,
        34–35
Growth:
    economic constraints, 45
    management, 157, 158, 160–162
Groundwater:
    contamination, 124
    Pearl Harbor Aquifer, 120–122
    protection strategy, 122
    quantity, 120–121
    Use Act of, 121
    *See also* Water

Hall, Jack, 240
Hall, Peter, 157
*Haole,* 246–251
Harbors, 15
Hargrove, Edwin, 93
Hawaiian:
    attitudes towards voting, 74
    culture, 244, 251
    depopulation, 246
    Homes Commission, 23

Homes Trust, 250–251
    Kingdom, land policy of, 136
    land movement, 247–251
    nationalist movement, 242
    reparations, 254–256
    self-governance, 253, 261
    sovereignty, 253–261
    Sugar Planters Assoc., 234–235
Hawaiian Affairs, Office of, 16–17, 23,
    251–256
Hawaiian Constitution. *See* Constitu-
    tion, Hawaiian
Hawaii, county of:
    crime in, 206
    marijuana in, 206
    police department, 204
    police recruit training, 205
    population of, 213
    prisons on, 210
    Visitor Bureau, future of, 198
Hazardous waste, 126
Health, Department of: 118, 120, 122, 124
    statistics, vital, 59–60
        health risk factors, 60
        life expectancy, 59
Heftel, Cecil, 72
Heptachlor epoxide and milk contami-
    nation, 124
Home Rule Party, 24
Homestead Commission, 23
Honolulu:
    City and County of, 14, 24, 26, 160
    central Oahu, 159, 160, 161
    charter, 156, 160
    council, 159, 161
    crime in, 204–206
    police department, 204
    population of, 213
*Ho'oponopono,* 113
Hotel Employees and Restaurant
    Workers, 241
House of Representatives. *See*
    Legislature
Housing:
    affordable, 142, 150, 159, 162, 163
    Coalition, 162
    construction, 150, 154
    costs, 150, 152, 157
    off-site infrastructure, 156
    regulatory, 157

demand, 150
government-developed, 150, 153, 154
Hawaii Housing Authority (HHA), 154
home-ownership, 151, 152
low-income, 163
market-priced, 150, 151, 152
needs, 160
non-resident, 151
policy, 161
privately-developed, 153, 163
production process, 155
programs, 151, 153
public, 15
rentals. *See* Rental housing
rent supplement program, 155
resales, 150
single-family, 151
subsidies, 153–155, 163, 238
supply, 150, 152–153, 155, 160, 163
Housing Finance and Development Cor-
     poration (HCDA), 153, 154, 163
Dwelling Unit Revolving Fund
     (DURF), 154
Homes Revolving Fund, 154
Howard, Kenneth S., 85, 87, 96, 99
Hula, meaning of, 247
Human Services, Department of, 96,
     211–212
H-3, 177

Impact fees: 140–142, 181
national nexus requirement, 141
Incumbents, 82–83
*See also* voting
Inequality, social, 60–64
*See also* Population
Initiative and referendum, 20
and land use, 143–146
Inouye, Daniel K., 80–81, 254–256
Insecticide, Fungicide and Rodenticide
     Act, 119
International Commercial Dispute
     Resolution, Center for, 106
International Longshoremen and Ware-
     housemens' Union (ILWU),
     240–241
*An Island Community,* 53

Japanese-Americans, 71–73, 75–76,
     78–81

Japanese labor, 234
Jones-Costigan Act (1934), 238
Judges:
     number of, 209
     recruitment of, 209–210, 214
     sentencing by, 210, 212, 214
Judicial function, 15, 21
     *See also* Courts
Judicial Selection Commission, 22,
     209–210
Judiciary, 20–22
Jury, summary trials, 104

Kauai, county of:
     crime in, 205
     police department, 204
     population of, 213
Kaho'olawe Island, 250
Ka Lahui Hawaii, 253–257, 261
Kalama Valley, 249
Kamehameha. *See* Monarchs
Kealoha, Jimmy, 80
Keir, Gerry, 75, 81
Key, V. O., Jr., 100, 101
Kido, Mits, 80
King, Jean, 101
Kings. *See* Monarchs
Koloa Plantation, 232
Koreans, 79
Kuhio, Jonah Kalanianaole, 78
Kupa'a 'aina, 244

Labor:
     Asian Workers, 237
     legislation, 235
     market, 38, 39
     mechanization of, 241
     question, 232
     strikes, 232, 234, 235, 240–241
Land and Natural Resources Depart-
     ment of (DLNR), 110, 119, 120,
     121, 129, 137
Landholding:
     Bishop Estate, 159
     Campbell Estate, 159, 161
     Castle and Cooke, 159
     chiefs, 230
     federal land, 230
     heritable property, 230

large landowners, 158, 159
privatization, 230
Land use:
  Commission (LUC), 137, 146, 158,
      159, 162, 163
  and Tourism, 197–198
  controls, 153, 155–158, 160–161, 163
  District Boundary Amendments,
      159, 162
  history of regulation, 136
  law, 136–137, 156, 159, 162
  planning, 160, 163
    City and County of Honolulu
        General Plan, 156, 160, 161
    comprehensive plan, 156
    development plans, 143, 156, 160
    functional plan, 163
    Hawaii State Plan, 158
    and initiative, 143–144, 145
  policy, 151, 157–162
  preservation of open space, 139–140
  public participation in, 143–146
  referendum, 143
  regulatory takings, 137–138
  state plan (Act 100), 136
Law enforcement, 204–205
Lead:
  in drinking water, 121
  Contamination Control Act, 121
Lee, Herbert, 80
Lee, Kehau, 244
Legislative districts, 19, 20
Legislature, state:
  general, 19, 20
  House of Representatives, 19, 20
  local government, 25, 26
  Senate, 18, 19, 21, 22
  territorial, 19
Lieutenant Governor, 17
Liliuokalani, Queen. See Monarchs
Lind, Andrew, 53
Liquor Commission, 25
Local government. See Government, local
Long, Oren, 80

Maka'ainana, 230
Malama'aina, 250
Maori, 257
Marijuana:
  legalization of, 207

plants destroyed, 207
  sentencing of offenders, 214
  value of, 206
Mass transit:
  buses, 172
  federal funding, 179
  fixed rail, 174–175
Masters and Servants Act,
    232–233
Masumoto, Harold, 163
Matsunaga, Sparky, 80–81
Maui:
  crime in, 205
  police department, 204
  population of, 213
McKinley Tariff (1890), 234
Mediation:
  Alternative Dispute Resolution
      (ADR), 104
  family, 106
  and local culture, 112
  and politics, 113
  process, 109
Medical wastes, 128
Meyer, John, 168
Migration:
  immigration, 54
  intra-state, 56
  See also Population
Missionaries:
  economic development,
      231, 232
  Hawaiian culture, 246
Missouri Plan, 209
Monarchs: 13, 14
  Kamehameha the Great, 13, 14
  Kamehameha II, 230
  Queen Lili'uokalani, 246
Motor vehicles:
  accidents, 171
  car sales, 170
  occupancy rates, 170
  registered, 170

Neighborhood Justice Center of
    Honolulu, 106
Niihau, 14
Nollou v. California Coastal Commis-
    sion, 141–142
Nukolii Case, 144

Oahu, 19, 26
Oahu Metropolitan Planning Organization, 177
Oahu Transportation Study, 169
Office buildings, development, 171
OHA. *See* Hawaiian Affairs, Office of
Oil:
  for energy, 127, 128
  spills, 127
  waste oil, 126–127
Open space, preservation of. *See* Land use
Organic Act of 1900, 13, 14, 19, 21, 234
Oshiro, Robert, 80

Palaka Power, 101
Parole:
  criticism of, 212
  Hawaii paroling authority, 212, 215
Pesticide use, 122, 124–125
Planned Program Budgeting System (PPBS or PPB). *See* Budgeting
Planning and land use. *See* Land use
Planning of Economic Development, Department of, 159
Plantation system: 14, 15
  mechanization, 239–241
Plea bargaining, 207–208
"Plunking", 20
Political economy. *See* economy
Political parties, 20, 24–26, 100
  Democratic Party of Hawaii, 24–26, 71–73, 76–77, 79–82
  Republican Party of Hawaii, 24, 71–73, 75–78, 80–82
Population: 15, 16, 24, 26
  decline, 232
  resident, 54–57
    age, 58
    ethnic groups, 58–59
    by island, 54–56
    migration, intra-state, 56
    precontact, 54
    primary language of, 58–59
    state, 55
  social stratification, 60–64
    by ethnicity, 64, 79
  Income, 61–63
    by ethnic group, 62
    mean, 62
    poverty threshold, 63
  statistics, vital, 59–60
    health risk factors, 60
    life expectancy, 59
  transient, 57–58
    military, 31, 57
    tourist, 57
Prisons:
  ethnic populations, 211
  overcrowding of, 210–212, 214
Privatization, 181
Prosecution, 207–208
Public disputes, general characteristics, 107
Public lands. *See* Lands, public
Public participation in land use. *See* Land use
Public Safety, Department of, 211–212

Quinn, William, 80

Rabinowitz, Francine, 182
Race relations, 242
Reciprocity Treaty, 30
Recycling, 126
Referendum. *See* Land use
Regulatory takings. *See* Land use
Rental housing, 150
  government-developed, 153
  Hawaii Rental Assistance Program, 155
  non-resident rentals, 153
  rates, 150, 152, 154
  subsidies, 155
  supplement program, 155
  supply, 152
  time-share, 153
  vacancy rate, 152
Republican Party of Hawaii. *See* Political parties
Republic of Hawaii, 13, 14, 21, 246
Richardson, William, 80
Roads and highways, 14, 15
Robinson, Charles Mulford, 169

Samoans, 79
Sandy Beach Case, 144, 145

School districts, 14
Semi-autonomous agencies, 22–24
Senate. *See* Legislature
Settlers:
  Polynesians, 117
  westerners, 117
Sewage Treatment:
  cesspools, 122
  treatment waivers, 122, 123
Sheriff, 204
Sierra Club, 110, 120
Soil conservation, 14
Solid waste:
  amounts of, 125
  collection, 15
  garbage incineration, 125
  H-power, 125
  landfills, 120
  recycling, 126
Special assessment districts, 180
Stannard, David, 54
Statehood, 17–19, 21, 23, 25
State Plan Act. *See* Land use
State Planning, Office of (OSP), 18,
  140, 163
State v. Kaluna, 208, 214
Strikes. *See* Labor
Sugar:
  and gross state product, 31
  historical production, 30
  recent production, 31
  subsidies, 238
Sugar Planters Association, 110

Tahiti, 257
Taxes:
  gasoline, 180
  property, 25
  taxation powers, 25
tax-increment financing, 180
Thielen, Cynthia, 73
Thompson, Frank, 240
Tokunaga, Mike, 77–78, 81
Tourism, 120, 241–242, 245
  cost sharing, 196
  county control over, 197
  diversification, 191–192
  foreign investment in, 199
  and Hawaii Visitor Bureau, 198
  history in Hawaii, 188–190
  impacts on environmental quality,
    118, 119, 120, 128, 131–132

and Land Use Commission, 197–198
  public opinion about, 196
  social impacts, 195
Trade:
  exports, 32, 33
  imports, 32, 33
  relative to gross state product, 33
Transportation and federal planning,
  176
Trask, Mililani, 244
Tungpalan, Eloise Kamashita, 76

United Cannery, agricultural and
    processing workers, 239
University of Hawaii, 17, 18, 22
Urban districts, state, 136–137, 139

Voting:
  ethnic patterns, 71–72, 76
  Hawaiian attitudes toward, 74
  registered voters, 19
Veto, executive, 18
Vietnamese, 81

Waihee, John, 72, 80, 122, 126–127,
    210, 214
Waste oil, 126–127
Water:
  Board of Water Supply, 120
  Clean Water Act, 122
  Commission on Water Resource
    Management, 26, 120, 121
  conservation, 120–122
  doctrine of prior appropriation, 111
  fresh supply, 119–120
  Water Code Roundtable, 109–112
  *See also* Ground water
Welfare, 15
Whaling industry, 233
Whitt, J. Allen, 185
Wildavsky, Aaron, 90, 99
World War II, 14, 25

Yoshinaga, Nadao, 80

Zoning, 20, 155, 156, 163
  park dedication ordinance, 156
  subdivision ordinance, 156
  urban district, 158, 162